T0311835

Television's Spatial Capital

This book launches a comprehensive detailing of the dramatic expansion of the geography of television production into new cities, states, provinces, and countries, and how those responsible for shaping the "landscape" of television have been forced to adapt, taking established strategies for engaging with space and place through mediated representation and renegotiating them to account for the new map of television production.

Modeling media studies research that considers the intersection of production, textuality, distribution, and reception, Myles McNutt identifies how the expansion of where television is produced has intersected with the kinds of places represented on television, and how shifts in the production, distribution, and consumption of television content have shifted the burden of representing cities and countries both locally and internationally. Through a combination of industry interviews, textual analysis, and in-depth consideration of industry and audience discourse, the book argues that where television takes place matters more today than it ever has, but that the current system of spatial capital remains constrained by traditional industry logics that limit the depth of engagement with place identity even as the expectation of authenticity grows significantly.

Representing a cross section of media industry studies, television studies, and cultural geography, this book will appeal to scholars and students within multiple areas of media studies, including production studies and audience studies, in addition to television studies broadly.

Myles McNutt is Associate Professor of Communication and Theatre Arts at Old Dominion University.

Routledge Studies in Media and Cultural Industries

For more information about this series, please visit: www.routledge.com/
Routledge-Studies-in-Media-and-Cultural-Industries/book-series/RSMCI

Television's Spatial Capital
Location, Relocation, Dislocation

Myles McNutt

LONDON AND NEW YORK

First published 2022
by Routledge
2 Park Square, Milton Park, Abingdon, Oxon OX14 4RN

and by Routledge
605 Third Avenue, New York, NY 10158

Routledge is an imprint of the Taylor & Francis Group, an informa business

British Library Cataloguing-in-Publication Data
A catalogue record for this book is available from the British Library.

Library of Congress Cataloging-in-Publication Data
Names: McNutt, Myles, author.
Title: Television's spatial capital : location, relocation, dislocation / Myles McNutt.
Description: Abingdon, Oxon ; New York. NY : Routledge, 2022. | Includes bibliographical references and index.
Identifiers: LCCN 2021033702 (print) | LCCN 2021033703 (ebook) | ISBN 9780367477516 (hardback) | ISBN 9780367477523 (paperback) | ISBN 9781003224693 (ebook)
Subjects: LCSH: Television program locations—Economic aspects. | Television program locations—Social aspects. | Television—Production and direction—United States. | Television viewers—United States.
Classification: LCC PN1992.78 .M35 2022 (print) | LCC PN1992.78 (ebook) | DDC 384.550973—dc23/eng/20211022
LC record available at https://lccn.loc.gov/2021033702
LC ebook record available at https://lccn.loc.gov/2021033703

ISBN: 978-0-367-47751-6 (hbk)
ISBN: 978-0-367-47752-3 (pbk)
ISBN: 978-1-003-22469-3 (ebk)

DOI: 10.4324/9781003224693

Typeset in Sabon
by Apex CoVantage, LLC

Contents

Introduction
Television's spatial capital

It was only logical that the USA Network drama series *White Collar* (2009–2014) would be set in New York City. Telling the story of a con artist-turned-consultant who liaises with the F.B.I. naturally lends itself to the island of Manhattan, with its corrupt CEOs and suspicious elites. Although technically there is white-collar crime in any major city across the United States, viewers would readily associate that crime with New York, making it the most productive backdrop for generating the episodic "crimes of the week" that would serve as the backbone of the series' narrative structure.

However, as a show that balances episodic storytelling with a serial narrative of Neal Caffrey's checkered past and complicated relationships with law enforcement, *White Collar*'s story eventually took it beyond the city where it was primarily set. In "Wanted," the fourth season's premiere, Neal is not in New York: he is on the run and has taken refuge in an unidentified island paradise where he is wooing a local shopkeeper and building sand-castle cities in honor of his former home. The episode turns his location into a mystery, but his friends at the F.B.I.—who are hoping to find him before a bounty hunter hot on his trail—solve the mystery mid-way through the episode: Neal is in Cape Verde, a series of volcanic islands off the coast of West Africa in the Atlantic Ocean.

This spatial shift requires more unpacking: whereas setting *White Collar*'s primary narrative in New York City sent a clear message to audiences about what kind of show it was and the kinds of stories they might expect to see, it is unlikely that audiences have many—if any—preconceptions about Cape Verde. I myself had no idea that Cape Verde existed until watching this episode, meaning that the show was serving as my first introduction to the archipelago country. On a basic level, Cape Verde was chosen for the purposes of the episode's plot: it has no extradition treaty with the United States, meaning, it is among the global locations where Neal would have hidden after becoming a fugitive. But in selecting a location that has had such little media representation, *White Collar* was shaping viewers' understanding of this country in a way that it was not with New York, where the show could merely draft off of an average viewer's existing impressions. Although Google Maps and Wikipedia could provide ample information for

DOI: 10.4324/9781003224693-1

those who seek it out, a mediated version of Cape Verde carries a different weight: when I watched this episode, I had no reason to question the show's representation of Cape Verde and thus largely accepted the show's depiction as a fair representation of the country.

But as I was in the early stages of research for this project, I was compelled to dig deeper into Cape Verde in the interest of understanding this choice; I discovered that the mystery of Neal Caffrey's location was more of a mystery than I had realized. The island where Neal was hiding out featured predominantly Spanish-inspired architecture, but Cape Verde was a Portuguese colony—it is even a plot point in the episode, as the characters note a Spanish bell overheard on a phone recording with Neal is out of place and discovered to be the result of a shipwreck. This confusion extended further, as almost all the extras and guest actors featured in the episode are Hispanic, despite the fact that the majority of Cape Verde's population is Creole; along similar lines, the characters on *White Collar*'s Cape Verde speak Spanish, despite the fact that Portuguese is the official language, and local Creole dialects represent the other widespread languages on the islands. What became immediately clear was that even if I had been an expert on Cape Verde, I never would have been able to solve the mystery of Neal's location before the F.B.I., because little of what appears onscreen in the episode in any way resembles Cape Verde.

The fact that this happened is not, I argue, in and of itself surprising: a mid-budget American basic cable procedural failing to accurately represent a small African country that most of the show's viewers were unaware of before watching the episode is far from news. All media are forced to balance the logistics of production with the story's needs, and an expectation of absolute verisimilitude is unreasonable, particularly when a show is only visiting a location for a single episode (as opposed to an entire series). But the question that drew my attention to this example is *why* it happened: for a nation's history, language, and people to be erased in this way requires either absolute ignorance—which we can rule out given that the writers had to do the basic research of knowing the country's extradition status—or a strikingly different set of priorities. How is it that a version of Cape Verde so removed from the truth of the country made its way to U.S. television screens?

The answers are, as is always the case, contextual to this case study, but this book's goal is to provide a framework for understanding television's inherent spatiality and identify key patterns shaping how space and place are articulated within the medium. I take as my starting point that the production and distribution of television functions as a complex negotiation of what I term "spatial capital," a value associated with the spaces where television is produced, set, and ultimately consumed. This is not a static value: it is ever changing, under constant renegotiation on a series-by-series basis and in this case an episode-by-episode basis. By analyzing television through the lens of spatial capital, this book will demonstrate that the medium carries an incredible capacity for place-making, one that is distinct from other media and also increasing rapidly through advances in technology, distribution, and production incentive programs around the world in an era of "Peak TV." However, while the potential spatial capital of television continues to grow, activating this capital requires navigating fundamental realities of the television industry that render spatial capital an inherently contingent form of capital: its mobilization depends on the various stakeholders involved, their investment in questions of space and place, and how they are able to negotiate hierarchies of power to ensure that—for example—a televisual depiction of Cape Verde has a connection to the actual Cape Verde.

As this book will demonstrate, it is now easier than ever before for the American television industry to "take place" in locations around the world, breaking through historical borders in terms of where it is produced, how it is distributed, or how audiences engage with it. Yet despite this clear expansion of television's spatiality, the contingency of spatial capital ensures that the hierarchies that limit and restrict the medium's sense of place remain active. The result is a process where locations from New York City to Cape Verde are not simply "put on the map" through television: they are constantly located, relocated, and dislocated, with significant consequence for how we understand spatiality's role in the media industries.

Mapping television

By introducing the notion of "spatial capital," I am drawing on the work of Pierre Bourdieu (1984), whose treatise on capital is foundational to any consideration of cultural hierarchy. His distinction between different forms of capital—social capital, economic capital, and cultural capital—offers a framework for considering one's social position within those hierarchies, while also identifying capital as a series of interconnected forms of value rather than a single, absolute one. In isolating spatial capital as its own framework, this book is not adding it to the existing three categories offered by Bourdieu. Rather, a "spatial capital" approach to the media industries seeks to understand how a text's sense of place is situated in hierarchies of social, economic, and cultural capital within given industries, and how it accumulates value within that process.

In this way, this book follows the lead of Michael Curtin, who studies geographies of production by framing different locations as "media capitals," arguing that doing so "directs our attention to complex interactions among a range of flows (economic, demographic, technological, cultural and ideological) that operate at a variety of levels (local, national, regional, global)" (2003, 222). What Curtin frames as media capital is a critical part of understanding spatial capital, but I make a distinction between the two given the limits of binding a term to a particular location. Moreover, media capital is primarily concerned with industrial questions of production and distribution; the stakeholders of media capital are predominantly localities and the corporations doing business in them. Spatial capital, by comparison, encompasses a wider range of stakeholders that push us to consider how spatiality shapes the granular ways individual industry workers and members of the audience engage with media.

For this reason, rather than thinking about spatial capital as a value associated with individual cities or even broader industries, this book considers spatial capital as a value attached to a given text, and constitutive of other forms of capital—this includes not only the media capital Curtin identifies, but also the cultural capital attached to particular cities and other texts related to those locations, as well as symbolic capital attached to particular landmarks within said locations. Doreen Massey (2005) argues that "if **space** is rather a simultaneity of stories-so-far, then **places** are collections of those stories, articulations within the wide power-geometries of space" (130, emphasis in original). Isolating and emphasizing the accumulation of spatial capital works to identify those articulations and explore how a text's relationship to space positions it within other television shows, other media, and other cultural discourses tied to location. The foundation of spatial capital is how a series consciously maps itself within overlapping hierarchies of industry and cultural geography, a process we can see firsthand in two very different efforts to draw a "map" of the U.S. television industry.

This first map, titled "America: The home of television," is a poster created by graphic designer James Chapman. The poster was originally made available on Chapman's Etsy shop in 2013 and plots over 130 television series across a map of the continental United States and Hawaii; it was subsequently updated in 2014 to include more than 170 series, including shows as recent as Netflix's *Orange is the New Black* (2013–2019) and HBO's *True Detective* (2014–). The map includes shows set in real cities like Los Angeles and Atlanta, along with fictional towns like Dillon, Texas, featured in NBC's *Friday Night Lights* (2006–2011). Although it does not feature *White Collar*, it does highlight more than a dozen shows set in Manhattan, alongside a dozen more set in the other boroughs of New York City. On his Etsy page, Chapman positioned his poster for TV lovers, asking a series of questions: "Have you ever wondered how far it is from *Breaking Bad* to *Arrested Development*? Or which coast has more crime drama? Or how many shows are set in Idaho? (Spoiler alert, it's none). Well, wonder no more." For Chapman, the map is the answer to the question of where television's spatial capital lies, and that answer is the United States.

Broadly speaking, this assertion is true, but thinking about the absences from the map reveals that America's spatial capital is not evenly distributed among all television series and not even among all series set in a particular location. If a show does not appear on the map, it means its relationship with space and place was not significant enough to merit mention: the fact that *White Collar* was not among the shows featured in Manhattan, for example, suggests that it failed to leverage its setting enough to meet the threshold for spatial capital Chapman was using when selecting which shows to

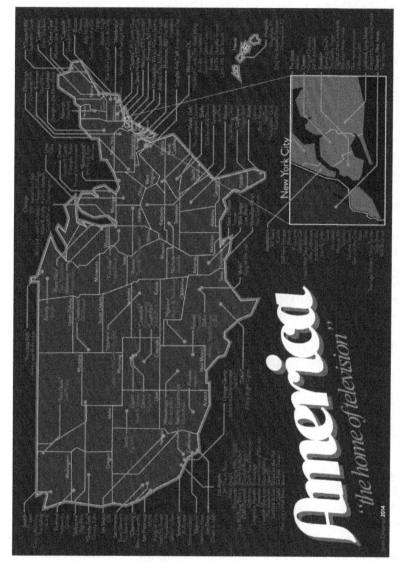

Figure 0.1 America: The Home of Television, a poster print created by graphic designer James Chapman and made available on his Etsy page in 2014.

Used with permission of creator.

include. However, it is unclear on what parameters Chapman based this decision: was it his own evaluation of how important a show's setting was to its narrative, or was it simply derived from his own personal favorite shows, or perhaps the shows he felt his imagined customer on Etsy might enjoy? The construction of this map is subject to Chapman's understanding of hierarchies of cultural capital operating in the television industry, whether shaped by Nielsen ratings, channel branding, or industry awards, among other possible vectors. The fact that a show is not on the map does not mean it has no sense of place; rather, it suggests that the circumstances surrounding the show—where it was produced, how it was produced, how it was distributed, how it was received by audiences—failed to generate the spatial capital necessary for it to be perceived through this lens.

Chapman's description of the map also points to the fact that there are many states where there are no series at all: the description mentions Idaho, but North Dakota, Alabama, Wyoming, Iowa, West Virginia, Mississippi, Missouri, South Carolina, New Hampshire, and Delaware are also *not* the home of television according to the map. This is partially due to choices Chapman made in constructing the map, like excluding reality television, which has shot shows in many of these states, but it also reveals the absence of scripted series set in these locations. It suggests that the perceived lack of cultural capital attached to states that are too small, or too rural, or too southern functions as an impediment to spatial capital: while there are no doubt stories to be told about people living in these states, the industry does not believe people want to see stories set in these locations, thus excluding them from this mapping of spatial capital across the country.

The value locations do or do not hold with audiences is one significant factor shaping spatial capital, but an additional map is necessary to consider the complexity behind the decisions made regarding where television shows "take place," as it were. I received a version of this second map while attending the 2014 Association of Film Commissions International (AFCI) Locations Show, a yearly event where producers and others in the industry gather in Los Angeles and browse booths from locations across the world to help decide where to shoot their latest projects.

Like Chapman's map, this updated version from 2020 features the United States, and it is also an attempt to depict the "home" of television and other media. However, this map—by production consulting company Cast and Crew Entertainment Services—charts the country through the lens of economic capital, outlining the various incentive programs in U.S. states and territories that are influential in determining where television is produced. It is a complex labyrinth of economic considerations, with rebates, grants, and tax credits all set at different values depending on how much productions spend, how much local labor is utilized, and what kind of project is being made. Cast and Crew has built a business out of helping productions interpret this map, even creating an interactive tool on their website to help productions identify the best location to shoot their series.

These two maps do not present competing views of spatial capital, but rather, overlapping ones. If the maps are laid over each other, it becomes clear how many of the states that lack meaningful television representation on Chapman's map also lack incentive programs that would encourage shows to be produced in those locations. And if one begins investigating where each of the shows on Chapman's map are produced, it becomes clear how many of them are not produced in the states where they are set. Rather, many are "off the map" entirely in Canada, which Cast and Crew covers in a different map outlining each province and territory's efforts to draw production north of the border. Although the empty states on Chapman's map already disrupt the idea that we can think of the entire United States as the home of television, adding Cast and Crew's map further reinforces how hierarchies of capital—whether cultural capital tied to particular cities or the intertwined political–economic forces that create media capitals—shape industry practice and serve as boundaries on spatial capital accordingly.

Together, the maps reveal the foundational interplay of spatial capital: where a media text is produced and where it is set are at the core of understanding how it relates to space and place. These basic lenses help us to understand the failure of spatial capital in *White Collar*'s Cape Verde. The choice to set the episode in Cape Verde came down to its lack of cultural capital: the writers needed a setting that does not have an extradition treaty with the United States, but which viewers would not immediately recognize so it could remain a mystery to be solved. However, they also needed a production location that was economically viable, with an incentive system that would allow them to justify the expense of leaving their New York production base. Thus, although the island territory of Puerto Rico may not have much Portuguese-inspired architecture, and may lack Creole extras, in 2012 it did have a transferable tax credit of 40% of total local expenditures, 40% of resident labor, and 20% of nonresident labor. All of this made it a popular production location for any series looking to send its characters somewhere warm and exotic on a budget. It also made Puerto Rico the production location for *White Collar*'s Cape Verde regardless of its inability to realistically stand in for that location.

However, these two maps only explain the initial problem of spatial capital presented to *White Collar*'s production team. For story reasons, they desired to set their episode in Cape Verde, but Cape Verde carries no media capital, in terms of either economic incentives or production crews who could facilitate a major television series; this meant finding another location with media capital where they could film to achieve the same effect of traveling to what they intended to frame as an exotic, mysterious location. But there were tools at the producers' disposal to overcome this discrepancy and laborers whose jobs are either explicitly built on the construction of spatial capital or positioned to activate spatial capital if allowed or directed to do so. The spatial capital of *White Collar*'s trip to Cape Verde was not determined by its production location but was instead contingent on a series of stakeholders throughout the production process who failed to invest in spatial capital to avoid this misrepresentation. That spatial capital is then subject to its reception and interpretation by critics and audiences: if you Google "White Collar Cape Verde," the first search result is a blog post I wrote in the early stages of researching what would become this book, with the hopes of better educating viewers on the show's failure.

In other words, no one map—or two maps or three maps—will succeed at capturing the complexity of television's spatial capital. To develop a framework for this book, then, it is integral to leverage existing understandings of how media and space interact while also confronting limitations to how we understand the relationship between production, textuality, and reception within media studies writ large and television studies in particular.

Mapping media studies

By positioning spatial capital as a framework of television scholarship, this project builds on existing research into how media engages with questions of space and place and the very nature of place itself. As noted, spatial capital fits into what Roger Aden defines as the study of cultural geography and "the role played by the physical terrain in our development of a sense of community and culture" (2007, 53). But within media studies research, the role of media within this process has been contentious: Joshua Meyrowitz (1986) argued that media technology would erase the meaning of space and place due to its transcending of geographic boundaries, while postmodern (Baudrillard 1994) and supermodern (Augé 2009) readings of media culture identify television and other media as engines of the hyperreal and generators of "non-places." By contrast, David Harvey believes that media's collapse of traditional geographic barriers makes us "more sensitized to what the world's spaces contain" (1991, 294), a sentiment echoed by Nick Couldry, who argues that media "shape and reorganize [territory], creating new distances . . . and building new presences, new places of significance" (2000, 26). It is these latter approaches that best capture the goal of analyzing television through the lens of spatial capital—doing so will reveal evidence of postmodern and supermodern spatiality, but the end result is not the obliteration of place's importance, but rather an evolving understanding of how television stakeholders value place under changing circumstances.

Such an approach requires expanding the frameworks for how we analyze space and place within the context of media. In her 2005 book *For Space*, Doreen Massey writes,

> To uproot "space" from that constellation of concepts in which it has so unquestionably been embedded (status; closure; representation) and to settle it among another set of ideas (heterogeneity; relationality; coevalness . . . liveness, indeed) where it releases a more challenging political landscape.
>
> (13)

Within media studies, this first set of embedded concepts has often been the default, with scholarship investigating how a given place—whether a country, a region, a city, etc.—has been represented within specific media texts. Although these questions are relevant, Henri Lefebvre (1992) has argued against applying literary codes to social space, and other scholars have developed further ways of thinking about media in relation to spatiality: Edward Soja (2011) has productively proposed thinking of the text as a map in and of itself, while Shaun Moores (2012) suggests media analysis "has been focused rather too tightly on the symbolic and interpretive," rather than what he understands as "place-constituting activities" happening within media (46). This terminology from Moores is echoed in Tim Cresswell's definition of place itself in which he argues place happens when humans engage in "place-making activities" that lead them to become attached to those spaces (2004, 5).

A spatial capital approach to studying media industries is designed to focus on these place-making activities. It treats spatial capital as a live entity, perpetually constructed and reconstructed at various stages within the process of a television series being produced and eventually released to audiences. Although there are points at which spatial capital will appear concrete, as in considerations of textual representations, I assert throughout this book that it is always under negotiation, and that what might appear as clearly situated within hierarchies of economic or cultural capital is in fact the result of complex dialogue between industry stakeholders.

In addition to Curtin's work referenced earlier, my approach extends a body of media studies scholarship that embraces the principles of spatial capital, albeit not by name (see Massood, Matos, and Wojcik 2021; McCarthy and Couldry 2004). This is particularly true in the rich area of research into media tourism (see Hills 2002; Jackson 2004; Aden 2007). Nick Couldry (2003) argues pilgrimages that audiences take to locations featured in media contribute to "the key structural hierarchy of the media's ritual space: the hierarchy of places 'in' the media over those which aren't" (80). But to fully understand these hierarchies, it is important to merge such research into how audiences engage place with the textual strategies that inspired that engagement and to what Vicki Mayer (2008) productively refers to as "the cultural geography of production" (see Tinic 2005; Mayer 2017; Morgan Parmett 2019). In Lefebvre's (1992) framework for understanding the production of space, he distinguishes between spatial practice (in television, the space of production), representations of space (the television text itself), and representational spaces (here, spaces of distribution and consumption) (29). Rather than focusing on one of these areas, I locate spatial capital within the collective, collaborative, and contingent labor—the place-making activity—that happens within these spaces. In this book, through a combination of interviews with industry professionals, textual analysis, considerations of trade discourse, and audience research, I reveal how spatial capital is pivotal to understanding the past, present, and future of not just television's relationship to space and place but central questions of production, distribution, and reception central to the television industry.

Indeed, while this approach can—and should—be applied to any media texts, spatial capital is particularly relevant to the study of contemporary television. The contributing factors to a text's spatial capital are the same across both film and television, but the latter is produced over longer periods of time, during which spatial capital remains in flux. Over the course of its life, a show can completely change production locations and settings not only just for a single episode like in the case of *White Collar*'s trip to Cape Verde via Puerto Rico, but it can do so for entire seasons: HBO's *The Leftovers* (2014–2017) filmed and set its first season in upstate New York, but moved its second season to Texas, before filming significant portions of its third season in Australia. The logics underpinning such decisions are embedded within both the history of television production, and—as this book will explore—sweeping changes in the television industry that are inherently linked to spatial capital as a value.

As I have completed work on this book, these changes have moved to the foreground of television studies. The era of "Peak TV" has dramatically expanded the scale of American television production, in terms of both the number of shows being produced and the number of studios, channels, and streaming services vying for audience attention with original programming. But it has also expanded the geography of American television: limited resources in traditional locations for television production push producers to new locales, increased competition drives more acquisition of foreign-produced content to compete in the ongoing "content arms race," and streaming platforms with international footprints create the incentive for American companies to invest in producing content in those foreign countries. This book considers spatial capital as both a cause and an effect of these processes, shaped by the labor practices and discursive formations of this shifting landscape of American television. By analyzing television's spatial capital, this book offers a specific insight into the shifting landscape of the television industry and the contingencies it creates for all forms of capital. Although inherently limited in terms of both geography (focusing primarily on North America) and medium, this analysis is intended to have broader implications for how we study television and all media industries, within and beyond questions of space and place.

Mapping spatial capital

This book is organized into five chapters, moving chronologically through the circuit of television production and distribution in order to consider how space and place inflect each stage of this process. Although each chapter makes a distinct contribution to the study of spatial capital, the book also continues to complicate its own findings, as the labor done within each stage of production is subsequently renegotiated as a television series moves through both time and space. The final chapter in particular reconsiders case studies from earlier in the book to consider how prior discussions of their spatial capital are changed when they are analyzed through a different lens. Each chapter draws on existing scholarly work within these areas, but I argue that a fundamental understanding of television's relationship with space and place requires placing these areas of investigation in conversation with one another.

In the first chapter, I begin this process by exploring the labor involved in the expansion of American television production beyond its traditional borders, with a specific focus on the work of location professionals and other below-the-line laborers in enabling what I identify as a culture of "mobile production." The reality of mobile production is that any given TV show could be produced in an increasingly large selection of viable production centers made possible by the work of said laborers. The chapter explores the complex factors of spatial capital—which go beyond economic incentives to the presence of diverse extras, availability of production facilities, and flashpoint political issues—considered by stakeholders involved in this decision-making, with a specific focus on how labor capital is critical to this process. The chapter then considers how the inherent mobility of this production climate creates instability for those laborers, whose employment is both dependent on and subject to changes in the spatial capital offered by a given location amid a period of rapid geographical change in the American television industry.

In the second chapter, I examine the strategies used by producers to generate spatial capital within a particular text, focusing on production and post-production strategies that leverage the production realities of the previous chapter alongside new technological advancements. As locations become easier to access and replicate, it becomes possible to represent a larger number of locations more easily, but the chapter explores the restrictions that remain on complex place identity despite the increased capacity for spatial capital within contemporary production practices. In other words, it may be possible to set a television show in more places, but that does not necessarily mean producers are increasing what I identify as the "burden of spatial capital" they choose to take on. By considering case studies ranging from backlot-bound to globe-trotting, the chapter contrasts the spatial capacity of television production with the actual manifestations of spatial capital created by these practices, a foundation for the subsequent chapters.

In the third chapter, I shift focus to how the accumulation of spatial capital is contingent on questions of distribution, an increasingly important area of media studies research. Specifically, the chapter considers how distinct textual strategies have emerged to adapt to transnational and global forms of distribution, within both the historical reality of co-productions and the new reality of "global" production for streaming platforms like Netflix. These strategies often work to elide or in some cases erase spatial capital, with the ultimate goal of maximizing the show's value for producers and distributors. By considering these texts as inherently built to serve these distribution environments, the chapter pushes back against claims that such shows exist as "placeless," instead arguing they represent careful negotiations of spatial capital that could theoretically be read as local in multiple contexts. As the space of distribution shifts, producers are increasingly expected to navigate the cross sections of spatial capital therein. This chapter focuses on understanding how this is being achieved and the consequences of those forms of spatial practice.

The fourth chapter, meanwhile, extends the consideration of spatial capital to hierarchies of cultural capital operating in discourse around the television industry. By analyzing the types of shows praised for their authentic relationship to space and place, often articulated by suggesting that their location is "a character in the show," the chapter reveals how spatial capital has become an often empty claim to prestige, rather than an inherent value attached to the spatial practice outlined in the previous chapters. The chapter assesses the contingencies on which this discourse hinges and explores how its relationship to so-called quality television works to reify specific types of spatial practice—deployed in limited contexts—over others. I consider which stakeholders in spatial capital are allowed to participate in this negotiation of spatial capital and how "place as character" came to serve as an aspirational claim within both industry and popular discourses of television culture.

The fifth and final chapter brings the book to its conclusion by revealing how television's spatial capital is being reshaped by the rise of social media, through which previously localized responses to representations of particular places in television programming are made available to a general audience. Although audiences have always played a critical role in evaluating how a series confronts its burden of spatial capital, social media has made the spatial practice outlined throughout this book more visible, increasing the burden on productions set in distinct locations and creating ramifications for how shows negotiate spatial capital from the point of conception. By exploring tweets collected using show hashtags and selected search terms from both new case studies and those examined in the book, this chapter explores how spatial capital's ultimate value within the circuit of television production must reckon within the dislocating nature of convergent viewing practices.

Location, relocation, dislocation

"Location, location, location" is a phrase most commonly associated with real estate, but I have adopted it—and adapted it—here in the interest of acknowledging what happens when we approach television through the lens of spatial capital. As the maps in this introduction demonstrate, this mantra in some cases describes an existing preponderance on place within television culture and television production culture, such that one does not need to stretch significantly to say that every television show contains some form of spatial capital and can thus benefit from being investigated through this lens.

However, as the case of *White Collar*'s Cape Verde and the range of case studies in the chapters that follow demonstrate, a television series' spatial capital is not a set value. Although "location, location, location" reads as an answer to what is important to television culture, such a response is a dramatic oversimplification. There are strategic formations with television production that shape spatial capital, which are in and of themselves constantly in flux as the television industry relocates. Moreover, as how we consume television evolves, spatial capital is dislocated from its original context. Throughout my time working on this project, I have seen shows move from one production location to another or completely adjust their approach to spatial capital based on shifts of cultural or economic capital happening behind-the-scenes or within popular discourse around the series. From the people who make television to the people who consume it, and in the discourse in between, where a television show takes place matters. This project exists to better understand how this reality is shaping our understanding of television, place, and the spatial capital that maps out their relationship to one another.

References

Aden, Roger. 2007. *Popular Stories and Promise Lands: Fan Cultures and Symbolic Pilgrimages*. Alabama: University of Alabama Press.

Augé, Marc. 2009. *Non-Places: An Introduction of Supermodernity*. London: Verso.

Baudrillard, Jean. 1994. "The Precession of Simulacra." In *Simulacra and Simulation*, translated by Sheila Faria Glaser, 1–42. Ann Arbor: University of Michigan Press.

Bourdieu, Pierre. 1984. *Distinction: A Social Critique of the Judgment of Taste*. London: Routledge.

Chapman, James. 2014. "Map of US TV Shows (A1) Updated 2014." *Etsy.com*. Accessed July 1, 2019. www.etsy.com/listing/125086059/map-of-us-tv-shows-a1-updated-2014?ref=shop_home_active_7.

Couldry, Nick. 2000. *The Place of Media Power: Pilgrims and Witnesses of the Media Age*. London: Routledge.

———. 2003. *Media Rituals*. London: Routledge.

Cresswell, Tim. 2004. *Place: A Short Introduction*. London: Wiley-Blackwell.

Curtin, Michael. 2003. "Media Capital: Towards the Study of Spatial Flows." *International Journal of Cultural Studies* 6.2: 202–28.

Harvey, David. 1991. *The Condition of Postmodernity: An Enquiry into the Origins of Cultural Change*. London: Wiley-Blackwell.

Hills, Matt. 2002. *Fan Cultures*. London: Routledge.

Jackson, Rhona. 2004. "Converging Cultures; Converging Gazes; Contextualizing Perspectives." In *The Media and the Tourist Imagination: Converging Cultures*, edited by David Crouch, Rhona Jackson, and Felix Thompson, 183–97. London: Routledge.

Lefebvre, Henri. 1992. *The Production of Space*. New York: Wiley-Blackwell.

Massey, Doreen. 2005. *For Space*. London: Sage Publications.

Massood, Paula J., Angel Daniel Matos, and Pamela Robertson Wojcik, eds. 2021. *Media Crossroads: Intersections of Space and Identity in Screen Cultures*. Durham: Duke University Press.

Mayer, Vicki. 2008. "Where Production Takes Place." *The Velvet Light Trap* 62: 71–72.

———. 2017. *Almost Hollywood, Nearly New Orleans: The Lure of the Local Film Economy*. Oakland: University of California Press.

McCarthy, Anna, and Nick Couldry, eds. 2004. *Mediaspace: Place, Space and Culture in a Media Age*. London: Routledge.

Meyrowitz, Joshua. 1986. *No Sense of Place: The Impact of Electronic Media on Social Behavior*. New York: Oxford University Press.

Moores, Shaun. 2012. *Media, Place and Mobility*. London: Palgrave Macmillan.

Morgan Parmett, Helen. 2019. *Down in Treme: Race, Place, and New Orleans on Television*. Stuttgart: Franz Steiner Verlag.

Soja, Edward W. 2011. *Postmodern Geographies: The Reassertion of Space in Critical Social Theory*. New York: Verso.

Tinic, Serra. 2005. *On Location: Canada's Television Industry in a Global Market*. Toronto: University of Toronto Press.

1 Spatial capital in the era of mobile production

Here, there, and everywhere

Why does a television series shoot in one location as opposed to another?

This chapter outlines a comprehensive understanding of the stakeholders within the process of deciding where a television series is produced, a decision that becomes the primary contingency on which a text's ability to generate spatial capital is determined. The ongoing, collaborative nature of television production creates a distinct production culture that maps onto shifting political and economic circumstances differently from film, necessitating a focused framework that pulls together multiple lines of inquiry and adapts to changing dynamics at local and national levels. Although the chapter will not argue against the thesis that production incentives are a significant factor in enabling a state or province to lay claim to media capital, and in convincing a production studio to make the commitment to produce a television series in that location, I am primarily interested in the cultural negotiations—and negotiators—that emerge from such decisions, which are at times obscured in scholarly, trade, and industry discourse. In other words, while hierarchies of economic capital may be the most visible and at times dominant reason why a television series films in one location rather than another, they cannot be separated from other dimensions of spatial capital being negotiated by the stakeholders involved.

In the spring of 2012, independent production company Gaumont International Television was in preproduction of *Hemlock Grove* (2013–2015), a supernatural drama series from producer Eli Roth that was set to debut on Netflix in 2013. The series is based on a novel by Brian McGreevy set in the fictional town of Hemlock Grove, Pennsylvania, with McGreevy serving as a producer on the adaptation, a role that gave him input into the decision of where the series would be filmed. Having grown up in Pennsylvania, and having set his novel there, McGreevy's goal was clear: speaking with *The Pittsburgh Post-Gazette*'s Rob Owen, McGreevy explained how

> in our first meeting [with] . . . Gaumont, they presented us with options for Vancouver and Pittsburgh, and I made a very long argument for why it had to be Pittsburgh. And it turned out I was completely wasting my breath. They said, "Cool, it's Pittsburgh. Moving on."
>
> ("Author. . . " 2012a)

DOI: 10.4324/9781003224693-2

On its surface, this seems logical: with a novel and series both set near Pittsburgh, shooting in the city is common sense.

However, the decision meant that *Hemlock Grove* would be the first television series to film in Pittsburgh since the introduction of Pennsylvania's film tax credit program in 2004. Although numerous feature films had filmed in and around Pittsburgh to take advantage of the incentives offered, *Hemlock Grove* signaled a major turning point in Pennsylvania's efforts to establish itself as an emergent media capital. As Pittsburgh Film Office director Dawn Keezer told the *Post-Gazette*, *Hemlock Grove*

> illustrates everything we've been working toward since the beginning of the film tax credit program. We've always wanted a series. Series mean long-term employment opportunities, and the icing on the cake for this one is it's written by a local Pittsburgher. He gets his first deal and brings it home. We're extremely grateful to Gaumont and Brian McGreevy.
>
> ("Author. . . " 2012a)

It was as close to a home run as you could imagine for the intersection of production studio, creator, and local film commission. Gaumont praised Keezer and the Pittsburgh Film Office, with head of production Andy House admitting, "I've always found big state and federal applications to be daunting to say the least and Dawn explained the process and held our hand to guide us through" (Owen "More. . . " 2012b). In the same article, Pennsylvania Department of Community and Economic Development press secretary Steven Kratz touted the importance of his government's role, pointing out, "It's safe to say without tools like the film tax credit, it would have been difficult to have a project like this." Meanwhile, after suggesting that "to film in Vancouver would not convey the notion of place as a character," McGreevy gets his wish of shooting a series in his hometown and maintaining the sense of place established in his novel. In the *Post-Gazette* coverage of the news, all parties were already looking forward to the show filming in Pittsburgh for multiple seasons, imagining the impact it could have on the city's local workers and its capacity to compete with other locations like Louisiana, Georgia, and North Carolina. A production office opened in late April, McGreevy and Roth were scheduled for a local reading from McGreevy's book in mid-May, and *Hemlock Grove* was set to help put Pittsburgh and Pennsylvania on the map as a prime location for television production.

There is just one small problem: *Hemlock Grove* never filmed in Pittsburgh. In mid-May, the production office was closed, the local reading was canceled, and Gaumont packed up production and moved to Toronto, Ontario ("Pittsburgh-set" 2012c). Keezer, the individual praised for walking Gaumont through the tax incentive system, wrote in a letter to the Pittsburgh Film Office board of directors that the change was the result of Gaumont simply not understanding how the Pennsylvania Film Tax Credit program worked—specifically, Gaumont did not realize that the transferable tax credits would not be available until each episode of the series was actually aired. This conflicted with Netflix's plan to hold all episodes until they could be released at once for binge viewing, thus delaying their ability to transfer the tax credits and recoup that portion of their investment. Although McGreevy had convinced Gaumont on the merits of Pittsburgh, it was at a time when the production company saw the state's incentives as comparable to those in cities like Toronto or Vancouver (where no such delays would exist); when their misunderstanding was revealed, McGreevy's argument no longer carried significant capital in their decision-making. McGreevy called the decision "heartbreaking" but told the *Post-Gazette* that "it just comes down to economics. There were complications that, frankly, I don't completely understand" ("Pittsburgh-set").

These economic complications have often been identified as the primary answer to the question of why a television series shoots in one location as opposed to another. In trade journal conversations about the rise of media capitals like Pittsburgh, incentive programs are the dominant narrative in how states like Louisiana or Georgia emerged as competitors to Los Angeles and New York, dating back to Vancouver's emergence in the early 1990s. In preparing to interview industry professionals regarding this project, I was forewarned by an executive that decisions of where to film a series "ultimately come down to money." At the 2014 Association of Film Commissioners International Locations show in Los Angeles, where film commissions from around the world gather to pitch themselves as a media capital, nearly every city, state, or country with a booth had their percentage incentive prominently displayed, and industry professionals speaking on organized panels knew those percentages to the point where accountants had detailed spreadsheets that could run comparisons between different locations at a moment's notice.

However, the case of *Hemlock Grove* reinforces that such decisions are not wholly economic in nature. The decision to film *Hemlock Grove* in Toronto may have been the result of economic considerations, and the decision not to film in Pittsburgh was the result of political confusion surrounding the state's film tax credit program. But critically, at stake in that decision was the cultural capital associated with a locally set series created by a "local boy" being filmed in the state of Pennsylvania. Moreover, the estimated 150 jobs provided by the production were a foundation for what the community hoped would become an established production culture sustained by multiple seasons of one-hour drama production, which Keezer characterizes as the "Holy Grail" of local film production ("Author. . . " 2012). Although these may be direct consequences of political–economic dimensions of the television industry's relationship with geography, there are cultural dimensions to this negotiation that reverberate throughout the production chain, from above-the-line creatives like McGreevy—whose goal of being true to his local roots was valued until it was financially infeasible—to below-the-line laborers who would make up the vast majority of the 150 local jobs lost in Pittsburgh (and the 150 jobs that were subsequently gained in Toronto, and in many cases likely maintained when Gaumont moved forward with second and third seasons of the series in 2013 and 2014).

This chapter outlines a comprehensive understanding of the stakeholders within the process of deciding where a television series is produced, a decision that becomes the primary contingency on which a text's ability to generate spatial capital is determined. The ongoing, collaborative nature of television production creates a distinct production culture that maps onto shifting political and economic circumstances differently from film, necessitating a focused framework that pulls together multiple lines of inquiry and adapts to changing dynamics at local and national levels. Although the chapter will not argue against the thesis that production incentives are a significant factor in enabling a state or province to lay claim to media capital, and in convincing a production studio to make the commitment to produce a television series in that location, I am primarily interested in the cultural negotiations—and negotiators—that emerge from such decisions, which are at times obscured in scholarly, trade, and industry discourse. In other words, while hierarchies of economic capital may be the most visible and at times dominant reason why a television series films in one location rather than another, they cannot be separated from other dimensions of spatial capital being negotiated by the stakeholders involved.

By applying this framework to a series of case studies not unlike that of *Hemlock Grove*'s aborted production in Pittsburgh, the chapter will outline how the U.S. television industry has become defined by what I have previously identified as a state of mobile production (McNutt 2015), a reality that has dramatically expanded the number of locations where television can be produced while simultaneously destabilizing productions and the workers employed by them. This reality has fundamentally transformed how we understand television's spatial capital. The basic question of where television is produced and the issue of who within the decision-making process does or does not carry agency over the spatial realities of producing television becomes a key concern in this complex landscape. Through a consideration of location professionals, this chapter outlines the labor crucial to negotiating spatial capital and the circumstances in which other forms of capital—economic or otherwise—outweigh their contributions and make their jobs inherently precarious in an ever-changing television landscape.

The spatial capital exchange

When exploring why television is produced in one location or another, my research brought me to the aforementioned 2014 AFCI Locations Show. Held in a Los Angeles-area hotel, the event draws attendees—who range from top-level industry executives to minor producers—looking for more information about where to film their next projects; they are presented with myriad options. In the registration area, large ads for the state of Illinois cover the sign-in desks, while Hawaii and Iceland sponsored a coffee and snack bar, respectively. The swag bags available at the registration desk are emblazoned with a logo for one state/province/country or another, while every attendee is carrying some form of paraphernalia that they have picked up from one of the dozens of booths scattered across two large rooms. The UK brought the Iron Throne from Northern Ireland-filmed *Game of Thrones* (HBO, 2011–2019), while Utah hired a caricaturist to help keep people at their booth for a longer period.[1] On industry panels, producers and executives spoke to attendees about broad shifts in the dynamics of where film and television series are produced, after which Q&A periods often devolved into representatives from different locations taking over the microphone to ask why there was not more discussion of the great local incentives offered by, for example, their own state of Massachusetts.[2]

Walking through the show floor as a researcher, I saw television's spatial capital come to life. The AFCI Locations Show is far from the only place where decisions are made regarding where a particular film or television series will film, given that the internet has made most of the information available in pamphlets or printed onto signage readily accessible without needing to travel halfway across the country or the world to be in attendance. However, the event offers a rare opportunity to see these stakeholders sharing one space, engaging in networking that forms the foundation for how these decisions are made. We could think of it as the Spatial Capital Exchange, a shared space for companies like Hilton Hotels, the studios that make decisions, the producers who work within those decisions, the state/ provincial film commissions that govern incentive programs, the smaller film commissions that help facilitate local production, and even specific locations like warehouses, universities (Yale and Penn State shared a table), and the Battleship Iowa, located on the Los Angeles waterfront.

This book primarily frames spatial capital as a value attached to a particular text, but activating that capital depends on it being accessible within a specific production location, which requires a range of resources that each of the localities at the AFCI Locations Show highlighted in their respective booths (see Figure 1.1). For some, attending the Locations Show is a long-standing ritual that reinforces the spatial capital available in their region and reaffirms their place in the conversation of where media is produced; for others like Canada's Northwest Territories or the Battleship Iowa, 2014 was the first time announcing their presence, hoping to get noticed by industry professionals and articulate the spatial capital available if one were to choose to produce media content—which would include films, television shows, commercials, music videos, and so on—there in the future.[3]

However, by the time the event concluded, I was no closer to a definitive or simple answer to my question regarding where television is filmed. Not unlike the floor of the New York Stock Exchange, there was almost too much information to interpret in order to get a clear read on the spatial

Figure 1.1 A poster in Panama's booth at the 2014 Location show photographed
           by the author, highlighting various locations that could be successfully
           "doubled" in the country. The small print at the bottom reads "Just in
           case, all this (sic) pictures are Panama."

Photo by author.

capital being exchanged on the show floor. Was the absence of major players
like Georgia and Puerto Rico a simple concern regarding the budget necessary to attend the event or a broader sign of the Location Show's irrelevance
to certain groups in an era of easy online communication? Although individual cities and communities within Louisiana chose to attend, the absence
of the overarching Louisiana Film Commission meant those communities
were scattered throughout the exhibition areas, whereas the Texas and
North Carolina Film Commissions were in attendance and brought each
of the local groups together in one larger booth space. During the formal

presentations, representatives from Film Commissions spoke out against claims by producers that it was their job to make production cheaper, arguing that their responsibility to taxpayers outweighed the ease with which studios were able to save money—this drew applause from the crowd. Every corner was a moment of negotiation, with different representatives of various stages of production converging to engage with how location would influence the film or television show they were about to make. It was a reminder that even in a space where at times abstract negotiation of spatial capital was made readily visible, the process was not necessarily made more comprehensible as competing forces jockeyed for their place within the hierarchies of the media industries.

Understanding the spatial economy of television production

The one narrative regarding patterns of television production that was evident in this experience was that the historic answer to the question of where television is produced—Los Angeles—has fundamentally changed. I did not need to be at the AFCI Locations show to know this: researchers and journalists have spent the past two decades outlining the problem of "runaway production," in which film and television productions that would historically have been shot in Hollywood began traveling. The process has its origins in early moves to cities like New York and Chicago (Hall 1998), but the term gained traction as production began crossing the border to Canada (Gasher 2002; Tinic 2005), and later to states like Louisiana (Mayer 2017).

Runaway production was facilitated by both push and pull factors. The dissolution of the studio system has been identified as one driving force for expanding location shooting outside of Hollywood (Elmer and Gasher 2005). Other scholars have explored how a globalized media landscape and the mobility of both capital and production push the industry in search of the most advantageous spaces in which to complete their business (Miller et al. 2005; Hozic 2001). However, runaway production has been historically framed through its pull factors, as spaces outside of Los Angeles spend resources and create public policy designed to incentivize productions to leave the stability of Hollywood for their own localities. Such research follows the political–economic tradition, examining how runaway production is altering both the macro-level economy of the creative industries and the economies of the cities, regions, or countries in question (see Scott 2004, 2005; Christopherson and Clark 2007; Miller and Abdulkadri 2009; Liu et al. 2010; Connaughton and Madsen 2011; Hurt 2014).

Runaway production is destabilizing in two key ways. The first is that it threatens—without dismantling—the primacy of Hollywood within global media culture, particularly in the space of television. Runaway production affected film more so than television initially, with the relative stability of television production helping the local industry offset losses on the film side. But in 2012, only two of that year's 23 hour-long drama projects chose to film in Los Angeles, choosing instead to shoot in one of the many cities that had incentives on a scale not offered by the state of California at the time (Verrier 2012). This macro-level adjustment of spatial capital is a reordering of the map of television production. Each year, industry trade journals like *The Hollywood Reporter* and *Deadline* take an accounting of where pilots and series are being produced to explore the contours of an industry that has seemingly run a far distance from its origins bound to Hollywood backlots.

However, the primary destabilizing of runaway production comes in its impact on television labor. *The Los Angeles Times'* report on the 2012 "crisis" is full of stories from Los Angeles-based workers who can't find employment, forced to move to other states or pursue other industries based on the decrease in television production (Verrier). Kevin Sanson (2014) notes that media workers "exist in the midst of friction" between location and labor (57), with media workers subject to what has been described as "class warfare" (Curtin and Vanderhoef 2015) that forces workers into more temporary work environments and extends the burden of globalized labor to the individual laborers (Mayer 2011). The inherent contingency of labor (Ross 2010) in this environment is expanded by the inherent precarity of the primarily economic capital involved in the "pull" factors that drove runaway production in the first place: shifts in exchange rates can make shooting in Canada less advantageous, while some incentive programs have finite resources.

This reality reveals what I have argued elsewhere (McNutt 2015) represents the fundamental limitation of the term "runaway production" as it pertains to the contemporary landscape of U.S. television production. If we take the example of *Hemlock Grove*, Gaumont International never "ran away" from Los Angeles; they never considered shooting the series in Hollywood, always imagining it in one of the emerging production centers that Goldsmith, Ward, and O'Regan (2011) think of as "local Hollywoods" in their case study of Australia's Gold Coast. In the hopes of luring television productions, cities like Pittsburgh invested in infrastructure to mirror that of Los Angeles, building soundstages and training programs to create what Goldsmith, Ward, and O'Regan term "location interest," which become critical foundations for productions to be able to access spatial capital. As a result, rather than being pushed or pulled away from the stability of southern California, television series now enter a competitive location marketplace where any given television production could theoretically shoot in any given location depending on the financial, logistical, and geographical considerations involved. I therefore frame this environment not as "runaway production," but rather as "mobile production," as there is never a time when a production is inherently anchored in Los Angeles during the decision-making process. Doing so shifts away from a Hollywood-centric term that describes an industry perception, rather than lived reality, of contemporary television production practices.

Spatial capital in an era of mobile production: stakeholders

To understand the realities of mobile production, it is critical to understand the stakeholders who take an active role in negotiating and generating the spatial capital inherent to the process of television production. Like "runaway production," mobile production is defined by push and pull factors, but they are moving in a multitude of directions, and the stakeholders involved often approach these issues from cross-purposes in what John Caldwell has identified as "the borderlands of production culture" (2003, 164). In considering these stakeholders more carefully, we reveal the sheer multitude of points of negotiation for spatial capital within the geography of television production, ultimately leading us to a consideration of the price of the mobility achieved therein.

Politicians: Although it is an oversimplification to say that mobile production is an inherently political phenomenon, there is no question that it is built on a foundation of incentive programs established at local, state/provincial, and federal levels. For a location to be seen as financially competitive with the established media environment of Los Angeles, financial incentives—in the form of tax credits, tax rebates, and a range of other local- and state-level considerations—are considered a necessity for a state or province to establish enough economic capital to serve as a base for media production in general and ongoing television production in particular. Such programs therefore require political support, introduced by state or local legislators and then signed into law by governors or premiers.

That process involves other stakeholders convincing politicians that providing incentives for production will serve the interests of the state or province: while some of this results in economic capital contributed by the productions to the local economy, there is also the hope that if a text generates enough spatial capital, it will result in cultural capital being gained by the location, potentially drawing further economic revenue through tourism. For a state like Georgia, which offers one of the most lucrative incentive programs, politicians in support of the incentives could point to the tourism industry surrounding AMC's *The Walking Dead* (2011–present) as a productive return on investment, as the series' success has spawned economic spin-offs that bring visitors and attention to the locations where the show was filmed (Martin 2013). The hope of achieving this type of spatial capital was undoubtedly part of the decision-making for the state of Virginia when it provided production incentives to AMC for a spin-off of the show in 2019 (Owen 2019). Georgia believes in the potential benefits of spatial capital so much that as of 2021, it offers productions an additional 10% tax credit solely for including the state's iconic peach logo at the end of each episode of a television series or the credits of a feature film.

However, the capital benefit of these productions—whether in terms of their economic spin-offs or their cultural influence—is a contentious issue, and there are no guarantees of continued political support for incentives as elections or economic conditions change the balance of power or priorities within a given legislative body. If support disappears, incentive programs can be either reduced dramatically or removed entirely, at which point the infrastructure involved could evaporate. During negotiations to renew the state of Oklahoma's incentive program in March 2014, *The Hollywood Reporter* noted that those who supported the legislation argued it "brings the state revenue, taxes, and attention, and it is a boost to tourism," while the bill's detractors criticized the program for supporting films like *August: Osage County* that "portrayed the state in a negative light" (Block 2014). The process reinforced that the spatial capital generated by drawing productions to a given location may not necessarily be in line with the goals of the political stakeholders involved.

Politicians can also undermine a jurisdiction's capacity for spatial capital through policies unrelated to media production in the state. In Georgia, state legislators have thrice run into controversy with bills that drew significant criticism from the film and television industries: first in 2016 with the "Free Exercise Protection Act" designed to allow faith-based organizations and businesses to deny services to same-sex couples and other LGBTQ individuals, then in 2019 with the so-called Heartbeat Bill that banned abortion after roughly six weeks, and again in 2021 with a voting law deployed in the wake of false claims of voting fraud in the 2020 election. In the case of the Free Exercise Protection Act, Hollywood pressure led to former Governor Nathan Deal vetoing the bill (O'Neil 2016), but the latter two bills were allowed to move forward, with the majority of major studios criticizing the bills but resisting an outright boycott in the hopes that a court challenge would strike down the bills without forcing them to choose between the state's generous incentive program and taking an ethical and moral stance (Lee 2019). In 2019, at least, this gambit worked, as the "Heartbeat Bill" was ruled unconstitutional in July 2020. In these cases, the accruement of spatial capital is threatened not by a shift in the viability of incentive programs among state legislators, but rather tension between the political goals of those legislators and the necessary image management for the major studios taking advantage of those programs.

Production studios and networks: These moments of political tension between legislators and industry are not always surrounding ethical concerns. Studios and networks may be forced to take a public stance within conflicts that threaten their business interests, but they also take a more private role as lobbyists encouraging states to continue or expand incentive programs. The production studios who produce television content, and networks or channels who will eventually distribute that content, have specific financial baselines that they are expected to meet. Although there are various points within the production process—licensing fees, streaming rights, syndication sales—where production studios and networks negotiate to profit off a given television series, the cost of production is one space where they are in a position to control costs, particularly in an era of mobile production that enables choice between a wide range of locations based on the available incentives. The result is an incredible amount of leverage for these production studios and their affiliated networks. If states are unwilling to give them the desired incentives to continue production, that production can in most cases relocate to another location with a similar incentive program, taking with it the jobs and economic spin-offs on which the program is predicated.

Accordingly, there have been situations where studios have successfully lobbied for states to adjust their incentive programs in order to accommodate them. This is particularly true for capped incentive systems where only a limited amount of funds can be distributed through incentives to film and television productions in a given year. In 2014, both Netflix's *House of Cards* (2013–2018) and ABC's *Nashville* (2012–2018) challenged the states of Maryland and Tennessee, respectively, with their production studios threatening to move production elsewhere if incentives were not expanded beyond the scope of existing legislation. In Maryland, lobbying from *House of Cards* producer Media Rights Capital led the state to expand its available incentives from $4 million to $11.5 million (Johnson 2014a), while a combined consortium of the state of Tennessee, the city of Nashville, the Nashville Convention and Visitors Corporation, and Grand Ole Opry-owner Ryman Hospitality Properties were able to offer *Nashville* $8 million in incentives for its third season (Rau 2014). In both cases, political negotiations led to incentive packages below what the productions had received in previous seasons (and likely below the ideal level for the studios involved), but they were still able to force the states to expand their financial commitments based on the argument that the spin-offs from the shows' spatial capital would justify the costs involved.[4]

Although the expansion of television production outside of Hollywood through mobile production makes the threat of moving a television series easier for a production studio, the logistics of moving productions are still significant: while some key crew members may move along with a given series, and elements of certain sets could be moved to a new location, there is still an inherent disruption to the production culture of a television series if forced to move across borders in search of incentives. As a result, production studios approach the political dimensions underpinning the negotiation of spatial capital with a priority of leveraging their current location to offer them the incentives they desire, crossing the bridge of becoming mobile only if absolutely necessary or financially lucrative enough to justify the disruption.

Film commissioners and film offices: If productions are forced to move, they will be working closely with a critical intermediary within the negotiation of spatial capital. Although large-scale negotiations directly connect studios with figures like state governors or city mayors, typically studios interact directly with film commissioners from local- and state-level film offices. In New Mexico, for example, the New Mexico Film Office functions as a division of the state's economic development department, and according to their "About Us" page (n.d.) it is responsible for a range of tasks including "consult[ing] with productions regarding the financial aspects of their projects, guiding them through the incentives," along with "connect[ing] productions with the crew, vendor services and film liaisons throughout the state." Productions shooting in New Mexico will also likely have a relationship with a municipal film office, like the Albuquerque Film Office, which similarly works to walk studios through the city-level incentive programs while also facilitating production in other ways. In 2014, the Albuquerque Film Office won a Location Managers Guild of America award for Outstanding Film Commission, cited during the award ceremony for their ability—among other tasks—to get AMC's *Breaking Bad* (2008–2013) the proper permissions to film in crowded downtown locations in the city. As evidenced in the example of *Hemlock Grove*, these city film offices are often the direct points of contact for a production on a daily basis and are particularly important given that each state or province—or even city—has different procedures that would be difficult to navigate without assistance.

Foster, Manning, and Terkla (2015) identify local film offices as a key intermediary within emerging "production clusters," identifying their ability to "connect mobile creative professionals and boundary-crossing creative production networks to particular local settings and resources" (434). Local film offices are also crucial points of contact for the accountants and lawyers at a studio level who are crunching the numbers of the various complex incentive programs, which—as seen with *Hemlock Grove*—can create considerable confusion. As decisions are made at a studio level, film commissioners and film offices are called on to explain their systems while also selling the benefits of their location in a process not dissimilar to the sales pitch evident at the AFCI Locations Show. Mobile production would ultimately not be possible if not for the film commissions and film offices that facilitate such mobility.

Above-the-line laborers: Film commissioners and film offices are also intermediaries in the sense that they are simultaneously serving the production studios who are trying to balance their books and the creative laborers who are trying to generate spatial capital as part of their creative vision. In the case of *Hemlock Grove*, creator Brian McGreevy's ties to Pittsburgh were a crucial part of the film commission's messaging and were taken into consideration by Gaumont early in the process. Although financial considerations eventually outweighed the creative value of shooting in the state where the series itself was set, the creative needs of the production were nonetheless central to these negotiations of spatial capital. A series set in a large city requires certain types of locations that some cities would not be able to offer, while a series focused on rural areas has a similarly limited selection of production centers that will serve its needs. In this sense, while the wishes of above-the-line laborers like creators or showrunners may not often override broader financial concerns at the studio level, the content of a script will dictate what locations will be considered and therefore give the creator or showrunner some degree of authority over issues of spatial capital.

In some cases, the creative goals of a series could outrank financial considerations and foreground spatial capital, while in others, showrunners may be forced to compromise due to other contingencies. Both AMC's *Breaking Bad* and HBO's *True Detective* (2014–present), two series often lauded for their strong engagement with place and which will be discussed further in the fourth chapter, were both originally conceived in different locations, resetting the series to New Mexico and Louisiana, respectively, in order to take advantage of production incentives. Furthermore, as production continues to expand to locations beyond Los Angeles, the ability for writers to be hands-on with production becomes more challenging: as writer's rooms typically remain on studio lots in Los Angeles regardless of where a series is produced, they must rely on Skype for production meetings and rotate "on set" writers to ensure a presence should any rewriting or adjustments need to be done. If the writer's room is running during ongoing production, it becomes impossible for the showrunner to be in both places at once, requiring greater delegation to other executive producers. Moreover, this also requires greater confidence in the local labor whose work is under less intense supervision by those whose vision is being executed.

However, the primary force within considerations of where a television program is filmed in terms of above-the-line labor is in fact actors. *The X-Files* (Fox, 1993–2002, 2016–2018), one of the early success stories of so-called runaway production in television based out of Vancouver, British Columbia, famously moved production to Los Angeles for its sixth season after actor David Duchovny pushed to leave Vancouver. As he told the *Vancouver Sun*,

> However lovely this city is, and however wonderful the people have been, and however talented the crew that works here, and however perfect the city is for *The X-Files*, that hasn't really figured into the personal dislocation that I've felt.
>
> (Strachan 1998).

This personal dislocation also appeared to be behind the decision for *The Good Wife* (CBS, 2009–2016) to film in New York, rather than Chicago where the series is set: while Illinois has a solid incentive system and a strong local production crew, star Julianna Margulies—also a producer on the series—wanted to remain based out of New York, where she lived full-time (Parsi 2012), a decision that also served co-stars Alan Cumming and Chris Noth, who continued to balance work on the series with theater roles on and off Broadway.

Not all actors have the same ability to fight against this personal dislocation: in the case of an ensemble drama like ABC's *Mistresses* (2013–2016),

Alyssa Milano's choice not to follow the production to Vancouver from Los Angeles resulted in her departure from the series (Goldberg 2014), and *Supergirl's* (2015–2021) similar move in 2016 led to co-star Calista Flockhart shifting to a recurring role due to not being willing to commute to British Columbia (Brown 2016). In these cases, the financial considerations of the moves outweighed the concerns of members of the ensemble—most actors are required to move to find work, while other above-the-line crew like directors are required to dislocate themselves to follow different productions to the wider range of cities drawing television production. When I asked one TV director how shifts in the geography of television production had impacted his career, he indicated that it had likely destroyed his marriage as it forced him to be away from his family given that it was no longer feasible to stay in one location and make a living on episodic television. Although some above-the-line workers are in a position to have a direct impact on spatial capital, others are subject to the decisions of those at a higher pay grade, forced to make their labor mobile to continue working in television.

Below-the-line laborers and production facilities: Spatial capital places significant importance on the collection of below-the-line workers in a given location, as the strength of a labor pool is critical to the ability of that location to position themselves relative to spatial capital and draw mobile television productions. Given that many incentive structures offer a higher percentage rebate if local labor is used in the production, the quality and quantity of those laborers are crucial to any effort to take full advantage of a state or province's incentive system. While actors like Margulies and Duchovony hold individual power over spatial capital, a production would likely never make a decision based on the needs of an individual below-the-line laborer—as Vicki Mayer (2011) has detailed, below-the-line work in television production is historically marginalized, making it challenging for any one laborer to articulate their importance to the production. However, taken collectively, below-the-line labor is an integral part of how television confronts spatial capital, even if their individual agency may remain limited.

Television production in particular relies on a strong "crew base," a term typically used to describe a city, state, or region's labor pool—locations are often ranked based on how many "crews deep" they are, which refers to how many simultaneous projects can be in production at a given moment. At the 2014 AFCI Locations show, a producer spoke of being pushed by a network to shoot a television series in Shreveport, Louisiana, as opposed to Atlanta, Georgia, for the state's more lucrative tax incentives but then being forced to fly in crew from Georgia when the Louisiana crew base was not deep enough to support the project due to multiple other projects draining the labor pool. Such considerations were also central to the decision to move production of Syfy series *12 Monkeys* (2015–2018) from Detroit—where it shot and set its pilot—to Toronto: producers present at the 2015 Television Critics Association (TCA) press tour said they were willing to pay slightly more to shoot in Detroit, where Michigan's capped incentive pool would likely offer less money than Ontario's production incentives. However, the presence of Zack Snyder's *Batman v Superman: Dawn of Justice* (2016) in the city meant that there was not enough experienced local crew available during the window they needed to shoot the series.

Decisions like this one may on the surface appear to be financial, based solely on the incentive system. Yet, the labor pool becomes a crucial variable for balancing the different financial models with the logistics of actually producing a television series within that environment. Crew base therefore functions similarly to other forms of production infrastructure, such as sound stages or equipment rentals, which take time to establish but offer long-term value for supporting ongoing production. Consequently, as states, provinces, and countries seek to lure television producers to their locations, part of their goal is replicating the infrastructure available in Los Angeles. The plethora of sound stages located in Los Angeles is one reason why television production has remained comparatively stable in California compared with film production. More recently, however, states such as Georgia (where UK studio Pinewood invested in its first American facility) and New Mexico (where an additional tax incentive is offered to those filming on one of the state's sound stages) have consciously expanded their studio capacities as part of an effort to replicate Hollywood infrastructure. While any one single below-the-line laborer may not be critical to generating spatial capital, the existence of a significant crew base and a production infrastructure in which they can operate is critical to the stability of mobile production and the assurance that any given location could achieve the desired spatial capital.

Consequences of mobile production practices

This close accounting of the stakeholders of mobile production clarifies that the negotiation of spatial capital is, like television production as a whole, dependent on a collaborative process. Although the content of a series may set the initial terms of where a television show might be filmed, the decision-making process must account for all stages of the production process; depending on context, different stakeholders may carry more or less capital in any given example. Some projects may be dictated by economic capital, whereas in other cases labor capital becomes a deciding factor, and it's even possible that cultural capital—whether carried by an actor involved in a project or the perceived value of shooting in a particular location— could outweigh other concerns. By following projects from conception to production, we can see how the ongoing negotiation of these factors can have a tangible impact on a series' engagement with spatial capital.

Fox's short-lived *Red Band Society* (2014–2015) serves as a productive starting point to explore these impacts. The series, which is set at a Los Angeles children's hospital, chose to film in Atlanta, Georgia, to take advantage of the state's incentive system, but it remains set in Los Angeles as

Margaret Nagle's initial script had established—she based it on a UCLA hospital, and her research was based out of southern California, and so the show chose to engage in what is known as "city-for-city doubling" to make Atlanta into Los Angeles. It is a process that is inherent to the realities of mobile production: while Atlanta has emerged as a significant production center, the writers generating these stories remain based out of Los Angeles, and of the American broadcast networks only The CW has actually set shows being produced in Atlanta in the state of Georgia. Every other broadcast series shot in Atlanta has used the city to stand in for other cities like, in this case, Los Angeles. In this way, creative concerns drive the negotiation of spatial capital in the process of city-for-city doubling, with the cultural capital of the show's Los Angeles setting forced to co-exist with the economic capital of shooting in Atlanta.

However, this co-existence required changes to the pilot script as it was originally written (and as it was distributed on agency servers after being ordered to pilot). The first change was purely cosmetic but demonstrates the loss of specificity when not being able to access the actual location. Whereas three patients who break out on a joy ride originally traveled to Los Angeles staple In-N-Out Burger in Nagle's original script, they travel to a generic convenience store in the final version of the pilot, as there are no In-N-Out restaurants in Atlanta. From a production perspective, the loss of specificity was a necessary concession to take advantage of the incentive system, and it ultimately did little to change the storyline or the character development for those involved. Such small changes are necessary when a series is produced somewhere other than where it is set, which also goes for any series produced in Los Angeles, but which is set elsewhere. This demonstrates how accepting city-for-city doubling means losing access to the kinds of markers of authenticity that writers use to activate spatial capital in their scripts, which I will discuss further in the next chapter.

The second change is more substantial, though, and reveals the material impacts of mobile production on storytelling. In the original version of the script, the pilot episode opens with the character Jordi traveling across the Mexico–U.S. border with his cousin, Alex. Born in Los Angeles, Jordi had been sent to Mexico to stay with his cousins following his mother's death and was traveling across the border with a degree of risk in order to gain access to a medical specialist. Although the backstory is discussed in later scenes, the border sequence marks his cross-border journey and articulates his Latino background directly, emphasizing both the series' setting near the Mexico–U.S. border and the cultural dynamics of a multiracial part of the country. The choice to begin the show with a scene that contributes so much spatial capital—the landscape, the racial diversity—to the series shows a clear investment in location and in the way its characters are an outgrowth of that reality.

However, the scene is missing from the final version of the pilot: Jordi is seen in the truck with Alex outside the hospital, but there is no dialogue, and the episode only later—through dialogue—reveals the story of how he made the journey to Ocean Park Hospital. The pilot instead begins with the character of Kara, a white cheerleader, in a nondescript school gymnasium that carries no spatial capital and could be taking place in any location. When I first saw the pilot, I noticed the discrepancy, which is not unexpected: through issues of running time, test screenings, and network notes, pilots often change significantly during production, and I could imagine that the network thought that the show would connect better with an average viewer by opening on a white character as opposed to a border crossing. However, when I spoke with series creator Margaret Nagle about the pilot (2014), I learned that the scene with Jordi and Alex was not cut based on a network note or a test screening; instead, before shooting even started, Nagle and the producers were informed by local production crew in Atlanta that there was not a single feasible shooting location in or near Atlanta where they could have shot the border crossing. The choice to film in Atlanta would impact the production in many ways, limiting the pool of actors compared to a larger market and making it more challenging to garner on-set press coverage. The loss of this scene is a case where the creative goals of the script were fundamentally incompatible with the reality of producing the series in the location in question. As a result, the character's Latino identity is less central to the finished pilot, as the series' negotiation of spatial capital and embrace of mobile production made it more challenging—albeit not impossible—for the series to focus on this component of his character in subsequent episodes. The choice to use city-for-city doubling came with unintended consequences for the series' representation of its characters, a fact only made clear when the locations team became involved.

In this way, then, we see the key role of local below-the-line laborers in negotiating spatial capital. Although eventually writers, directors, and editors will make the final decisions regarding what we see onscreen, local labor like the location professionals who made the call on the impossibility of finding a location to double for the Mexico–U.S. border are crucial to keep production moving smoothly. They may not be the most powerful stakeholders of spatial capital, but location professionals in particular have the strongest connection to that spatial capital in terms of their labor, making them a critical point of negotiation with respect to how television manages that spatial capital during production. A close detailing of their labor demonstrates the symbiosis between location professionals and the culture of mobile production, which makes them both extremely valuable to and extremely vulnerable within the television economy.

Location professionals and spatial capital

Although those who work in locations for a production can be broadly termed as location professionals, the location scout and the location manager are the two primary roles that a location professional will be expected to perform over the course of their career. The location scout, according to one location professional I interviewed in 2014, is "a person whose basic job is to go out and look to find certain locations"; another adds "the scout finds where you film, or they find the options for the director to pick where they film." This second description captures the way the location scout functions within the process of preproduction, whereas the location manager then takes over by securing the use of a particular location (which may involve negotiating with a homeowner or getting the necessary permits from a local government), ensuring the required resources are in place to film in that location, and then supervising the restoration of that location once filming is complete. One location professional referred to location managers as "the face of the production," as they are responsible for ensuring a smooth relationship with the people in and around a particular location, which is crucial for the production to operate on schedule.

When it comes to the production itself, the location manager has been described as "first one in, last one out," a process that needs to carry over to each location that a production would use in a given week or even a given day. The location manager therefore must balance both space and time: as location manager Rebecca Puck Stair—who is based in New Mexico— notes, "it's a rolling thing, because the location manager is prepping one location while shooting in the second while cleaning up the one they shot in yesterday. You have to be able to think fluidly in time" (2014, Personal Interview). They are, in other words, the key manager of spatial capital on a practical day-to-day basis within the production of a television series.

Stair has worked as a location professional on a range of film and television productions based in New Mexico, entering the industry after switching careers from English teacher to production assistant during the early days of the state's incentive system, eventually transitioning into locations work. In order to complete this work, Stair has over the past 15 years developed an intense knowledge of the state of New Mexico that she is able to draw on when a production is looking for a location for a particular scene. Comparing location professionals to taxi drivers, Stair claims, "I pretty much know the entire state and if you show me a picture I will tell you where it is, anywhere in that state." This is a necessary skill to be able to find locations on the short time frames offered by productions and to ensure that those locations work logistically for the production in question. She explains that "there's some part of the location scout's brain that's always on that's off for most people most of the time, because we'll remember [locations we drive by] and exactly what it looks like, and where it was." Although she officially scouts certain locations, taking photos and building a library, she also relies on these mental pictures—and on technology like Google Streetview—to tap into her personal map of New Mexico and offer directors or producers a sense of her plan for a particular scene.

Given this self-representation, we can understand Stair's role as a location professional as being explicitly tied to the local geography and thus to the negotiation of spatial capital. Although the skills she uses apply to most location professionals around the world—and are skills she could apply in a range of different states—it takes a considerable amount of time to gain the knowledge necessary to quickly and easily find a location that could serve a particular scene or double as a different location entirely. Stair presents herself as being able to complete this work quickly based not on a unique set of skills among all location professionals, but on the locality of those skills within New Mexico, gained through personal experience scouting and managing locations in the state.

The emergence of workers like Stair has been crucial to allowing locations like New Mexico to benefit from the increased mobility of television production, as their labor replicates established location-based production cultures present in Los Angeles. Michael Meehan, a location professional who began his career working in television in Los Angeles before branching out into global film production, describes working in Los Angeles in the mid-1980s as a "plug-and-play" environment (2014). He explains that he would "run around to try to find a mansion and knock on the door and [hear] 'there's my agent's number.' Aw jeez—[I] might as well have just looked through the books." Meehan is referring to books filled with potential locations, which he notes many location professionals contributed to and contain "the usual suspects: where do you find this, where do you find that, who owns this, all that kind of stuff. That used to be the calling card of Los Angeles." A producer for *Brooklyn Nine-Nine* (Fox/NBC, 2013–2021) referred to location professionals as "unsung heroes" when I asked about their work shooting Los Angeles for New York, as their knowledge of the city gave them quick and efficient access to locations in downtown Los Angeles, which successfully stood in for Brooklyn when they needed something beyond the scale available on a backlot.

Meehan, reflecting on the rise in production outside of Los Angeles, observes "that's what [other cities] would do too—just show and tell. Where can you shoot New York? Where can you shoot the usual suspects there?" Stair's self-representation confirms this: while discussing her ability to serve as a local expert, she explicitly offers that "I can quite quickly think of doubles," and discusses the distinct challenges between "landscape for landscape doubling"—which would be common on a New Mexico-filmed series like A&E's *Longmire* (2012–2017), which was set in Montana—and "city-for-city doubling." She argues that the former is more challenging

> because we tend to hold the camera wider and be closer to 360 degrees if we can. It's easier to cheat an urbanscape with an interior or a city block—you need fewer degrees of sellability to make it work.

That Stair frames her work in the terms of doubling indicates the degree to which her knowledge has been constituted not simply in terms of places in New Mexico that would be ideal for shooting—she also translates those locations into practical terms expected by producers. These are also terms that emulate the type of institutional knowledge that has existed in Los Angeles for decades. She explicitly understands her labor capital in the terms of spatial capital and the specific negotiation of spatial capital necessitated by mobile production.

However, this knowledge takes time to generate and is not as easily acquired by a production as other forms of television labor. In a state with a nascent incentive system and the lack of an established crew base, a production has the option of bringing in more experienced crew from a neighboring state or from Los Angeles—it costs more money and may not hold the same production benefits depending on the state's incentive system, but those crew members are guaranteed to be familiar with the equipment and the process of making a television series. However, if little-to-no major production has been done in a particular state, there may be no location professionals who have exhaustively scouted that state to be in a position to facilitate a production expecting to double that state for another or to manage locations efficiently. That labor takes time to develop. Moreover, it requires professionals like Stair who enter the film industry as incentives create demand for local labor, latch onto locations as their area of focus, and then gain the local experience necessary to generate the same base of knowledge that exists in established media capitals like Los Angeles. In the case of the UK, where TV production was expanding rapidly in 2014 due to new tax incentives, the Production Guild of Great Britain even created an extensive training program specifically for location managers: as chief executive Alison Small explained, "Location teams pave the way for well-managed and smooth productions and play a key role in ensuring the UK film and television production sector maintains its competitive edge and excellent delivery" (Banks 2014).

In the absence of this labor, other stakeholders outlined earlier in this chapter are at times forced to step in. For instance, at the 2014 Location Managers Guild Awards, long-time Film Commissioner Sheri Davis was lauded for her years of service as part of the Ontario County Film Commission in California, and a producer told a story about sending her out into the field to take photos decades earlier, instructing her on the procedures expected from a location scout. While film offices will often offer some pre-scouted locations as part of their services, in other cases workers outside of the formal film industry can step into roles traditionally held by location professionals. A tourism bureau employee working in Louisiana when that state's incentive system was first introduced relayed her experience getting phone calls from producers asking for photos, requiring her to drive some distance to capture images of a particular home in her area. In these cases, professionals with different or indirect ties to the film and television industry have the type of local knowledge that is valuable to spatial capital and are at times asked to use this knowledge to play an informal role in the production process. This is further reinforced by the tourism bureau's presence at the

AFCI's locations show, with the employee's role having evolved to include facilitating filming that takes place in that area in a role supplemental to formal location professionals and film offices in the region. Location professionals are important enough to spatial capital that, in their absence, other local stakeholders are forced to perform the same labor, as opposed to outside workers being able to simply step into a new state and fill their shoes.

Whether through formal or informal laborers, locations work is the below-the-line labor category most distinctly tied to spatial capital. Although other below-the-line workers have a strong tie to local communities, such as casting directors with intense knowledge of local talent or production designers with strong relationships with local vendors, location professionals are responsible for directly negotiating a series' engagement with the location where it is produced, and therefore are the central force driving its negotiation of spatial capital during the initial stages of production. And while this is technically true for both film and television production, Stair's experience on the ABC drama *Killer Women* (2014) indicates the specific location challenges found when working on an ongoing television series in a period of mobile production and the importance of considering such below-the-line workers in any negotiation of a text's spatial capital.

Locating spatial capital in *Killer Women*

Killer Women is a crime procedural following a group of Texas Marshals and filmed its first and only season in Albuquerque after filming its pilot in Austin and San Antonio. By shooting in Albuquerque, the show took advantage of an expanded incentive system for television production in New Mexico that had an additional 5% incentive on top of the state's existing 25%—this was instituted in early 2013 in what became known as the *Breaking Bad* bill, so named after the hit AMC series that helped establish Albuquerque as a major benefactor of mobile production (Couch 2013). The series was one of two produced in 2013 to double Albuquerque for Texas, although NBC's *The Night Shift* (2014–2017) had the advantage of being set primarily inside a hospital. As a crime procedural, production for *Killer Women* spent most of its time traveling between different locations, requiring upwards of 40 different locations over the course of an eight-day shoot for a single episode, according to Stair.

As the location manager on *Killer Women*, Stair was responsible for finding locations suitable for the ongoing procedural storylines. It was her first ongoing television series and came with a distinct set of challenges compared to her work in films up to that point. Reflecting on her experience, she observes

> [I]t's harder to get away with things. In a feature, if one location doesn't quite work—first, you have more resources in terms of time and money, that kind of thing. And if one particular scene doesn't exactly sell itself,

it's okay, because you're not coming back there. It's like sleight of hand—they never do the same trick twice, because people will catch on. But in television, you have episodic characters, and you never know if we're coming back to a location. We don't know, because scripts are coming out as we're filming, so the standards are higher for finding believable locations.

Although Stair is speaking generally regarding the challenges of finding believable locations—which could include simply passing off one type of building for another—she is specifically confronting the challenge of city-for-city doubling Albuquerque for Austin. Acknowledging that this made locations more challenging than if the series had—like *Breaking Bad*—been set in Albuquerque, Stair notes that

[A]t the beginning of the season we found a lot of locations and we had our pick. But by the end of the season, by episode eight, we really had to stretch ourselves to see what we could get away with.

Location professionals are not the only below-the-line laborers whose jobs on series like *Killer Women* involve dealing with city-for-city doubling: Stair notes that she worked closely with the production designer, together reporting to the producers and directors who make the final decisions and jokes that "sometimes we'll shift the burden onto the shoulders of the DP— if you film this action scene correctly, no one will be paying attention to the buildings in the background. So there." At the same time, the process of city-for-city doubling starts with a location that can be realistically doubled for another, placing significant responsibility on Stair and her locations team. This must also be balanced by the other logistics of the production, including limited budgets and a finite amount of time to film each episode. Stair recalls that with "pretty much with every location there was the dream place that would have been gorgeous, but logistically with the time there was no way we could get there to shoot." Locations therefore become one of the many elements of television production that are prioritized or not depending on what else is happening in a given episode: according to Stair,

[T]he question I always ask producers is 'How much do we want it?' Because sometimes you really want it . . . so we pay the time and the money it takes to get to that particular location. But at times, eh—you don't care so much. We'll scrimp on that to save time and money on something you really do want.

This negotiation of spatial capital happened over the course of the series, involving not only the location managers and other below-the-line crew in Albuquerque, but also the writers back in Los Angeles. The job of the crew was to facilitate the scripts, which were all set in and around Austin and therefore established the specific parameters that the production 800 miles away would then have to translate into the locations available (and accessible) for the production's use. From Stair's perspective, the below-the-line crew in Albuquerque was very aware of the limitations, and "knew from the beginning that there were certain iconic Austin landmarks we just couldn't do." This included the Austin State Capitol and its proscenium dome: as Stair notes in very plain terms, "there is no such building in New Mexico." However, the series included the character of Jake, who was a state senator, and so the crew in Albuquerque received scripts early on with scenes set in front of the Capitol building, which had been used as a location in the pilot produced on location in Texas. Although Stair notes that they "would do their best to find what was available," she recalls "it started dawning on the producers earlier and earlier with each episode that they'd have to kick the script back. 'We can't have this scene outside the state Capitol, can we put it in Jake's office instead?'"

This form of negotiation returns to the aforementioned case of *Red Band Society* and reinforces that spatial capital within the context of a given production is the result of this negotiation between above-the-line and below-the-line laborers, contingent on the resources available to them in the location where production is taking place. The writers' perception of what elements of the Austin setting were doable in Albuquerque was established over the course of the production in close coordination with workers like Stair, who felt personally responsible for the series' engagement with spatial capital. In fact, Stair reports that all involved were concerned about ensuring that the doubling was successful: "All the time we're thinking about who's going to be watching, and whether our double is close enough to fool them." This included having to replace locations that were unsuccessful in capturing the script's sense of place according to the series' producer, as well as other instances where Stair was forced to explain that there was no other option, at which point their producer would have the script changed. Therefore, the end product's relationship with "Austin" is the result of the Albuquerque crew's interpretation of the original script, which in some instances would change the show's relationship with place based on their input.

The example of *Killer Women* outlines the crucial role of location professionals like Stair in navigating spatial capital within mobile production, which has turned city-for-city doubling into an increasingly common practice in a wider range of locations. Without a locations team capable of finding doubles on a hectic television schedule, the production would be forced to accept a lesser standard of city-for-city doubling or move the production to Texas and sacrifice the incentives. In fact, this was a possibility had *Killer Women* been picked up for a second season: reflecting on the challenges they faced toward the end of the season, Stair explains that

> [T]he consensus on the crew was that if there was a season two, it would have been extraordinarily difficult to continue to cheat and film

it in New Mexico. We and the production designer agreed that we really
needed to go to Texas to pull it off again.

This remains a hypothetical situation, given that ABC canceled *Killer
Women* before it aired its eight produced episodes, but whether or not ABC
would have been willing to take Stair and the production designer's professional opinion into account when choosing a production location for a
second season is unclear. On the one hand, as laborers whose work is critical
for television production to be sustainable when doing this kind of doubling, they are the category of production laborer best suited to make such
a judgment—without them, mobile production would be significantly more
difficult for a city like Albuquerque to sustain, giving them greater value
in negotiations of spatial capital than the average below-the-line laborer.
On the other hand, however, they remain decidedly below-the-line laborers
whose recommendation that the production lose a significant percentage
of its tax incentives is unlikely to override the studio or network's bottom
line. As important as their labor capital might be within television's spatial
capital, issues of economic capital could overrule their determinations. For
instance, if Stair and her team had expressed their belief that a second season in Albuquerque would not be possible, producers could have brought in
another locations team to do their jobs, thereby absorbing the consequences
to spatial capital as a necessary cost of doing business.

With great mobility comes great instability

Stair's experience working on *Killer Women* reinforces the symbiotic relationship between mobile production and below-the-line laborers that is
essential to television's spatial capital, but it also reveals the limitations of
that symbiosis. The work that below-the-line workers find on television
series in cities like Atlanta or Albuquerque is contingent on the existence
of mobile production, as well as the expansion of television's footprint to
states that have begun competing with strong incentive systems. The ability
for mobile productions to survive is contingent on the strongly localized
workforces created by those initial productions, who allow a given location to compete with other states offering similar incentive programs or
resources. And yet the reality of that competition, in which an increasing
number of locations have successfully generated enough media capital to be
perceived as a viable production location for an ongoing television series,
makes these laborers particularly vulnerable to the fluctuations inevitable as
other stakeholders—politicians, studios—make decisions that disrupt existing production circumstances.

Take, for example, the Fox drama *Fringe* (2008–2013). The show shot its
pilot in Toronto to take advantage of that province's incentive system, but
then moved production of the first season to New York to take advantage
of that state's incentive program. When the New York system ran out of

money after the show's first season, they moved to Vancouver in search of incentives to keep the expensive science fiction series afloat. Mobile production made these moves possible, but it resulted in inevitable turnover among the local production crews, who were forced to find new work opportunities not based on their own skills but rather the flows of media capital happening around them. When *Hemlock Grove* left Pittsburgh right before beginning production, the most significant impact was the loss of 150 jobs, nearly all of which would be considered below-the-line. Given that mobile production is characterized by a consistent reexamination of media capital in order to potentially move if costs need to be reduced or incentive systems fluctuate, the end result is the inherent precarity of this labor force: while discourse around runaway production pointed to the loss of stable jobs in Los Angeles, mobile production is creating a whole generation of laborers across U.S.—and North American—television production whose jobs are built on an inherently unstable foundation.

As referenced earlier, this means that mobile production necessitates the mobility of labor. When North Carolina Governor Pat McCrory eliminated the state's existing 25% tax rebate in 2014 and replaced it with a capped grant system, it meant that ongoing television series like CBS' *Under the Dome* (2013–2015) or Fox's *Sleepy Hollow* (2013–2017) would lose millions of dollars in incentives if they continued to shoot in the state. Quoted by the *Wilmington Star News* in an overview of the impact this change will have on production, Wilmington Film Commission director Johnny Griffin boiled it down to a simple truth: "I don't care how much somebody likes you and loves you, they are not coming going to come here and spend 25 percent more than they can spend somewhere else" (Ingram 2014b). The decision resulted in both *Sleepy Hollow* and Cinemax's *Banshee* (2013–2016) leaving the state for Atlanta and Pittsburgh, respectively, with *Under the Dome* choosing to stay and claiming half of the state's production grant money in the process. *The Hollywood Reporter*'s coverage of the situation cites local production studios and other laborers considering leaving behind their homes and experience because they "have to go where the work is" (Block 2014). The workers in Georgia in the wake of Hollywood backlash against state legislation would face the same kind of decisions, as shifts in capital outside of their control fundamentally alter their ability to make a living in the case of a potential boycott. Whereas above-the-line laborers have remained largely centralized in Los Angeles, below-the-line workers are expected to be willing to move to find work, sacrificing their personal stability to meet the expectations of the industry's broader financial and logistical interests.

All below-the-line workers face the expectations created by mobile production, but those whose role in shaping spatial capital makes them critical to that mobility are particularly vulnerable as a result. The case of Stair's work on *Killer Women* reinforces the distinct spatiality of location professionals' labor: their value to a production is in their ability to generate the required spatial capital within that location, which is specialized knowledge. Although there are basic attributes that give someone the capacity to become a location professional, their central asset is their quick recall of a city, state, or region, which is something that would need to be recreated in each new location to which they travel. If a state's incentive program were to collapse, most workers would be asked to uproot their lives, but a camera operator's skills would be instantly transferrable to another state. The same is not true for location professionals, who would need to learn an entirely new location in addition to disrupting their personal life to make such a move. Mobile production necessitates mobile labor, yet the impacts of this mobility are felt differently when a state like North Carolina's incentive system is put into a position of political uncertainty, placing workers with strong ties to spatial capital in a precarious position.

The potential departure of *Under the Dome* would have meant personal sacrifices for many laborers given the option of moving to remain with the production, but its location professionals likely did not have that choice to make. *Under the Dome* locations coordinator Charlie Courter, facing the potential loss of the series, argues "you can't just move to a place and have that knowledge. It takes time to build that base of information" (Ingram 2014a). This means that even if the production had been willing to allow its workers to follow them to Georgia or Louisiana, Courter and other location professionals would be unable to replicate their knowledge base in the new location quickly, likely leading the production to hire local location professionals in its new production location with the knowledge necessary to serve the needs of the mobile production. Location professionals' role as a key stakeholder in spatial capital allows them to assist locations in attracting mobile productions but makes it far more challenging for them to become mobile themselves.

Any worker who has a family or is tied to a particular location for other reasons has a stake in the politics of tax incentives, but this is especially true for location professionals: Stair, who in May 2014 became a board member of the advocacy-focused Location Managers Guild of America, argues

> part of my job is being political [and] being in contact with my legislators educating them about what the film industry does and who I am and how it's benefitted me, and how it's benefitted the state. I consider that as my job when I'm not working on a project.

Although not all location professionals are as politically engaged, they are more keenly aware than most about the political side of incentive structures, given that their work is so attached to the geography on which those incentives are mapped by the studios producing content and considering that they work so closely with local film commissions in completing day-to-day labor on a given series. The time they spend connected to the local community gives them incredible value to productions, but only in circumstances where other elements of the television economy within a given state or province give the knowledge gained value.

For this reason, Stair argues that mobilizing one's labor is a requirement for someone in her line of work. She said in 2014 that she was

> actively working right now to be able to work in other places as a sort of insurance against [the possibility of the New Mexico incentive disappearing]. It probably will happen. That's my choice, and my personal family situation. Many other crew will have to choose between the work they love and the place they love.

As much as the incentive system made it possible for Stair to break into the film and television industry and develop into a location professional, the loss of that incentive system could just as easily make it impossible for her to find sustainable work in the state, thus pushing her to expand beyond the single state while she is in a personal position to do so. Although there were no clear signs in 2014 that New Mexico could lose its incentive system, and it has remained in place ever since, the situation in North Carolina and the threats of a boycott against Georgia underscore that the mobility of television production has been defined by a state of precarity, which has been transferred primarily to the below-the-line laborers whose work is critical to but also dependent on the subsequent negotiation of spatial capital necessitated by that mobility.

Timeless and the shifting flows of mobile production

The preceding cases have demonstrated how mobile production necessitates the negotiation of spatial capital, a process contingent on political–economic capital associated with tax incentives designed to activate the cultural capital of a show's setting. Mobile production is also dependent on the labor capital of the workers whose labor is critical to spatial capital but also rendered precarious as a result. By considering the interplay between the stakeholders involved in these various stages of decision-making, it becomes clear that while below-the-line workers such as location professionals or even above-the-line workers like writers may have strong feelings about the importance of filming in one location over another, the realities of mobile production dictate that these perspectives are unlikely to guide that decision-making. Although these examples have revealed the complex negotiations of spatial capital happening within the labor involved in making mobile production possible, there remains a very clear hierarchy in which economic capital is the primary consideration, as those in the industry warned me when I began this research.

At first glance, a different trend within mobile production would appear to support this thesis. Los Angeles has not stayed passive in the push-and-pull of mobile production: the state expanded its own incentive program in 2009 in an effort to compete with the incentive programs being offered in other states; in 2015, they expanded it even further to $330 million per year, which has been guaranteed through 2025 (Johnson 2014b). Although the program offers incentive to all film and television productions, it also specifically embraces the realities of mobile production by providing its highest television incentive—a 25% non-transferable tax credit—for "relocating television series" that filmed their most recent season outside of California, with the credit reduced to the normal 20% for any additional seasons. On the surface, the existence of this particular incentive reaffirms the priority of economic capital within this decision-making; despite all of the media capital that Los Angeles has in terms of its soundstages, established crews, and proximity to above-the-line laborers, it still needs to compete financially in order to reverse the impacts of runaway production and participate in the culture of mobile production that has redefined the geography of television.

Yet, an investigation into one relocating television series reveals how it is misleading to overstate the importance of economic capital within mobile productions' relocation to Los Angeles. NBC time travel drama series *Timeless* (2016–2018), which ran for two seasons and a TV movie series finale on the network, made the decision to shoot its first season in Vancouver based on economic capital: Shawn Ryan, the series' co-creator, told me that it was close to $700,000 per episode cheaper to film in Canada than in Los Angeles (2018). This made for an easy decision for the show's production studio, Sony Pictures Television, which sought to keep costs low to reduce the deficits of upfront financing in order to more quickly profit from international and streaming rights in addition to ancillary products like DVD box sets. When *Timeless* became one of 22 productions as of 2020 to become mobile and relocate to California since the 2015 expansion (Sakoui 2020), it suggested that California's relocation incentive had successfully bridged this gap in economic capital and allowed for the series—in which three leads travel through history to stop a renegade organization with their own time machine from destroying history as they know it—to remain economically viable.

However, according to Ryan, producing the second season of *Timeless* in California likely cost more on paper than if they had stayed in Vancouver, although at less of a discrepancy than before. In fact, the production had been looking to move to Los Angeles regardless of whether or not they received the relocation incentive based on struggles they found in negotiating media capital on the ground in Vancouver. Ryan paints a picture of a Vancouver that has clearly established itself as a prominent location for television production but still faces challenges of media capital as it relates to key stakeholders. Although the Vancouver incentives are much more stable than those in many U.S. states, the huge number of series filming in the city means that there are limited resources available. *Timeless'* soundstages were actually a converted warehouse without proper insulation, meaning that any time it rained—and it rained often—they were forced to halt production due to the sound echoing through the stages. Meanwhile, the vast number of productions in the city meant that there was intense competition for experienced crewmembers, such that numerous workers were drawn away by higher paychecks or shows that were better established and carried less risk than a first-season broadcast series. This lack of "crew depth" meant that *Timeless* had many workers in key positions who had little-to-no experience in the industry, such as a person wrangling 250 extras who had never been on a film set before; in other cases, the lack of local labor meant Ryan and the producers had to fly in workers like costume designer Mari An-Ceo from Los Angeles, which created additional costs. As Ryan describes it, "we were facing unexpected costs all the time," and Vancouver is "kind of a victim of their own success," with too many productions vying for a finite supply of resources.

These concerns related to media capital were not evident in the initial balance sheets that studios use to decide where to shoot a series, but they were among many reasons why the producers eventually made the request to shift filming to Los Angeles. Shooting in Los Angeles meant that the writers could attend weekly table reads in person (as opposed to virtually) and be on set to make any additional changes. It was also easier on the cast, who were all based out of Los Angeles and in fact lived within 20 minutes of the studio where season two was filmed. Ryan recalls boarding a flight to Vancouver during the filming of the first season and seeing one of his lead actors on the same flight, mentally piecing together their call time with their flight time and noting the sacrifice they were making by managing the distance, something that moving to Los Angeles rectified. Combined with the lack of rain and the larger crew base to draw from, these factors made the logistics of shooting in Los Angeles worth the additional cost from the perspective of Ryan and the producers. This example reinforces why even productions that do not receive additional relocation funds often choose to shoot in Los Angeles despite potentially higher costs. Although mobile production has threatened Los Angeles' place at the center of television production, its claims to media capital have never disappeared, and the expansion of the state's incentive program successfully bridged the gap necessary to draw shows like *Timeless* back to Los Angeles even if the costs remain higher than shooting somewhere like Vancouver.

These elements of media capital—soundstages, below-the-line crew depth, above-the-line livability—would be comparably relevant for other relocating series like NBC's *Good Girls* (2018–present), which left Atlanta for Los Angeles ahead of its second season (McNary 2018). Yet, Ryan's explanation for *Timeless*' move also identified creative issues that had problematized the Vancouver filming location in terms of the show's ability to generate spatial capital within its storytelling. The series' focus on history meant that each episode required new locations, often wildly geographically and demographically diverse. Vancouver served the former requirement well, with Ryan referencing an episode featuring Jesse James that benefited from some striking snow-covered forests. However, demographically, Vancouver proved more limiting: while the city is extremely diverse, it lacks certain groups of people within its extras population that would allow the show to explore specific historical events. Ryan cites the lack of extras of African and Latinx descent as a limiting factor, noting that it forced them to abandon a planned episode about César Chávez because their people on the ground in Vancouver admitted they could not pull it off. Here, then, the spatial capital of the show itself became limited by realities of media capital, a problem that was less of an issue in Los Angeles, where extras coordinators had a more diverse and established pool from which to pull.

Ryan admits that, despite all of their issues in Vancouver, it is likely that Sony would not have allowed the production to move if not for the relocation incentive: Sony was absolutely willing to continue limiting the production and facing unexpected costs if it meant keeping the base cost of the show down, especially given that it had been barely renewed for a second season after being initially canceled by NBC during the spring of 2017. But this deeper exploration of the decision-making behind *Timeless'* move to Los Angeles reinforces the chapter's argument that these choices are never solely driven by economic capital. Moreover, this example showcases how the negotiation of spatial capital is an ongoing and highly contextual process within a culture of mobile production. Trade stories regarding California's relocation incentive work to frame this as a decision of economic capital, yet the truth reveals an interplay of forces for both above- and below-the-line stakeholders whose labor is central to spatial capital and without whom the procedures of mobile production would be impossible.

Conclusion

This chapter opened with a question: why does a television series shoot in one location as opposed to another?

Rather than offering a single answer to this question, the chapter has outlined the interplay of a range of stakeholders who shape the contemporary environment of mobile production, creating contingent conditions for any negotiation of spatial capital. We cannot simply use the case of *Hemlock Grove* as evidence for the inability for Pittsburgh to sustain ongoing television production, as the circumstances that led the series to shift production to Toronto were based on a conflict between a distinct incentive structure, a distribution strategy dictated by a "network" (in that case Netflix), and a specific set of expectations from the production studio; other shows have filmed in Pittsburgh in the years since, and others will continue to film there provided the incentive structure remains viable. The inability to generalize regarding where a television series is produced is the result of the sheer complexity of mobile production, which is continually evolving as incentive systems are introduced, changed, eliminated, or misinterpreted and as other forms of capital beyond economic considerations vacillate in concert with or opposition to those changes.

These fluctuations have material consequences for workers across the television industry, in particular those who are most crucial to the negotiation of spatial capital: workers like location professionals whose labor is critical to an emerging media capital are also the first workers whose jobs are threatened by shifts in mobile production, a reality that makes it an inherently destabilizing force within the television industry. However, it is also a fundamentally stable source of instability: while any given location may be removed from the map of television production due to a loss of incentives, there are now enough locations vying for those mobile productions that there is no returning to a time when Los Angeles is the default, even with Los Angeles retaining its historic media capital and incentivizing production at levels comparable to its competitors. Television production has settled into a new normal of media capital where productions are mobile when they are conceived and mobile as they continue production, making it more difficult than ever to answer the question of where television is produced.

This chapter has focused on the way that this new normal is reshaping television labor and the industrial dynamics of television production, but the example of *Timeless* reinforces that these changes don't simply impact what goes on behind the scenes: Vancouver's limited extras pool fundamentally shaped the show's ability to depict certain locations, while the work of location professionals like Rebecca Puck Stair generates representations of locations that must "sell" the city-for-city doubling forced by mobile production practices. Material conditions of media capital are embedded within the decision of where to film a television series, but the ultimate value of spatial capital attached to a particular series is shaped by a longer negotiation happening throughout the circuit of television production, beginning with the production and post-production processes that seek to overcome the challenges created by mobile production's expanded footprint.

Notes

1 The effectiveness of this strategy was fairly limited, though, as the caricaturist knew little about the film industry, and therefore couldn't offer much insight.
2 The answer was weather: the presenter suggested we should "let global warming have a few years," after which point Massachusetts would become more competitive.
3 The representative from the Los Angeles-based Battleship Iowa felt he left with some good leads, although he noted that the prominence of the word "Iowa" on their signage gave some people the wrong impression regarding where the Battleship was located. He intended to change that the following year.
4 These efforts are not always successful: I spoke with a state Film Commissioner who refused a request for increased incentives from a series trying to make a second season financially feasible due to the series' negative depiction of their police infrastructure. The show was not renewed.

References

"About Us." n.d. *New Mexico Film Office*. Accessed April 5, 2014. www.nmfilm. com/About_Us.aspx.

Banks, Paul. 2014. "Production Guild: Location Manager Training." *The Knowledge*, June 6. www.theknowledgeonline.com/the-knowledge-bulletin/post/2014/06/16/ Production-Guild-launches-location-manager-training-scheme.

Block, Alex Ben. 2014. "North Carolina Kills Film Incentives: Which States Benefit?" *The Hollywood Reporter*, August 22. www.hollywoodreporter.com/news/ north-carolina-kills-film-incentives-726966.

Brown, Scott. 2016. "Hollywood North | Flockhart Chooses Reduced Role on Supergirl, Midler Backs Menzel, and Thurman Merman Returns." *The Vancouver Sun*, August 4. https://vancouversun.com/entertainment/movies/hollywood-north-flockhart-chooses-reduced-role-on-supergirl-midler-back-menzel-and-thurman-merman-returns.

Caldwell, John T. 2003. "Industrial Geography Lessons: Socio-Professional Rituals and the Borderlands of Production Culture." In *MediaSpace: Place, Scale, and Culture in a Media Age*, edited by Nick Couldry and Anna McCarthy, 163–89. London: Routledge.

Christopherson, Susan, and Jennifer Clark. 2007. *Remaking Regional Economies: Power, Labor and Firm Strategies in the Knowledge Economy*. New York: Routledge.

Connaughton, John E., and Ronald A. Madsen. 2011. "The Economic Impact of the Film and Video Production and Distribution Industry on the Charlotte Regional Economy." *Journal of Business & Economics Research* 9.4: 15–26.

Couch, Aaron. 2013. "New Mexico Governor Signs 'Breaking Bad' Subsidy Bill into Law." *The Hollywood Reporter*, April 4. www.hollywoodreporter.com/news/ new-mexico-governor-signs-breaking-433168.

Curtin, Michael, and John Vanderhoef. 2015. "A Vanishing Piece of the Pi: The Globalization of Visual Effects Labor." *Television & New Media* 16.3: 219–39.

Elmer, Greg, and Mike Gasher. 2005. "Introduction: Catching Up to Runaway Productions." In *Contracting Out Hollywood: Runaway Productions and Foreign Location Shooting*, edited by Greg Elmer and Mike Gasher, 1–20. Lanham, MD: Rowman and Littlefield.

Foster, Pacey, Stephan Manning, and David Terkla. 2015. "The Rise of Hollywood East: Regional Film Offices as Intermediaries in Film and Television Production Clusters." *Regional Studies* 49.3: 434–50.

Gasher, Mike. 2002. *Hollywood North: The Feature Film Industry in Vancouver*. Vancouver: UBC Press.

Goldberg, Lesley. 2014. "Alyssa Milano Exits ABC's 'Mistresses'." *The Hollywood Reporter*, October 1. www.hollywoodreporter.com/live-feed/alyssa-milano-exits-abcs-mistresses-737178.

Goldsmith, Ben, Susan Ward, and Tom O'Regan. 2011. *Local Hollywood: Global Film Production and the Gold Coast*. St Lucia, QLD: University of Queensland Press.

Hall, Sir Peter. 1998. "The Dream Factory: Los Angeles 1910–1945." In *Cities in Civilization*, 520–52. New York: Pantheon Books.

Hozic, Aida A. 2011 [2001]. *Hollyworld: Space, Power, and Fantasy in the American Economy*. Ithaca: Cornell University Press.

Hurt, Amelia. 2014. "Hollywood on the Bayou: An Optimal Tax Approach to Evaluating and Reforming the Louisiana Motion Picture Investor Tax Credit." *Louisiana Law Review* 74: 581–612.

Ingram, Hunter. 2014a. "'Dome Crew Faces Dim Outlook as Season Finale Set to Air." *Star News Online*, September 19. www.starnewsonline.com/article/NC/20140919/News/605046461/WM/.

———. 2014b. "Grant Program Darkens Chances for TV Series, Indie Productions in N.C." *Star News Online*, August 13. www.starnewsonline.com/article/20140813/ARTICLES/140819864/1177?Title=Grant-program-darkens-chances-for-TV-series-indie-productions-in-N-C-.

Johnson, Ted. 2014a. "'House of Cards' Receives Maryland Tax Credit." *Variety*, April 25. http://variety.com/2014/biz/news/house-of-cards-maryland-filming-1201164393/.

———. 2014b. "Governor, Legislative Leaders Reach Deal on California Film and TV Tax Credit." *Variety*, August 27. http://variety.com/2014/biz/news/governor-legislative-leaders-reach-deal-on-california-movie-and-tv-tax-credit-1201291914/.

Lee, Chris. 2019. "Hollywood's Future in Anti-Abortion Georgia, Explained." *Vulture*, May 30. www.vulture.com/2019/05/hollywoods-future-in-anti-abortion-georgia-explained.html.

Liu, Cathy Yang, Ric Kolenda, Grady Fitzpatrick, and Tim N. Todd. 2010. "Re-Creating New Orleans: Driving Development Through Creativity." *Economic Development Quarterly* 24.3: 261–75.

Martin, Jeff. 2013. "'The Walking Dead' Is Turning Small Georgia Towns into Popular Tourist Destinations." *Business Insider*, October 7. www.businessinsider.com/the-walking-dead-is-turning-georgia-into-a-tourist-attraction-2013-10.

Mayer, Vicki. 2011. *Below the Line: Producers and Production Studies in the New Television Economy*. Durham: Duke University Press.

———. 2017. *Almost Hollywood, Nearly New Orleans: The Lure of the Local Film Economy*. Oakland: University of California Press.

McNary, Dave. 2018. "TV Series 'Good Girls,' 'You,' Relocate to California to Receive Tax Credits." *Variety*, July 2. https://variety.com/2018/tv/news/tv-series-good-girls-you-relocate-california-tax-credits-1202863215/.

McNutt, Myles. 2015. "Mobile Production: Spatialized Labor, Location Professionals, and the Expanded Geography of Television Production." *Media Industries Journal* 2.1. https://quod.lib.umich.edu/m/mij/15031809.0002.104.

Meehan, Michael. 2014. Personal Interview.

Miller, Stephen R., and Abdul Abdulkadri. 2009. *The Economic Impact of Michigan's Motion Picture Production Industry and the Michigan Motion Picture Production Credit Centre for Economic Analysis*. Ann Arbor: Michigan State University.

Miller, Toby, Nitin Govil, John McMurria, Richard Maxwell, and Ting Wang. 2005. *Global Hollywood 2*. London: British Film Institute.

Nagle, Margaret. 2014. Personal Interview.

O'Neil, Lorena. 2016. "Georgia Governor to Veto Anti-Gay Bill After Hollywood Pressure." *The Hollywood Reporter*, March 28. www.hollywoodreporter.com/news/georgia-governor-veto-anti-gay-bill-religious-liberty-878556.

Owen, Rob. 2012a. "Author Brian McGreevy Pulled to Have 'Hemlock Grove' Series Filmed Near Pittsburgh." *The Pittsburgh Post-Gazette*, March 28. www.post-gazette.com/ae/tv-radio/2012/03/28/Author-Brian-McGreevy-pulled-

to-have-Hemlock-Grove-series-filmed-near-Pittsburgh/stories/201
203280206.

———. 2012b. "More on 'Hemlock Grove,' the TV Series." *The Pittsburgh Post-Gazette*, March 28. http://communityvoices.post-gazette.com/arts-entertainment-living/tuned-in/32407-more-on-hemlock-grove-the-tv-series.

———. 2012c. "Pittsburgh-Set TV Series 'Hemlock Grove' Pulls Out a Month Before Filming." *The Pittsburgh Post-Gazette*, May 11. www.post-gazette.com/ae/tv-radio/2012/05/11/Pittsburgh-set-TV-series-Hemlock-Grove-pulls-out-a-month-before-filming/stories/201205110194.

———. 2019. " 'They Love Richmond': AMC's 'The Walking Dead' Spin-Off Will Film in Central Virginia This Summer; Production Office Opening in Richmond." *Richmond Times-Dispatch*, April 8. www.richmond.com/entertainment/television/amc-s-the-walking-dead-third-series-will-film-near/article_554eecaf-4ab0–5413-a323-2b9233857426.html.

Parsi, Novid. 2012. "Julianna Margulies on The Good Wife | Interview." *Time-Out Chicago*, March 8. www.timeout.com/chicago/tv/julianna-margulies-on-the-good-wife-interview.

Rau, Nate. 2014. "ABC's 'Nashville' Accepts $8 Million Incentive Package." *The Tennessean*, May 16. www.tennessean.com/story/money/2014/05/15/abcs-nashville-accepts-million-incentive-package/9154383/.

Ross, Andrew. 2010. *Nice Work If You Can Get It: Life and Labor in Precarious Times*. New York: New York University Press.

Ryan, Shawn. 2018. Personal Interview.

Sakoui, Anoushi. 2020. "Despite Surging Pandemic, TV Productions Return to California for Tax Breaks." *The Los Angeles Times*, November 18. www.latimes.com/entertainment-arts/business/story/2020-11-18/pandemic-tv-productions-return-to-california-film-tax-credits-hunters-the-right-stuff.

Sanson, Kevin. 2014. "Location and Labor: Critical Crossroads in Global Film and Television." *Creative Industries Journal* 7.1: 54–58.

Scott, Allen J. 2004. "The Other Hollywood: The Organizational and Geographic Bases of Television-Program Production." *Media Culture & Society* 26.2: 183–205.

———. 2005. *On Hollywood: The Place, the Industry*. Princeton: Princeton University Press.

Stair, Rebecca Puck. 2014. Personal Interview.

Strachan, Alex. 1998. "The Alienation of David Duchovony." *The Vancouver Sun*, February 17. www.mjq.net/xfiles/dd-sun-interview.htm.

Tinic, Serra. 2005. *On Location: Canada's Television Industry in a Global Market*. Toronto: University of Toronto Press.

Verrier, Richard. 2013. "Los Angeles Losing the Core of Its TV Production to Other States." *The Los Angeles Times*, August 15. http://articles.latimes.com/2012/aug/15/business/la-fi-ct-runaway-tv-20120814.

2 The textual burden of spatial capital

Strategies for dropping the pin

How do you communicate that a television show is taking place in a location distinct from where it was filmed?

This challenge is not new to television or other forms of media, which have long had to find ways to establish spatial capital despite the inherent restrictions on production or a particular program format, such as a multi-camera sitcom filmed in front of a live audience. However, while the task of transforming Los Angeles and its soundstages into locations around the world is part of television's institutional history, shifts in where television is produced are creating a wider range of such transformations. Strategies for turning west coast backlots into east coast city streets are well established, but the previous chapter revealed the distinct challenges found in turning Albuquerque into Austin; similar issues have been critical to emerging media capitals like Atlanta, Vancouver, and Toronto. Shows that are shot and set in the same location can take elements of spatial capital for granted, but this is not the case for a vast majority of television series. Simply put, each must confront this challenge if where a show takes place matters to the story being told.

There is no question that where a television show takes place matters, on some level, to any TV show. Nick Couldry (2003) observes that an audience's understanding of how place intersects with media production hierarchizes places that appear in the media over those that do not. However, many locations where media production takes place do not actually appear diegetically in the shows filmed there, hidden by cases of city-for-city doubling to present the audience with a different location entirely. The reality is that while production locations hold media capital due to incentives or crew bases, the writers and producers of the shows being filmed there do not believe they hold spatial capital from a narrative perspective, leading them to set shows in other locations that they believe carry more value. The producers of *Killer Women* could have theoretically redesigned the series—based on an Argentine format—to be set in New Mexico, but that would have meant abandoning the mythical allure of the lead character being part of the Texas Rangers. Although there is in fact a New Mexico State Police Special Investigations Division, it does not carry the same cultural capital as

DOI: 10.4324/9781003224693-3

Texas' equivalent with an average audience member. Austin, therefore, possessed more spatial capital than Albuquerque, meaning that it then became the responsibility of the entire production to sell the show's Texas setting within the limitations outlined in the previous chapter, with the ultimate goal of erasing any evidence of Albuquerque within the text for all but the most observant viewer (which I will return to in the fifth and final chapter).

In this chapter, I frame this task as a responsibility to a "burden of spatial capital," and explore how it extends beyond the initial decision of where to film a television series to the work of producing and editing that series. I detail strategies deployed by shows seeking to activate spatial capital, framing these strategies as textual based on their collective purpose to shape the final product that is consumed by audiences. If where a television series takes place matters to the story being told, then it is up to laborers throughout the production process to negotiate and activate that spatial capital by successfully "dropping the pin"—to use a phrase tied to marking locations in Google Maps—within the text; depending on the series, this means obscuring that the series was produced in a different location, amplifying that it was filmed in the actual location, or generating an entirely fictional location from scratch. What are the strategies that have been historically used to meet this burden, and how are those tools evolving (or devolving) due to larger shifts in the television industry? How is the reality of mobile production reshaping the affordances available to productions to generate spatial capital? And how do these strategies, taken collectively, define the shape and scale of a text's "burden of spatial capital," for better or for worse?

To address these questions, the chapter begins by considering how television has historically signified location within the confines of production—and how those strategies are being threatened by contemporary realities of the industry—with an investigation of the ABC family comedy *Full House* (1987–1995) and other multi-camera sitcom production practices. After outlining the tools available to set a series in a given location, the chapter shifts focus to two case studies in which individual laborers challenge the difficulties of their production circumstances to expand their relationship with spatial capital. First, a close investigation of the post-production team for The CW drama *Hart of Dixie* (2011–2015) shows how a backlot-shot series set in a fictional location (Bluebell, Alabama) can create a "sense of place" without leaving the backlot but in ways that are dependent on individual laborers and distinct circumstances that are unlikely to be replicated in the current production climate and still restricted within this case study. Bluebell represents the possibility of spatial capital being negotiated successfully within the space of post-production, but it also reveals that the burden of spatial capital is not set by any one individual worker, limiting their capacity to push beyond both the contingencies of media capital outlined in the previous chapter and the boundaries set by producers, executives, and others with more authority over a television text's final form.

The second case study explores how burdens of spatial capital are shifting as a result of mobile production and advances in production technology. I focus in particular on the ability for shows based in one location to expand their geographical footprint. After a brief overview of virtual solutions, I turn my attention to the case of NBC's *Blindspot* (2015–2020), which began regularly engaging in what I term "strategic location shooting" in global locations beginning in its second season. Through interviews with the production team, I reveal the labor necessary to leverage the possibilities of mobile production in this context, while also highlighting the self-regulation of both production and post-production strategies that make this type of filming feasible. This analysis details how this globe-trotting production is predicated on a reduced burden of spatial capital that reinforces rather than breaks free from the presumed restrictions on such representations.

The first chapter was an investigation into why television series are filmed in one location and not another; this chapter considers the terms under which television workers confront the challenges created when production location and diegetic setting do not align. It reveals that this process has evolved to efficiently articulate spatial capital through a range of textual and production strategies but has simultaneously entrenched limits placed on television's spatial capital prior to these innovations.

TV textuality and the burden of spatial capital

In his book *Postmodern Geographies: The Reassertion of Space in Critical Social Theory*, Edward Soja (2011) argues that we can understand the text as a map. A map is a form of representation, but it exists as a symbolic representation of a given location, rather than an attempt at simulation. To suggest that we consider the text as a map is to argue for the process of producing a television text as a cartographical one, in which a variety of strategies are used to give the viewer an understanding of a given space. The accumulation of spatial capital becomes a process of giving the viewer enough understanding to successfully read the location into a series' storytelling, allowing them to map the action of a given series onto a suggested backdrop.

Historically, media studies scholarship has centered on evaluating and critiquing the resulting representations but often from perspectives that ignore or oversimplify the mapping process itself. Much research in this area focuses on close textual analysis of how a particular text represents a specific location, typically through analysis of narrative and the image itself rather than the production strategies behind it (see Rhodes and Gorfinkel 2011). Such work is valuable, but often offers little insight into the production dynamics underlying the textual representation. Helen Morgan Parmett (2018) pushes back against this with her analysis of IFC's *Portlandia* (2011–2018) as "site-specific television," linking its location shooting to both its narrative and narratives of urban renewal and gentrification. By framing questions of representation through the lens of meeting a burden of spatial capital, I aim to formalize this interplay between production practices and textuality, which remains underexplored. In Kristen Warner's work on television casting (2015), she considers the procedures by which diversity is achieved within a television series and how strategies like colorblind casting meet a basic burden of featuring more diverse bodies but fail to generate meaningful representation of racial difference. By applying these same principles to issues of spatial capital, I explore not just how locations are represented through a given television text but also the production and post-production practices that generate those representations. In other words, strategies for generating spatial capital shape our understanding of where television takes place much as casting shapes our understanding of who gets to appear on television.

The burden of spatial capital, on a basic level, is the ability for a television series to successfully convince the audience that a series is taking place in a particular location, regardless of where it is actually being produced. Although this book as a whole will explore a range of additional contexts that act upon and influence spatial capital, this chapter focuses on the text itself as the central site of meaning attached to location. While this includes the script, I also consider production and post-production decisions that are made specifically in relation to that script as a form of textuality, given that they are ultimately experienced as part of the text by audiences. Many of these decisions are contingent on the negotiation of media capital outlined in the previous chapter, yet my interest here lies in those directly responsible for the text—the writers and showrunners who craft the story, the editors and post-production workers who turn filmed footage into a final product—and how they understand their responsibility to issues of spatial capital. This serves to expand the book's definition of spatial capital's stakeholders to workers whose jobs are not explicitly tied to spatial capital in the same way as location professionals but who nonetheless are often completing labor with clear intent to generate spatial capital. This chapter explores how these laborers make sense of their relationship to the burden of spatial capital and the strategies they use in order to meet whatever responsibility is assigned to them as it relates to place's significance to a given text.

The question of who is responsible for the generation of spatial capital and how this work is completed has been oversimplified in existing media studies research. In *Places of the Imagination: Media, Tourism, Culture* (2011), Stijn Reijnders offers a circular model for understanding how a media text generates what I am framing as spatial capital, suggesting that "physical places inspire artists," and that those artists then "construct imaginary places" (17) that subsequently inspire audiences to become media tourists. However, Reijnders's understanding of artists is limited, understood only as "authors, scriptwriters and film directors" (17). This constitutes the mapping of spatial capital as an above-the-line creative task rather than a series of strategies I will demonstrate as being—in many circumstances—embedded within below-the-line production and post-production labor. Moreover, and more critically, the broadness of Reijnders's model fails to account for the fact that the process of constructing those places varies depending on the style of a particular television series. If a series shoots exclusively on location, its mapping strategies will be fundamentally different than a series that shoots exclusively on a backlot, with location series relying more on production laborers to capture existing spatial capital and backlot series relying on post-production departments to generate that spatial capital. Similarly, a single-camera series that shoots on a backlot will face different spatial challenges than a multi-camera series that shoots on the same backlot but using primarily indoor, three-walled sets. In other words, there is no single cartography that allows a television series to successfully be set in a given location: depending on the variables of where it is produced, the location where it is being set, and the specific mode of production, the burden of spatial capital will shift.

This means confronting the fundamental limitations of certain modes of television production, whether the budgetary or logistical decisions outlined in the previous chapter or the unavoidable realities of particular production forms. To take the multi-camera sitcom as an example, it is a form that has been historically separated from many investigations of television style, with John Caldwell (1995) arguing it embodies a "zero-degree style" that ties TV to its theatrical roots and creates a world that is "set-bound [and] dialogue driven" (56). Accordingly, in a guide to production design for television, it is suggested that multi-camera audiences must be "willing to meet their entertainers halfway in suspending their disbelief and allowing their imaginations to fill in the blank spots" (Byrne 1993, 9). The guide suggests that "the scenery in most sitcoms is rather badly painted—the level of detail anything but realistic—and the furnishings and props only those that are actually used in the action of a typical episode" (18). These production realities are designed to exclude the show from discourses of realism and authenticity that would, under many circumstances, be used in order to meet the burden of convincing an audience that a show is taking place within a particular city.

However, it is wrong to place the burden of spatial capital solely on notions of realism and authenticity. Such discourses do offer a clearer path to spatial capital: in a *Variety* feature ahead of the 2013 Art Directors Guild awards highlighting nominated work in a range of categories, Dave Blass (2013) highlights Derek Hill's work on History Channel miniseries *Hatfields & McCoys* (2012), writing that

> [W]ith grit, dirt, and hewn timbers as his tools, [Hill] and his team paint the deeply immersive landscape of Appalachia for the miniseries. . . . Each wooden shanty, cabin and barn is layered with a rich veneer of antiquity that creates a unique sense of place for each of the families, and the culture around them.

But despite the fact such a "rich veneer of antiquity" is not present in another profiled series, CBS multi-camera sitcom *2 Broke Girls* (2011–2017), Raf Lydon's (2013) analysis nonetheless explores its relationship to spatial capital, arguing that "in a city where space is limited but style is limitless, Glenda [Rovello] and her team expand on life in today's New York." In both cases, the basic burden of spatial capital—convincing the audience a series is taking place in a particular location—is the same, but the practical realities of their production mean that they rely on different strategies, with the authentic recreation of Appalachia and the symbolic evocation of New York through the three-walled soundstage sets working toward the same goal albeit through different means.

This focus on the symbolic raises the specter of the simulacrum, the postmodernist term Jean Baudrillard (1994) uses to lament the death of the real in the wake of an age of simulation. The multi-camera sitcom is built on symbolic capital that Baudrillard would read as a descent into hyperreality, and in the proliferation of the "effect of the real" in place of the real itself, which has been obliterated by simulacra. However, as noted in this book's introduction, such postmodernist dismissals of media's spatial capital are limiting, as seen in David Harvey's analysis of "spaces of individuation" that people make even within a postmodern spatial environment (1991). Following Harvey's logic, I argue that we should consider the spaces of different television series as spaces of individuation, through which characters and audiences engage with place-identity and the identity categories attached to it. There are strategies for activating spatial capital that are consistent across all modes and genres of television production, yet variations mean that such strategies are deployed in distinct ways, resulting in shifting burdens of spatial capital. I frame this as a form of distinction, rather than a hierarchy, as it is not productive to think of this as an evaluation of a series' *potential* spatial capital: any type of show can successfully generate meaningful spatial capital, but certain modes of production do make this more challenging, requiring greater responsibility to be taken by those involved with the production.

For the multi-camera sitcom, with its inherent disregard for verisimilitude, this means leaning more heavily on editing and post-production strategies that locate and dislocate the backlot sets into a desired setting. In order to identify key textual strategies used across television programming, the multi-camera sitcom offers the most transformative understanding of the capacity for textuality to generate spatial capital, given that the backlot sets lack authentic markers of place identity that are afforded single-camera series that film on location. Production design does give multi-camera series a tool for an expositional form of spatial capital: by having a "New York City" sign in a bar or featuring pennants from a local sports team in a character's bedroom, a series is able to remind the audience where a series is taking place even in the absence of scenes that physically situate characters in that location. However, to establish more meaningful forms of spatial capital with symbolic value beyond basic signification, more work is necessary to map those sets onto the desired landscape in a way that is both legible and memorable for audiences.

If one were to perform a Google image search for "1709 Broderick Street," for example, there would appear numerous images of people standing outside this attractive San Francisco Victorian. Those same people might also have taken photos outside of Alamo Square Park's famous "Painted Ladies" row homes on the city's Steiner Street. These individuals are often participating in practices of media tourism detailed in this book's introduction, and this is frequently an indicator that a series has met its burden of spatial capital: if viewers actively seek out locations related to the series, it implies that a strong connection has been made between the series' setting and its narrative. But in this particular instance, the media tourists in San Francisco are not traveling to a space where a television series was produced on a weekly basis—instead, these individuals are traveling to spaces that were used to construct place outside of the traditional space of production, through the use of the opening title sequence and establishing shots in the ABC sitcom *Full House* (1987–1995). The series, filmed at Warner Bros. Studios in Burbank, California, but set in San Francisco, uses these locations to gain access to spatial capital and to relocate the series for audiences from its space of production to where the series was set by its creators.

Everywhere you look, there's a [place]: opening title sequences and establishing shots

Although ultimately attached to the text itself, opening title sequences are an example of orienting paratexts in their function of framing an audience's understanding of the text itself. The orientation in question depends on the series and the sequence, but they are capable of introducing the viewer to a series' tone, plot, themes, characters, and—most relevant here—setting. Although one can distinguish between these functions, which may or may not be among the tasks of a specific title sequence, one of the key capacities of a title sequence is to map them in relation to one another. Through the choice of images, music, and style, opening title sequences integrate characters with plot and setting or any other combination of the qualities in question. The resulting paratexts are discursive spaces of identity formation, in which representative work is completed often before—or at least shortly after—the text itself has begun. They have also historically remained embedded within the text as a weekly reinforcement of what kind of show the audience is about to watch and where that show takes place.

Scholars have touched on this orienting function of opening credit sequences, whether as part of Jonathan Gray's (2010) larger theorization of paratextuality or through specific engagement with ideological questions of identity—specifically blackness—in Robin Means Coleman and Andre Cavalcante's (2013) investigation of the opening title sequences for *A*

Different World (1987–1993). Tied to this project's concerns, Victoria Johnson's (2008) work on the opening credits for *The Mary Tyler Moore Show* (1970–1977) is a thorough investigation of how the series' credits construct an image of Minneapolis as "a glamorous, vibrant city wherein Mary Richards can 'graduate' . . . to a 'free woman' of the 1970s," using analysis of the theme song's lyrics, the use of color and graphics, and the way different views of the city are used to frame Mary and her experiences (120). Specifically, Johnson identifies how an extended title sequence in the second season expands from Mary's arrival in Minneapolis to "further detailing Mary's day-to-day, happy, full integration within the life of the city," while the third season further emphasizes location through the superimposed image of a "Minneapolis/St. Paul" freeway sign (120).

In addition to identifying the capacity for opening titles to generate spatial capital, Johnson's analysis rightfully highlights integration as a key goal for a credit sequence. The opening title sequence for *Full House* is a strong example of this, as its goal is not simply to establish that the series takes place in San Francisco, but rather to emphasize that the Tanner Family *exists* in the space of the city. The sequence used in the series' first season begins with a shot of the entire Tanner family driving in a convertible, with the camera gradually pulling out to a helicopter shot revealing the convertible is driving across the Golden Gate Bridge. The characters are shown playing soccer in a park and are then each introduced through individual title cards—some of these shots feature the characters outdoors in what the rest of the sequence codes as San Francisco, while others place them inside the home, beginning to link the two spaces. A sign for Fisherman's Wharf begins the next segment, in which Danny and his two eldest daughters, D.J. and Stephanie, are placed in the San Francisco landmark before being shown fishing as the camera not-so-subtly pans to reveal Alcatraz in the background—we also see the two daughters, along with younger sister Michelle, in the back of the convertible as one of the city's iconic streetcars passes behind them. The sequence then shifts to an image of Danny with Michelle on the back of his bicycle, with the next shot showing the character riding the bike down San Francisco's famous Lombard Street. The opening title sequence concludes with the family in their kitchen, before shifting to an exterior shot of their home at 1709 Broderick Street, then a wider shot of the neighborhood around them, followed by an even wider view of San Francisco.

As is the case with multi-camera sitcoms set outside of Los Angeles, and as noted earlier, *Full House* is not filmed on location—the series was produced in sound stages at Warner Bros. Studios in Burbank, California. However, primarily through its title sequence, the series has become one of the most iconic shows to be set in San Francisco, as it successfully integrates the characters and their home within the broader geography of the city. The opening titles are a carefully mapped construct designed to attain spatial capital, relying on editing to bridge the spatial gap between the studio backlot and the streets of San Francisco. At closer examination, the constructive nature of the credit sequence is apparent: while the shots of San Francisco locations are clearly shot in the city, those shots appear to have been taken with body doubles (their faces are conspicuously never seen), with the actors being filmed separately on or near the backlot. Editing combines these shots to create the effect of presence; the same goes for the opening—and iconic—convertible shot, where the shot featuring the actors lacks any of the bridge-work in the foreground that is visible in the wider shot (where the actors are no longer legible). Although the shot of the three sisters in the convertible is obviously a product of a green screen, the other work is more subtle in its spatial subterfuge and yet productive in crafting a relationship between these characters, their lives, and the series' setting in San Francisco.

It is also a relationship that is reinforced—and allowed to evolve—over the course of a series' run. Although the opening title sequence is not exclu-sive to television (see Straw 2010), the way that it recurs week after week makes it function distinctly from the opening titles of feature films. By air-ing with the series every week, the setting is consistently reestablished, lest audiences forget where the show takes place. In the case of a long-run-ning sitcom like *Full House*, as with *The Mary Tyler Moore Show*, analy-sis can extend to consider how the sequence changes over time. As *Full House* became more successful, it began to engage more directly with its location, bringing the actors to San Francisco to more effectively integrate them into the city's landmarks and landscapes through both actor title cards and footage of the Tanner family out and about in the city. Starting in sea-son four, the title sequence shows the entire family on a real San Francisco streetcar rather than in front of a green screen, and the final image of the family together moved from the studio space in Los Angeles to the now iconic Alamo Square Park with the Painted Ladies in the background. By the eighth and final season, each cast member had their own title card shot on location in San Francisco, embracing the connection between the series and the city it claims to call home.[1] Although the *Full House* credits intro-duce the actors, characters, and the familial themes of the series, those are all elements also accessible through the production of the show on a weekly basis. By comparison, the show's sense of place is more difficult to reinforce within the confines of the studio, making the location-based work of the credit sequence a crucial component in engaging spatial capital and laying claim to the San Francisco setting.

This consideration of the opening title sequence can be extended to the function of establishing shots, which complete similar work within the text itself. Establishing shots offer brief contextual images of where a scene is taking place, generally used either to remind the audience of a broader sense of setting or to signal to audiences that a scene is taking place in a different location. In the case of *Full House*, these establishing shots work to reiter-ate images established through the opening title sequence, as the exterior of 1709 Broderick Street and the Painted Ladies of Alamo Square Park are consistently echoed within the text.

Establishing shots are common in films as well, but on television they can create a dynamic relationship with the audience, gaining familiarity over the course of a series' run; whereas the basic function of an establishing shot is to signal a change in location, or using a location to signal a change in time of day, they also have a cumulative potential in television to become constitutive of a series' sense of place. This accumulated spatial capital is evident when, in the case of *Full House*, audiences are making pilgrimages to locations that became associated with a television series almost exclusively through the work of these textual strategies—it was through the text, and not through production, that an intense connection between series and a location like the house on Broderick Street was mapped out for audiences.

However, although opening title sequences have been analyzed in a variety of different contexts, establishing shots have received comparatively limited analysis in academic work on television. This stems in part from a general lack of attention to television style and form comparative to similar work on film, outside of a few central texts (Caldwell 1995; Butler 2009). There is also the fact that establishing shots are often delegitimized through their reliance on stock footage, with some series reusing establishing shots from studio stock libraries, creating situations where viewers can recognize the same establishing shots across different shows. Rather than adding to a text's spatial capital, then, this practice positions establishing shots as an efficient and non-creative way to set a series in a particular location, with no engagement with the type of spatial capital this book examines. I therefore seek to reframe these textual and paratextual strategies as critical sources of spatial capital, deployed not randomly or thoughtlessly but rather as a conscious form of mapping over the course of a given series.

That being said, these strategies come with their own contingencies that restrict the labor of the title sequence designers—who have an Emmy category and a website, *Art of the Title*, to highlight their work—or editors who take on this responsibility. Both opening title sequences and establishing shots have over time become less common in ad-supported television shows like *Full House* as the time allotted for commercials within an hour has increased, and the running time of a series has been considerably reduced. The average broadcast sitcom used to run roughly 24 minutes when *Full House* debuted in 1987, whereas contemporary sitcoms run closer to 20 or 21 minutes. Although this truncation has required shorter scenes and smaller stories, it has also become common practice to cut down on the use of establishing shots and the length of opening title sequences in order to avoid having to cut jokes or other story content. *Full House*'s opening title sequence ran a minute and 26 seconds in its first season, along with 30 seconds of closing credits in which many of the shots of San Francisco from the opening titles were reused. When *Full House* airs in syndication on Nick@ Nite as of 2021, its title sequence is cut down to 41 seconds, while the closing credits are—as per contemporary standards—consigned to the bottom of the screen and sped through during previews of upcoming content or the beginning of the following episode.

In current primetime broadcast series, even 40 seconds would be considered a luxury: some shows have eschewed title sequences entirely in favor of title cards, which run roughly five to 15 seconds. Although these are still capable of laying claim to spatial capital, or completing specific ideological and representational work, they must do so with considerably less time and thus with a reduced capacity. *Mike & Molly* (2010–2016), a Chicago-set sitcom also filmed on the Warner Bros. backlot, used a five-second title card in its first two seasons, featuring the show's title over a shot of the city's skyline. The idea of a 90-second sequence featuring the series' actors walking around Chicago is an artifact of a televisual past, inaccessible to broadcast sitcoms in today's industry. Establishing shots have become similarly less common, as it is now far more likely that an episode will need to be trimmed than padded, creating less of a need for transitional material—it also increases the likelihood that series will rely on preexisting stock footage rather than shooting their own establishing shots on location, as they may not be used often enough to justify the expense associated with them.

Technically, these limitations need not apply in the realm of streaming television, where episodes can be released with varied runtimes. However, in the case of opening title sequences, their integrative function is being challenged by distributors' efforts to streamline the user experience; whereas DVRs and DVDs have always given users control over their viewing experience, potentially leading them to fast forward through the opening title sequence of a given series, Netflix has normalized this practice by introducing a "Skip Intro" button that has been emulated by nearly every other streaming media provider (McNutt 2017a). Although some series still develop opening title sequences, the producers must now operate with the understanding that viewers are not guaranteed to have access to its integrative function, pushing some Netflix-produced series to forego one entirely, or switch to a title card following the first episode of a given season (where, in some cases, the credits are not skippable). The title sequence may still exist in these examples, and can serve its integrative function initially, but the lack of reinforcement over the course of a series removes the ongoing integration historically provided by the form, limiting its capacity as it relates to spatial capital.

Full House was able to use dialogue and production design to reveal the show's San Francisco setting, although their ability to develop significant spatial capital—the kind that creates indelible links to a city where they filmed only a handful of episodes—required additional strategies with a stronger integrative function. Opening title sequences and establishing shots not only contain spatial capital in their own right but can also through their design and placement connect the events of a series to those locations in memorable ways. However, it is nonetheless important to consider how the spatial capital generated by these images intersects with the stories they are designed to support, which is where a show's burden of spatial capital is ultimately found. Elsewhere (McNutt 2017b), I have argued that place's relationship with narrative exists on a spectrum between two core strategies: place as a narrative engine, where the setting of a series serves as a generator of tension or conflict, and place as a narrative backdrop, where symbolic meaning is attached to setting action within a particular landscape. Both of these approaches rely on strategies like opening title sequences and establishing shots to engage with spatial capital alongside the production locations chosen. Nonetheless, where shows fit on this spectrum fundamentally shapes the stories being told and their relationship to the show's setting (see Griffis 2021). For place to function as a narrative backdrop, audiences need to only see and recognize a particular location; for place to function as a narrative engine, audiences need to understand the complexities of place-identity attached to that location or be made to understand those complexities as a storyline progresses, requiring a much deeper form of engagement beyond visual cues like those used by *Full House*.

For this reason, although *Full House* is perhaps the single most iconic television series to be set in San Francisco, it fails to offer a meaningful representation of life in the city in the stories it tells and the characters it features. The show spends almost no time exploring the specific social dimensions of San Francisco, in particular its racial diversity or significant gay community, predominantly because those topics were unlikely to make their way into a "T.G.I.F. sitcom"—as ABC branded *Full House* and other Friday night sitcoms—in the early 1990s. The show's studio-bound multi-camera sets belie its disinterest in realism as a mode of address. Moreover, the continued reinforcement of the show's San Francisco setting creates a burden the show is not interested in answering, as lived realities of the city are continually unexplored by the Tanner family in the series' episodic storylines. If the show had been less successful at setting itself in San Francisco, the absence of such stories might be less noticeable. Yet the fact that *Full House* may be many viewers' most significant exposure to the city within popular culture points to the consequences when limited forms of spatial capital are prioritized due to industrial context, perceived audience, or disinterest on the part of those producing the series.

The *Full House* example details the complications attached to generating spatial capital within an ongoing television series. On the one hand, one could point to *Full House* as a successful negotiation of spatial capital, given that viewers continue to associate the show with the city and vice versa: its opening title sequence and establishing shots successfully integrate the series' conflicts into the backdrop of San Francisco, pointing to the capacity for textual/paratextual strategies to complete this basic symbolic work. However, on the other hand, one could identify *Full House* as a failed negotiation of spatial capital, as its engagement with the city refused to evolve beyond basic symbols of place toward real engagement with place identity, accepting a reduced burden of spatial capital based on the writers' disinterest in using the show's setting as an engine for meaningful storylines. In either case, however, such analysis reinforces spatial capital as a negotiation, wherein those working behind the scenes must collectively address a burden of spatial capital that shifts in accordance with the collaborative process of making a television series. In the following case study, I explore how the responsibility for spatial capital landed unexpectedly on workers within one such collaboration, and how their own understandings of the burden of spatial capital intersected with those of the people in charge of the story being told.

Building Bluebell: the CW's *Hart of Dixie*

Debuting on The CW in 2011, *Hart of Dixie* (2011–2015) tells the story of Zoe Hart (Rachel Bilson), a New York City doctor who takes over her estranged father's medical practice in the fictional small town of Bluebell, Alabama. The following seasons document her predictable transition from fish-out-of-water to an integral member of a tight-knit community, as she comes to appreciate the appeals of small-town living. The series presents what we could categorize as a regional idyll of the South, a town where everyone knows one another, everything is in walking distance, and strolling by the town square gazebo means running into someone you know. Before Zoe first travels to Bluebell, she knows it only from postcards sent by her estranged father, foreshadowing that Bluebell is perhaps best described as a postcard come to life.

For that postcard to come to life, however, *Hart of Dixie* needs to negotiate the series' filming location or, rather, locations. Bluebell is enchanting enough to inspire numerous online commenters to express their desire to visit or live in the town per a Yahoo Answers page asking for an equivalent in the real world. Yet the series' primary filming location was the Warner Bros. backlot, in soundstages not far from where *Full House* was being produced two decades earlier, thereby sharing the same streets as *Mike & Molly* and other productions filming "on the lot." Backlots are designed to be devoid of distinct spatial capital, instead consisting of component parts—city streets, town squares, suburban roads, forested pathways—that can be turned into specific locations through combinations of production design and the textual strategies outlined earlier. A set of stairs to an El Train can turn a city street into Chicago, for example, while an establishing shot of the bayou can turn a cabin in the woods into Louisiana. However, the challenge of this work is that those same locations were likely used to represent entirely different places in other productions, meaning that new attempts to negotiate spatial capital may be competing with audience's recollections of other films or television series. If an audience member watched shows like The WB's *Gilmore Girls* (2000–2007) or ABC's *Eastwick* (2009), they saw the same town square and the same iconic gazebo that *Hart of Dixie*'s producers would need to convince viewers was actually the heart of a new town they have never visited before.

Some of this work was handled at the level of production, with Warner Bros. choosing to produce the show's pilot in North Carolina to take advantage of both regional tax incentives and, more importantly, the opportunity to film the series on location in the southern United States. By placing characters in landscapes with symbolic ties to the South as a region, the series more easily meets the burden of spatial capital by using authentic locations distinct from what one would see in a show shot in Los Angeles. This is particularly effective in the case of a pilot, which is designed to impress executives and test audiences, and where the higher costs of filming on location are worth it for a more conspicuous claim to spatial capital that might catch the attention of those who will directly or indirectly control a pilot's fate. However, shooting a pilot on location before moving the production to the backlot—which was always the intention behind *Hart of Dixie* if picked up to series, in order to save costs—also necessitates further negotiation, as the production must now reconcile "authentic" southern locations within the more generic spaces on the Warner Bros. backlot which are limited, for example, to a single body of water that had to double for any number of lakes, rivers, and ponds over the series' run.

These circumstances establish the basic burden of spatial capital for *Hart of Dixie*: the series must reconcile its pilot locations with the backlot where the series itself will be shot, while simultaneously addressing the intertextual bleed with past series and making Bluebell feel not only geographically specific to the South but also geographically diverse enough that audiences are not constantly reminded the town is just a corner of the Warner Bros. backlot that they have seen countless times before. Although the series' art department is central to how viewers experience Bluebell, and narrative developments focused on the town are present throughout its four-season run, it is in the work of post-production laborers where this negotiation primarily takes place, and where Bluebell is most clearly being constructed for audiences. Their work reinforces the capacity of textual strategies to gain access to spatial capital, yet their experiences with that work simultaneously show how forces outside of their control define the burden of that spatial capital.

Establishing Bluebell: paratextual and textual strategies

In line with contemporary practice, *Hart of Dixie*'s opening title sequence is only ten seconds long and features no location shooting; in spite of these limitations, it gains access to spatial capital through its shrewd engagement with locations featured in the series' pilot. During the series' pilot, two locations are given particular attention, captured both through wide angle establishing shots and through specific location work featuring the series' actors. One is a plantation home, surrounded by large trees with Spanish moss hanging from their limbs and branches, which is meant to stand in for the home of Bluebell mayor—and former professional football player—Lavon Hayes. The second is a gazebo, extending out into the water, on which Zoe and potential love interest George Tucker share a climactic, golden hour conversation that contributes to her decision to stay in Bluebell rather than return to New York. While the entire pilot was shot on location, these were the settings chosen to represent key moments and storylines, used to most clearly signify the South and the location shooting therein; consequently, they became symbols of Bluebell, and thus the shots that most clearly articulate the value gained by shooting in North Carolina.

The opening title sequence for *Hart of Dixie* is designed to reiterate this value on a weekly basis after the show no longer had access to those locations while filming on the backlot. The sequence opens with a high-heeled shoe in New York City, before zooming into the sky to show an airplane transforming into a bird, charting Zoe's journey from big city surgeon to small town doctor. Using entirely computer-generated imagery, the sequence shifts from these symbols of urbanity—high fashion, skyscrapers, air travel—to symbols of the southern small town. However, these symbols are neither random nor generic, but rather reconstructions of the iconography seen within the series' pilot. The sequence first reveals a sign for the town of Bluebell, reiterating the specific location, before then panning past a plantation house, a large tree with Spanish moss hanging from it, and then finally a gazebo extending out into the water.[2] Zoe Hart herself is then seen integrated into the space through green screen, occupying not a generic set of symbols, but rather a specific collection of images that viewers could associate with the locations from the series' pilot. Although only ten seconds long, the sequence uses advances in technology and the specific spatial capital accumulated in the series' pilot to complete work not dissimilar from that seen in the *Full House* credits; in subsequent seasons, the entire cast joined Rachel Bilson's Zoe in the sequence's final shot, all of them brought together within this virtual reality cobbled together from locations with real significance to the series and—potentially—its audience.

This is also work being completed by establishing shots, which are used throughout the series to link locations from the pilot to the sets constructed onstage at Warner Bros. The series continually shows different angles of the plantation used during production on the pilot when cutting to action happening in Lavon's home, which existed only as a limited collection of rooms on Warner Bros. Stage 11. The series also uses establishing shots captured in North Carolina by a second unit to connect other standing sets on the backlot to the pilot shooting locations, including the Breeland estate (where the other town doctor lives with his daughters) and the doctor's office.[3] Although the interiors shot during the pilot do not match those constructed on the backlot, where spatial limitations necessitate separate floor plans to best facilitate production, this connection to the exteriors shot on location enables *Hart of Dixie* to maintain a persistent connection to its pilot's spatial capital; this is further reinforced through the title sequence, and works to resolve the show's spatiality between North Carolina, Burbank, and the series' fictional Alabama setting.

However, in addition to establishing shots that link specific spaces on the backlot with particular images shot on location, *Hart of Dixie* uses also what I refer to as non-specific establishing shots. Although the series—some would argue conspicuously—never returned to the gazebo on the water, it continued to be used as an establishing shot to transition between scenes throughout the series' run. Shots like these are designed less to signify what building or location a scene is taking place in and more to provide a sense of scale that is impossible to capture in the spatial dynamics of the backlot. In the series' pilot, these images were used to build on location shooting: although no scenes take place at a derelict roadhouse, and no characters cross either of the two bridges featured in these establishing shots, they nonetheless work to sketch in the space around the characters and the locations that they occupy. One shot maps Bluebell more explicitly, offering what we presume is an overhead view of the town itself, placing it relative to the water and giving audiences a read of its basic geography. Although this particular shot is never repeated in the series proper, its work is continued by other non-specific establishing shots interspersed throughout the series' four seasons. Their proliferation runs counter to the broader trend wherein such shots are becoming less common, making them a conspicuous negotiation of spatial capital as compared with *Hart of Dixie*'s televisual contemporaries.

Although the symbolic work of these non-specific establishing shots is negotiated through the text itself, it is equally important to consider the labor that went into making these shots possible, in terms of both who produced these images and who is responsible for where they are placed within the text. In visiting the post-production facility for *Hart of Dixie*—itself located on the Warner Bros. backlot in Burbank—in 2014 and performing interviews with those responsible (the cartographers, if we extend the consideration of the text as a map), I discovered that the conspicuousness of Hart of Dixie's use of establishing shots was not an accident but rather the result of two individuals' unsolicited personal investments in the burden of spatial capital.

Bluebell town planners: the labor of establishing shots

Hart of Dixie's establishing shots come from three separate production cycles. The first is a collection of second-unit footage captured during the production of the pilot in spring 2011, in which members of the production crew traveled in and around North Carolina to capture images that could eventually be used as connective tissue and help mask the limited capacity of backlot production. These are primarily non-specific establishing shots, capturing scenes like a covered bridge in a wooded area. They are also constructed images, chosen and in some cases manipulated by the production crew: in the case of the covered bridge, I saw during my visit a longer version of the shot (which only ever appears for a few seconds in the series) showing a member of the production crew throwing an object into the water to create ripples, offering a sense of movement to give the image greater interest.

These images are generally attractive, but they were not well received by the editorial staff that would use them. Editor Brandi Bradburn, who worked on all four seasons of the series, characterized this footage as "sorely lacking," both because the production was more focused on the pilot itself and because "the tone of the pilot is not the tone of the show." Cite your interview here. As the series went through development, its aesthetic shifted toward a specific, idyllic version of the South that is not reflected in the aesthetics of the pilot, where the North Carolina locations offer a grittier angle of the region. There are some striking images among the footage captured by the second unit, but much of it—from the perspective of a viewer of *Hart of Dixie*—feels as though it belongs to another series entirely, something the editors realized when they began looking for footage for episodes beyond the pilot and finding nothing among the second-unit library that fit the tone of the stories they were telling. Although one could likely create an impressive video essay on abandoned buildings of the South or a regional variant on the credits to a grittier series like *Deadwood* (2004–2006) out of these images, the spatial capital they held was ultimately ill-suited to the show for which they were made. This is logical given that when the second unit was shooting them, the series did not exist yet, and thus the generic set of images they collected lack an explicit connection to the material while nonetheless having an explicit connection to the region.

Instead of using this footage, the editors primarily used the second round of establishing footage shot for *Hart of Dixie*, which was produced under circumstances in stark contrast to the second unit footage out of the pilot production. This footage was shot in Alabama by Lafe Jordan, who would serve as the post-production coordinator and then post-production supervisor over the course of the series' run.[4] Jordan was working on the pilot as a post-production assistant when its sense of place was being negotiated and told me that he felt Bluebell "had been well-establishing throughout working with producers in post during the pilot because that's when they're really hammering that out anyway." As this process was concluding, Jordan was discussing a trip to Alabama—to visit his grandmother and complete research for a writing project—with co-producer Ben Kunde, who according to Jordan "kind of half-jokingly said 'Hey, you should shoot stock footage for the show.'" Although the series had not been officially picked up, Jordan traveled to Alabama and shot his own collection of establishing footage—according to Bradburn, that footage was "basically . . . all we used because it was the only stuff that worked."

This footage differs from the previous establishing footage in two important ways. The first is that it was produced after the pilot existed, and therefore after the tone of the show had been more closely conceived; whereas those who shot the original footage were shooting with no sense of the final product, Jordan's footage was completed after producers had debated and considered the tone of the show relative to the pilot footage. As Jordan explains, "I knew what 'Bluebell' looked like, and what the feel was of it, that it's this happy, perfect Southern town." Given that he was directly involved with the post-production process, Jordan was able to capture not generic stock footage of the South, but rather footage explicitly designed to construct images meaningful to the series and connected to its sense of place. In this sense, Jordan could construct a better map of Bluebell because he knew what Bluebell looked like—and what its burden of spatial capital was, something that the second unit could not have accomplished.

The other reason this footage is different is that it was produced outside of the standard production process. Jordan shot his footage with a Canon T2i, a consumer-grade SLR digital camera that is more often associated with tourists than television production (where SLRs and even smartphones are becoming more common, but in the form of professional models and the help of professional tools augmenting the cameras themselves). But although the footage lacks the sophisticated lighting and high image quality produced by the second unit during the pilot's production, the quality was good enough for broadcast, and the perspective gained from working on the pilot created footage that the editors and producers felt better reflected the series they were making. As technology becomes more accessible, more members of the production process can engage in place-making activities like the construction of establishing shots; Jordan attended film school and learned the basics of composition but had no formal filmmaking experience from which to draw. Although Jordan admits he did not stray far from his grandmother's home in capturing his establishing shots and characterizes his work as "just kind of shooting pretty things," the process produced footage that would over the course of the first season comprise the audience's primary understanding of Bluebell and its surrounding geography. Shifts in technology mean that spatial capital can now be generated outside of the traditional production process, which would not have been the case a decade earlier.

Jordan followed this with the show's third set of stock footage, which was captured between *Hart of Dixie*'s first and second seasons during spring and summer 2012. After completing an entire season as post-production coordinator, Jordan explains that "we really, really knew what Bluebell's look was at that time," which created greater certainty from editors regarding what kind of footage they were lacking to meet the burden of spatial capital they were setting for themselves. According to Jordan, "there were things throughout the season the editors were like 'Oh, it'd be great if we had a night shot of this or a magic hour shot of this.'" Jordan met with each editor and made a list of the specific requests and then planned a road trip through Louisiana, Mississippi, and Alabama, doing research on towns and areas where he would be able to find specific images. However, at the same time, Jordan had been involved enough in the post-production process, and talked enough with the editors, that he also curated other establishing shots as he drove through the region:

> I knew stuff that they liked to use, and what they would like to use if they had it, and things like that. There were some things along the way, along the trip, that I'd see it and I'd be like "Oh, that's pretty, I'm going to shoot that" or "That's very Bluebell, I'm going to shoot that." You stop, it takes a minute and a half, and then back in the car.

The incentive for Jordan to return was undoubtedly personal: although not compensated for his time or travel during these trips, he was compensated each time the footage was used, providing a secondary stream of revenue. However, Jordan describes it as a "mutually beneficial" arrangement, as the editors gained access to material that better served their needs, created to their specifications. This material features prominently throughout the second, third, and fourth seasons, drawing from a collection of small towns and areas in the region, including the town of Fairhope, Alabama, which Jordan describes as "literally Bluebell."

The impact of this third round of footage is evident throughout the second season, as the expanded collection of non-specific establishing shots enables more thorough negotiation of spatial capital. In "Baby Don't Get Hooked On Me," an episode edited by Bradburn, Jordan's footage becomes a key factor in negotiating *Hart of Dixie*'s distinct production context. In the episode, Bradburn uses combinations of three establishing shots—two non-specific followed by one specific—in quick succession when transitioning between scenes. Repeated four times in the episode, the technique enables Bradburn to draw clear connections between different locations, and in the process map those locations together. In the first sequence (see Figure 2.1), two images of town streets are featured, the first outside a courthouse and the second outside of a beauty salon; this is then followed by a shot of the Butter Stick Bakery, a storefront located in the town square on the Warner Bros. backlot.

By linking together two similar town shots—it is unclear whether they were shot in the same town—and then linking it to the backlot, the images create a sense of travel for the viewer, who moves from location to location with no discernible evidence that there are nearly 2,000 miles between the second and third images. Although a single non-specific establishing shot would have worked to associate the backlot location with the spatial capital attached to the "authentic" locations in Jordan's footage, it is the combination of shots that most successfully expands the scale of Bluebell beyond the confines of the backlot. The same technique also works to bridge the gap

Figure 2.1 Three consecutive establishing shots used by editor Brandi Bradburn to transition between scenes in "Baby Don't Get Hooked On Me," the seventh episode of *Hart of Dixie's* second season.

Screenshots by author.

between the different collections of footage existing within the series' library. In one sequence, Bradburn connects shots from both of Jordan's trips to the south with an establishing shot located on the backlot, while in another, Bradburn uses similar shots to set up an establishing shot of the plantation from the North Carolina pilot shoot; while the aforementioned description reveals the different time frames and geographies of these images, their close proximity and relation to one another nonetheless achieves a basic sense of spatial cohesion, which is a critical part of the burden the show faces given its production context.

We can also observe here the negotiation of the Warner Bros. backlot's history, as *Hart of Dixie* lays its own claim to backlot space that has been similarly featured in other series. In another sequence of establishing shots in the episode (see Figure 2.2), two images on the water featuring fishing boats lead into an image of the Dixie Stop, the generic grocer/convenience store location in the backlot's town square.

This building may remind viewers familiar with The WB's *Gilmore Girls* of Doose's Market, an association that *Hart of Dixie*'s producers likely valued on some level given both its generic claims to that network's reputation for family drama and specific episodes that would appear to directly call attention to this intertextuality.[5] However, the establishing shots work to create a new association with the show's distinct spatial capital, attempting to make a similar connection that would need to be negotiated by the next series to take over the space. Although these sets may have been transformed into a snow-covered Chicago city street for *Mike & Molly* days later, as they were when I visited the backlot in early 2014, in the context of these images they are explicitly located in Bluebell, or at least in the geographic markers of Bluebell created by Bradburn's use of the footage available to her. This work reinforces that below-the-line laborers like Bradburn and Jordan can—in making their contribution to the collaborative process of television production—take on the burden of spatial capital on an individual basis, even if not explicitly directed to by their above-the-line counterparts. Bradburn, in particular, cites the use of establishing footage on the show as instinctive for an editor working on a series confined to the backlot: "When you're on an 'on the block' show, and you never leave the lot, the first impulse is 'Oh shit, we better put something in here that doesn't look like the backlot.'" In this sense, the negotiation of spatial capital through establishing shots is explicitly framed as a way of addressing the burden tied to a show's specific production context, albeit by workers who are often marginalized from creative control over a television series.

Bradburn acknowledges that establishing shots are not solely tied to spatial capital and elaborates on her investment in meeting this burden: while scripts written with transitions in mind or episodes with directors who shoot transitions into and out of scenes are generally light on establishing shots, they are more common in episodes where scenes "smack up against each other," requiring some form of transitive material. As a result, one cannot

Figure 2.2 Bradburn's strategy of using three establishing shots continues, here connecting the landlocked Warner Bros. backlot to the Alabama coast near
the fictional Bluebell.

Screenshots by author.

necessarily claim that each and every non-specific establishing shot outlined earlier is exclusively designed to negotiate Bluebell's sense of place, even if their function in the text contributes to the series' spatial capital regardless of the logic behind their use. This being said, Bradburn nonetheless emphasizes her connection to Bluebell's sense of place in framing her labor on the series, acknowledging the burden of representation the show has taken on through its choice to place its small town in the South. She suggests that, for her, "there's a responsibility to keep reminding people where we are—this isn't your neighbor's backyard." This responsibility is heightened by the fact that Bradburn lived in the South and has a personal connection to the region, which potentially explains why she uses so many more non-specific establishing shots than her counterparts: in the show's 22-episode second season, Bradburn averaged 9.1 of such shots in her eight episodes, while her counterparts Jeff Granzow and Les Butler averaged only 4.8 and 1.5, respectively, in their seven episodes each. Although this could simply be due to her episodes happening to require more transitive solutions—as in the case of the show's second season finale, where the need to indicate travel required 17 of such shots—Bradburn admits that

> [C]oming from that region, especially, there's shots that I've fallen in love with from that area, and for me it grounds it better. . . . I might be guilty of finding the beauty shots of the South [more often than my colleagues].

Although this reinforces how below-the-line workers can be critical to the burden of spatial capital of a given television series, it is important to acknowledge that this case study is distinctly tied to these particular laborers: Jordan's ties to the South initiated his involvement in the creation of establishing shots, while Bradburn's personal experience with the region made her relationship to spatial capital distinct from her counterparts (who, although completing similar labor, did so without the same investment). Jordan's experience in the region shaped the footage captured, and Bradburn's personal investment in Bluebell then worked to construct the town through her careful selection of specific images evoking her impression of the region. Drawing from her own personal library of establishing shots, Bradburn collated them together from the three phases of shooting. Explaining one of her favorite shots—which she identifies as "Brandi's Faves"—Bradburn reveals how her own connection with the show and specific shots is framed through the audience's experience:

> But I think there's a comfort to the viewer when they see the shots, because I use the same ones over and over. I don't go digging for new, because the ones that work, work great. So there's a shot of the blue truck, a turquoise bright blue truck, going over the bridge—I love that shot, I think it's a season one shot, and it's just the best shot. And to me,

as a fan of the show as well, it's a comfort to me—it's like "Oh, the blue truck goes here."

Although only one of three editors, Bradburn's more extensive use of the shots as well as her choice to use the same shots consistently makes her one of the laborers most responsible for negotiating spatial capital on *Hart of Dixie*. Bradburn's requests to Jordan reflected not simply practical use but a goal of mirroring her own experience in the area: "Because I have experience in the South, I'm like 'Well we definitely need to see this, and we definitely need to see that.' These were things that were part of my everyday life there." In requesting shrimp boats like the teal one used in one of the series' most-utilized establishing shots (and one of her "Faves"), Bradburn pushed Jordan to capture images that she subsequently used to heighten the series' connection to the region. Her commitment to the series' sense of place is also dynamic, as evidenced by the fact that her approach to using establishing shots changed when the town was literally put on a map in season two—with the reveal the town was closer to Mobile Bay than she had realized, she amplified her use of water and adjusted her philosophy to reflect her understanding of the series' reality. More than any other worker, Bradburn has tied her labor on *Hart of Dixie* to a responsibility to meeting the burden of spatial capital set out by the series' creation, even if an average viewer of the show may not be aware of her contributions as compared to the writers and directors more commonly associated with authorship of a series and, thus, its relationship to space and place.

Figure 2.3 The "Blue Truck," one of Bradburn's "faves" that she used extensively throughout her time as an editor on *Hart of Dixie*.

Screenshot by author.

Bluebell town founders: limits of post-production place identity

Characterized by her co-workers as one of the workers most invested in the series, Bradburn exhibits a clear connection to Bluebell. She speaks with pride that some viewers think they shoot on location in Alabama and describes interactions with Twitter users about what the show gets right and wrong about the South. However, if we expand to consider the show's greater burden of spatial capital tied to issues of place-identity related to states like Alabama and towns like Bluebell, we find that others involved with the production—those who audiences would consider the "founders" of Bluebell—do not necessarily match Bradburn's investment in spatial capital.

Although Bradburn and her fellow editors have the authority to choose establishing shots to place into their edits, those edits remain subject to the approval of the series' producers, specifically series showrunner Leila Gerstein. Bradburn describes one of her favorite shots, an image of two rusted-out trucks on the side of the road with "Roll Tide" written across their windshields, which first appeared in the series' pilot. From Bradburn's perspective, it's an image emblematic of the region: "That's the South! That's what it looked like when I lived there." However, after using the shot multiple times—usually when characters were leaving or coming back to Bluebell—Bradburn was told by producers not to use the shot again: it was "too sad." Subsequently, the shot was removed from her "Faves" and never appeared in any of the series' remaining episodes.

Bradburn was able to create her selection of shots to represent Bluebell, but the representation they constituted had to match that of the producers, whose vision for the show informs the labor of all of their employees. In the instance of place, however, this is complicated by the fact that Gerstein had—by her own admission, according to Bradburn—never been to the South when she created the series. It is unclear how the South is being defined here, or how literal this might be, but during a panel for the series at the ATX Television Festival in Austin, Texas, in 2013, Gerstein explains the genesis for the show's location, coming entirely through indirect exposure:

> The show was always going to be set in the South. Bluebell felt like a place that hadn't been seen before. When I was coming up with the pilot, the BP oil spill was going on, and I was hearing all these amazing stories coming out on *This American Life*. News pieces on small little towns, where everyone was working together, seemed so beautiful to me.
>
> (Gabrielle 2013)

Whereas Bradburn draws her perceptions of the South from her experience there, Gerstein comparatively draws from mediated representations of the region (in this case the personal interest stories of radio program *This*

American Life). The result is two different conceptions of the region, creating conflict with images like the Roll Tide trucks: as Bradburn explains, "from the showrunner's point of view, this is the ideal place—everyone in the world should want to live there. So nobody wants to live where rusted out trucks are."

Bradburn made clear efforts to capture the South in her contributions to representations of Bluebell, yet the focus on an idyllic South limited her capacity to do so. She had established a burden of spatial capital pushing toward realism—the rusted-out cars revealing evidence of class structures the series otherwise ignores—but Gerstein's burden of spatial capital was utilizing these textual strategies to construct an idyllic and symbolic South with less relationship to reality, reinforced by the use of computer-generated graphics in its title sequence. In the process, various shots that Bradburn might have used based on their capacity to reflect her own experience in the South were off limits by default: while I explored the series' library of footage with a member of the post-production team, a number of images of fishing boats feature the Confederate flag as a form of symbolic capital that raises significant issues of race and racism still prevalent in that region. However, these shots have never been used by the series, as it would acknowledge a complicated set of racial politics still operating in the South—and throughout the United States—that *Hart of Dixie* consistently avoided.

In this way, *Hart of Dixie*'s version of the South is similar to *Full House*'s version of San Francisco, wherein potential conflicts related to issues of race or sexuality are largely elided within the show's narrative, thus requiring them to also be elided in its negotiation of spatial capital. Unlike *Full House* that pushes toward diversity on television in the intervening decades, there are prominent African American characters on *Hart of Dixie*, including Bluebell's mayor, Lavon Hayes (Cress Williams). Despite this, the series struggled to introduce other African American characters, with both Ruby Jeffries and Lynley Hayes introduced and abandoned in the second and third seasons, respectively. The series also shied away from exploring racial politics in their stories, even in cases where there was a clear opportunity to do so: when Lavon began dating Bluebell resident Annabeth, her white parents objected to the relationship, but only on the grounds that he played for Alabama as opposed to their favored Auburn, in what played as an attempt to playfully wink at "outdated" racial conflict and assert a post-racial South. Similarly, although some establishing shots reveal fishermen and other seasonal workers whose livelihoods are continually in jeopardy, the series rarely acknowledges the class politics evoked by the rusted-out trucks; in considering the series' realism, Bradburn admits that "the shrimp boats and the crab on the dock—all of that stuff is the only real reality that we can afford to have." Because the series' narrative is designed to obscure the politics of race and class, the series' establishing shots must equally steer away from implying those politics exist in and around Bluebell, as the burden of spatial capital shifts away from an authentic representation to the idyll desired by those in charge.

For these and other reasons, Bluebell is not an "authentic" representation of the South, as its idealized perspective on the region glosses over significant politics of race and class that need to be unpacked to gain a real understanding of the past, present, and future of a small town in Alabama. Its burden of spatial capital was formed in the writers' room by a showrunner with limited experience with the region, but it was also reinforced by a network who picked up the show based on that representation; when the series was picked up in 2011, The CW had no history of addressing issues of race in their storytelling, although this began to change later in *Hart of Dixie*'s run with series like *Jane the Virgin* (2014–2019), *Black Lightning* (2017–2021), and *All American* (2018–present). Through the process of development, a set of guidelines was established for the town of Bluebell, and then enforced throughout the production and post-production processes, shaping the labor of those involved and the maps they created. While the aforementioned examples demonstrate the potential for post-production laborers to negotiate the spatial capital of Bluebell through their capturing and deployment of establishing shots, their capacity to bring their own experience in the South to bear is contingent on their place within the broader hierarchy of television production.

In speaking about the series' authenticity, or lack thereof, Bradburn largely accepts that the show is limited by its context as both a CW drama and a series created by someone who has no experience in the region. She explains that "our goal from the get-go in terms of the show is this idyllic place, and so my responsibility to that is to make it idyllic but with responsibility to that region too." None of her superiors asked her to add this sense of responsibility to her work: Bradburn acknowledges the realities of the series' relationship with the South, which keeps the show from embracing deeper complexities of southern life, and instead works to redefine "authenticity" within the limitations of the series' idyllic framework and the structural limitations of production more broadly. In the third season, Bradburn directed an episode of the show and brought her sense of responsibility into a role with greater influence over the production itself. However, although she was now in a position to instruct the art department on how to create a location set in the bayou, she was still limited by the small scale of the series' budget: when she requested Spanish moss, a common image in the establishing shots she used on a regular basis to sell the South on the backlot, she was told it was too expensive. She eventually settled on a dilapidated pier falling into the water as the production design element that signified her vision of the South, then worked with the episode's editor to find establishing shots that would meet her own burden of spatial capital within the confines of limited resources. Ultimately, she was still working within a show that narratively and stylistically adhered to a limited burden of spatial capital based on producer and network perceptions on what version of Bluebell was most salable to their audience.

Considering the labor of Jordan and Bradburn reveals, on the one hand, the potential for establishing shots to map out a fictional town through the careful negotiation of spatial capital by post-production laborers. Through efforts to engage with the real South—efforts framed by their own experiences with the region—*Hart of Dixie*'s workers established a substantial library of images to negotiate the spatial realities of backlot production and create a strong connection between audiences and the fictional idyll of Bluebell, Alabama. Without this work, the town would not have been as memorable for audiences and would have been far less specific to the region if not for Bradburn's investment in particular. However, while Bradburn and Jordan's personal connection to the region instructs and shapes their participation, that connection is also inherently limited by the production's focus on a broader representative framework informed by logics of network branding and audience demographics. Indeed, it seems unlikely that The CW—or Warner Bros. Television as the series' producer—would have prioritized the shooting of new establishing shots if not for Jordan's initiative, while the likelihood of the editorial department pushing for authentic representations of the South without Bradburn's influence seems slim. Although the show's burden of spatial capital was limited, one imagines how much sketchier the map of Bluebell would have been without the presence of folks willing to do the work to represent more than just the idyllic town in Gerstein's imagination.

New frontiers: virtual spaces and strategic places

Hart of Dixie reveals the constructive capacity of post-production practices to generate spatial capital for series restricted by their choice of production location, while simultaneously highlighting the functional limitations of that capital due to how the burden of setting a series in a particular location is understood by those in charge. No matter how much Bradburn and Jordan might have worked to meet their own burden of representing the South, the show was always going to be operating with a much simpler form of symbolic representation. The fact that the show's fictional location nonetheless resonated with audiences provides positive reinforcement for this industrial practice. The notion of efficiency being prioritized over complexity is, after all, a constant across television production, in no way limited to forms of spatial capital.

Accordingly, television production has searched for more efficient ways to signify location that extend beyond traditional editing into the realm of visual effects. Expanding the work that would be traditionally done by backdrops on soundstages, visual effects workers are increasingly active in television as technology evolves beyond "plates" (two-dimensional backdrops transposed into the background of scenes using blue- or green-screen processes) to what Stargate Studios refers to as a "Virtual Backlot." In a 2016 video detailing their Virtual Backlot service, Stargate executives walk through a technology wherein detailed computer-generated environments are built and then deployed as shows are being shot, allowing for directors to see the environment as they are shooting it. Al Lopez, vice president of creative services, claims that "the first thing we learned was that there were no limitations in the virtual world," a bold claim consistent with the messaging across the video. The technology is used to create locations ranging from the fantastical (the parting of the Red Sea) to the mundane (a character sitting on a park bench in a public square), demonstrating the immense (and allegedly unlimited) constructive potential of computers to activate spatial capital in a way that goes far beyond what we might traditionally think of as "green-screen." Although we may not associate such post-production work with textuality, the ultimate goal of such work is to integrate the action filmed on sets into key locations, such that the resulting text is as seamless as possible. Rather than using establishing shots to transport a generic studio soundstage to a location, these visual effects work to transform the soundstage into the location itself.

However, the deployment of this technology has been met with resistance in light of the expectations regarding realism and authenticity within live-action, single-camera television production. The visual effects work on ABC's *Revenge* (2011–2015)—a Hamptons-set drama filmed largely on sound stages in Los Angeles—is among the projects featured in Stargate Studios' 2013 compilation of their work across film and television production. On the one hand, the series represents an impressively extensive use of the technology, constructing a virtual set based on a location used during the production of the pilot in North Carolina (returning to the challenges faced on *Hart of Dixie*). Whereas the location—the beach-side veranda of the lead character—would typically be shot from the outside in to obscure the soundstage and avoid having to try to capture the surrounding landscape, Stargate worked with producers to construct a virtual version of the location, with the production using blue screens in order to place the characters against a dynamic landscape approximating that which appeared in the pilot. Whereas *Hart of Dixie* relies on establishing shots to retain access to the spatial capital of its location-based pilot shoot, *Revenge* uses the virtual backlot—along with establishing shots—to answer the burden of spatial representation as they have chosen to define it.

The problem was that the resulting shots failed to meet the burden set by the audience. The location was not just used occasionally: it featured heavily in the show's first season, and whether due to budget or time the producers struggled to generate images that successfully integrated the actors into the landscape, calling attention to the virtual set and its shortcomings. As a result, *Revenge*'s use of virtual sets reverberated in popular discourse around the series in ways that damaged its claims to spatial capital. Margaret Lyons at *Vulture* (2012) observed "the weird green-screen effects for scenes shot on Emily's porch are laughable," while Maureen Ryan at *AOL Television* (2011) described the "terrible green-screen" as "like something from a Syfy Saturday night movie." In an interview with *The Daily Beast* (Lacob 2012), creator Mike Kelley attempts to argue the "weird" visual effects were on purpose: "There is this lovely, surreal quality about the show: something doesn't feel quite right, but it's still beautiful to look at . . . We like keeping the viewer trapped in our world." Although he lays claim to a form of cinematic authenticity with a comparison to Alfred Hitchcock's *Marnie* (1964) and its use of painted backdrops, the fact remains that Stargate frames the virtual backlot through its realism and not through its stylistic flair. The technology is designed to negotiate spatial capital without having to leave the soundstage, but in cases like *Revenge* the technology was apparent enough to call attention to its artificiality, directly affecting the critical reception of the series.

Stargate's technology can create more elaborate virtual environments than backdrops and allow for a show's actors to appear "on location" in a way that offers an explicit form of integration compared to the orientation work evident on *Hart of Dixie*. Yet the reality is that the spatial capital of such locations is inherently static. Stargate's value to production is a searchable database of environments based on global locations, to be deployed as an efficient way to communicate that a scene is taking place in a particular location: while they suggest that certain series commission specific sets like *Revenge* did in order to deploy the technology more significantly, Stargate is still primarily positioning its spatial capital as a collection of iconography that can cheaply sell that a scene shot in Los Angeles is taking place in New York, using assets that are ready-made and available to a production on a budget. In this way, then, spatial capital becomes more accessible to a wider range of productions, but that spatial capital is a new form of stock footage, with productions restricted to whichever areas of a given international location that Stargate has deemed valuable. If a series intends to hold itself to a higher burden of spatial capital within the virtual backlot system, they must work with a company like Stargate to construct a location from scratch, which would likely destroy any cost savings and run the risk of threatening a show's budget. To generate spatial capital that goes beyond the most basic forms of symbolic capital built into Stargate's system, they are forced to sacrifice additional economic capital, which—as this book has thus far demonstrated—is an unlikely circumstance within the economics of television production.

However, such efforts are still historically understood to be cheaper than the alternative, which is abandoning soundstages to shoot on location. Whatever it might cost to construct a virtual version of a location like Paris' Champs de Mars near the Eiffel Tower, as Stargate Studios did for the ABC drama *Missing* in 2012, logic suggests it would be even more expensive to shoot the same scene on location in Paris. However, in the same year, USA Network drama *Covert Affairs* (2010–2014) sent series lead Piper Perabo and her co-star Richard Coyle to the Champs de Mars, and it was neither the first time nor the last time that the basic cable series—likely operating on a smaller budget—sent Perabo and her co-stars to global locations. It happened so often that the show's website featured a "Globe Tracker" map where audiences could keep track of all the spatial capital that the show accumulated on trips to locations like Cuba and Buenos Aires over the course of its run. These temporary pilgrimages of production, which I refer to as "strategic location shooting," represent an alternative path to spatial capital that pushes beyond the artifice of establishing shots or virtual sets. The following case study explores the labor necessary for strategic location shooting to be executed and also how the same limitations on place identity faced by Bradburn on *Hart of Dixie* are reinforced in their execution.

"The network tv show that actually goes places": the burdens of strategic location shooting

In October 2019, as the writers' room for the NBC drama *Blindspot* (2015–2020) finished breaking the story for their 100th and final episode, a commissioned cake featured various Post-it notes referencing the common tropes that the writers used in constructing the FBI drama's five seasons. On one of those Post-it notes was the following: "International location goes here."

The Post-it reflects the series' significant relationship with strategic location shooting, which actually emerged as a direct result of the work done by *Covert Affairs* in the years leading up to *Blindspot*'s debut. Creator and showrunner Martin Gero, reflecting in a 2020 interview with me on the decision to begin shooting internationally in addition to the show's production base in New York (which was also where the show was primarily set), speaks of jealousy toward global productions like *The Night Manager* (2016), and remembers "hearing there was this show, *Covert Affairs*, that set the infrastructure in place for us to then supercharge it, essentially." Over the course of its second, third, and fourth seasons, *Blindspot* would set significant parts of episodes in Thailand, Italy, Spain, South Africa, Japan, Peru, and Iceland, in addition to short scenes in the Netherlands, Australia, England, and Switzerland. This was achieved with the help of a company called MasterKey, an intermediary designed to assist U.S.-based productions navigate the complexities of local incentives and filming permissions. The resulting strategic location shooting allowed *Blindspot* to become, in Gero's words, "the network TV show that actually goes places," although only by regimenting the process of strategic location shooting to maximize its value. Although such work is obviously a production-based practice, drawing on the negotiations of media capital outlined in the previous chapter, the ultimate purpose of strategic location shooting is textual: the goal is that audiences tuning in to watch the story of Jane Doe, her mysterious tattoos, and her unknown past will believe that the characters are operating on a global scale. The shift in production might be crucial, but it is through textual practices that the show will translate this production into legible spatial capital for the show and its storylines.

Not coincidentally, given *Covert Affairs*' role in inspiring the development of strategic location shooting, MasterKey actually got its start working internationally on the USA Network series. Rhett Giles, one of MasterKey's executives, was working on a project with director Rajeev Dassani, who also ran the visual effects company contracted to work on *Covert Affairs*. When producers gave the company $1,500 and 48 hours to find a background "plate" for a visual-effects shot of Paris, the company chose to fly to Paris and shoot footage themselves, rather than buying a preexisting plate. The decision, Giles explained to me in an interview (2020), made the show's producers realize what was possible in light of increasingly mobile production, whether in the increase of experienced film crews in a wider range of locations (as described in the previous chapter) or in the increased availability of professional camera technology at a commercial level (to speak to Lafe Jordan's work shooting establishing shots for *Hart of Dixie*). Giles became involved when Rajeev and his brother Elan encountered logistical challenges as they expanded their work on *Covert Affairs* to filming full scenes, as their guerilla-style production approach lacked the proper paperwork required by the studio producing the series, necessitating a more robust infrastructure. MasterKey's current form emerged from this collaboration, offering full-service production assistance to any show seeking to leave its established filming location and expand the scale of their show in a foreign country.

MasterKey has found no shortage of interested clients but convincing them to commit to such projects can be difficult in an industry driven by the prevailing wisdom of how spatial capital intersects with economic capital. It is a widespread belief—as evidenced by the choice to shoot *Hart of Dixie* on a backlot—that shooting on location is, by nature, more expensive than shooting on soundstages. Ryan Johnson, one of the writers on *Blindspot* who worked extensively on its strategic location shoots, previously worked on the USA Network drama *Burn Notice* (2007–2013), and said in our interview (2020) that

> [T]he reason [*Burn Notice*] never [explored this option] was that if I would've walked into the line producer's office and said, "instead of shooting this seven pages in South Beach, let's shoot it in Colombia," I would've been laughed out of the office. They wouldn't have even let me put the numbers together. It would've been "listen, stupid young writer, we've been doing production for 25 years. Not possible."

Johnson blames this misconception on the belief that studios perceive international shooting as extra, as opposed to seeing it as a replacement for filming an equivalent number of days in New York or Los Angeles. MasterKey addresses this thinking on its website: on the "About" page, they claim

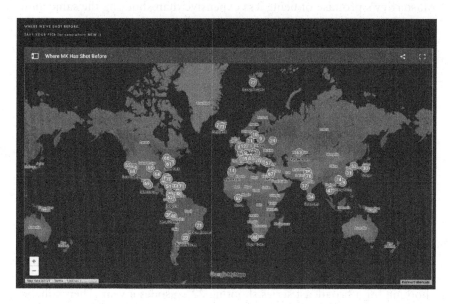

Figure 2.4 A map on MasterKey's website highlighting the different locations where the company has operated, either filming second-unit footage or facilitating first-unit location shooting.

Screenshot by author.

that they can shoot on location "typically for less than the cost of shooting in their home city," but they follow this with "Need a reference [or don't believe us?]" to acknowledge the skepticism this claim might generate. Johnson recalls that after MasterKey met with Gero to discuss the possibility of *Blindspot* going international during its second season, they believed that Warner Bros. (the show's producing studio) would never allow them to do it. Even when Gero eventually decided it was worth the risk, "Warner Bros. still said 'it's going to be way more expansive than you think, guys, it's not going to work how you think it's going to work, you should not do it.'" *Blindspot* moved forward anyway, designing a storyline for the second season's villain that included a car chase through the streets of Bangkok, Thailand, facilitated by MasterKey.

The ability to generate meaningful spatial capital with limited economic capital—Giles emphasizes that they actually delivered Thailand under budget—was pivotal to *Blindspot*: Martin notes that the show "took a pretty big haircut on our budget in season three," and so extending their use of location shooting with an expanded relationship with MasterKey "was a way for us to essentially increase our production value as the budget of the show decreased," with the shoots typically living up to

MasterKey's promise of being less expensive than shooting the same number of days in New York. This was achieved through a combination of the labor practices instituted by MasterKey and story choices made by Gero and the show's writers. In terms of labor practices, MasterKey kept costs low through a simple if controversial strategy of using local, non-union labor, which they were able to do because they sit outside of formal guild relationships. Although key crew—directors, directors of photography, stunt coordinators, main cast, and others as necessary—are flown over, MasterKey primarily looks for "competent and hungry" crews that will work for cheaper rates than commercial crews in a given market.[6] From a story perspective, Gero and the writers developed a shorthand to make the three-day shoots as efficient as possible: "we made it so it was all outside, all day, so that it keeps your footprint really small for the lighting package and the grip package you need." As the cost reports from this strategy started coming in, Gero recalls calls from the studio: "Holy shit, why isn't everyone doing this?"

The answer, according to Gero, Johnson, and Giles, has a lot to do with the amount of legwork required to pull off the logistics of strategic location shooting for a broadcast series shooting 22 episodes a year. Their collaboration speaks to the level of personal investment required for a series to engage in this form of spatial capital, particularly from a creative perspective: this would not have happened without Gero's approval and MasterKey's production strategies, but it also depended on Johnson stepping into a role mediating between the creative and production sides of the equation. Johnson became the de facto writer in charge of *Blindspot*'s strategic location shooting due to circumstance: Johnson was one of a handful of writers recommended by the show's line producer who could be trusted to represent the writer's room on the set based on his time spent in New York on *Blindspot*. These were skills Johnson developed based on his experience on previous projects that were byproducts of mobile production (and that were shot outside of Los Angeles, including the aforementioned *Burn Notice*).

For Johnson to take on this role, however, he needed to be willing and able to take on the burden of spatial capital, which went beyond being present on set to adding new job titles to his day-to-day work on the series. In addition to traveling for the international shoots, Johnson also became a de facto location scout, working with Giles to determine viable locations in each new city. This work began remotely using Google Earth, but after a series of difficulties during a shoot in Barcelona, Johnson pushed heavily to begin doing in-person location shoots:

> When [the next shoot in] Morocco came up, I was like "I will fly coach just to prove how valuable this is." We were so lucky we did, because the initial location they were going to show us didn't work at all, and we had to cold scout a brand new place which was perfect. But there's no way we could have done that the day before the shoot.

Returning to Brandi Bradburn's investment in Bluebell, Johnson's personal sacrifice is positioned as critical to the show's ability to pull off its strategic location shooting: Gero credits the show's success at executing these shoots to the shift to Johnson and Giles scouting long in advance, allowing the writers to craft stories with the confidence that they would have the locations necessary to pull them off.

While location scouting was a key part of Giles and Johnson's collaboration, Johnson's other role on set was ensuring that the show would successfully capture the value of strategic location shooting in how it was shot. This began with selecting the locations themselves, with a priority on those that gave the production the most "bang for your buck," in Gero's words. This often involved rooftops, which allowed the show to stage lengthy scenes of dialogue that would not be feasible at street level with larger crowds and that also featured 360-degree views of a city and its iconography. But after a location had been settled on, it became Johnson's responsibility to ensure that the directors were shooting the location to highlight the spatial capital on display. Although Gero did not have a strict "bible" for the visual style of *Blindspot*, his rule was "I need a massive wide shot and extreme closeups of everyone that's talking, because for whatever reason this show works there really well." When shooting overseas, however, Johnson—or Gero, who directed several of the international shoots himself—would ask the director to adjust the formula to introduce more medium shots that better established the space that the characters were occupying (see Figure 2.5).

Figure 2.5 A screenshot from *Blindspot*'s trip to Machu Picchu in season four's "The Tale of the Book of Secrets" showcasing the type of medium shot dictated by Gero and Johnson to best highlight the spatial capital of the logistics of filming in foreign locations.

Screenshot by author.

They also introduced more lateral movement to the camera in an effort to convince a skeptical audience conditioned to the use of virtual sets or blue-screen plate work that they had actually done the work of traveling to these locations. This was also achieved through the consistent use of drone shots, which the show was not able to legally use when shooting in New York, but which became a key signature of the show's international episodes. Gero points to these drone shots as a prime form of integration of story and location: multiple international episodes feature drone shots that first register as establishing shots, but as the drone moves closer, the viewer realizes that the show's characters are actually part of the shot, disrupting the audience's expectation that the show is going to use stock footage to trick them into thinking that they had traveled to the country in question.

Johnson's job on the set was to ensure these strategies were being deployed, and that audiences at home would recognize that the scenes were really shot in that location, which is the basic burden of spatial capital determined by the production. Johnson never directed *Blindspot* himself, but his role as the writer on the set in these instances meant that he was there to ensure the production's commitment to these international shoots would translate to the audience visually, making him a crucial figure in the negotiation of spatial capital within the final text even if he was not the one doing interviews with press about the show's globetrotting.

However, even with all of these forces prioritizing and facilitating spatial capital as central to *Blindspot*'s textuality in these episodes, strategic location shooting remains restricted by the same limitations found in *Hart of Dixie*'s use of textual strategies to articulate spatial capital on the backlot. Mobile production makes it possible for a network series like *Blindspot* to make pilgrimages of production and strategically shoot in international locations, but the only way this is feasible is if the burden of spatial capital remains consciously simplified. Where these storylines take place is not incidental to the episodes: although the production did choose locations based on practical logistics like cost and access to experienced crews in areas like stunts and practical effects necessary to deliver a successful episode of the series, they did this work well in advance, which meant that the writers had time to adapt their storytelling to the result of the location scouting done by Johnson and Giles. However, in selecting locations for scenes to take place, their priority was not to position the cities as narrative engines and draw on the local culture in order to tell specific stories: the priority was to find narrative backdrops that would be evocative and conspicuously perform the spatial capital of filming on location to the audience.

Blindspot's approach to these locations is touristic, both in terms of how the story intersects with the places themselves along with the specific types of locations that the production team chose to highlight in their selection of locations. Speaking to France as an example, Johnson notes that

[H]owever much the south of France is awesome, it looks like Iowa to the common viewer. To them, there's nothing distinct where they can go like "Oh, that's France!" But you shoot down the street from the Eiffel Tower, and you have the cars, and you have all that free production value, now you're instantly there. That's what we're always looking for: which shot says "No, they went there."

The explicit reference to production value points to how spatial capital is being foregrounded, but it is also being framed exclusively through how the audience experiences that value. Given that the priority rests on the efficiency of that process, the key question when choosing a location for Johnson was, "What are the fewest seconds we can take to show where we are," as opposed to what information about that location might be communicated in a given scene.

The result, ultimately, is forms of spatial capital that are no more complex than the computer-generated virtual backdrops used by companies like Stargate to construct fake scenes in those locations. *Blindspot*'s episodes still rely on recognizable iconography, and while the cinematography patterns identified earlier do a much better job of integrating the characters into the landscapes in question than computer-generated backdrops, they say nothing more about the landscapes themselves than digital solutions. Although there are circumstances—like the crowded streets of Bangkok and Tokyo—where the location shooting achieves a depth of shot that would be almost impossible to replicate successfully via a computer, the fact remains that the spatial capital at play here is built on existing forms of symbolic capital that audiences already implicitly understand, tied only to convincing viewers that they really were filming in Bangkok or Tokyo. Strategic location shooting, then, is also conspicuous location shooting, because its strategic value in relation to spatial capital is eliminated if the audience questions whether a scene was actually shot in that location. The result is that regardless of how much time the show spends in a particular location, and how much personal investment someone like Johnson might make to facilitating location shooting, the burden of spatial capital never expands beyond this basic form of signification: the value of the handful of shots that a freelance videographer who had the same camera used in the production shot of actor Luke Mitchell in Australia while he was there for a wedding to sell a scene set in Sydney may be considerably less than a boat chase through the Venice canals that required special permission from the city, but the difference of magnitude is not matched by any deeper exploration of the city in question. The principles of these two location shoots are the same, meaning that their overall impact on the burden of spatial capital is identical: to reframe these global locations as impressive backdrops, but denying them any additional value to the series' narrative.

This is not to suggest that the practices developed by MasterKey and *Blindspot*'s writers to execute strategic location shooting failed; in fact, this reduced burden of spatial capital is why they were considered successful. In order to expand the map of broadcast television production and "drop a pin" in new locations around the globe, Gero, Johnson, and Giles pro-actively limited what they expected to accomplish on location to the con-fines of their production schedule and the logistics of shooting in a foreign country. The touristic principles they used to choose locations may have decreased the ability to generate spatial capital beyond an audience's precon-ceived understanding of a given city, but it improved the chances that local film commissions would be willing to give them permits for such locations. While the on-site location shooting could have given Giles and Johnson an opportunity to explore beyond well-known iconography in a given city, the short three-day filming window meant that the locations chosen had to be efficient to access in addition to being recognizable, with exceptional spaces—a shoot at Machu Picchu, skydiving onto a glacier in Iceland—needing to carry massive spatial capital among audiences to be worth the additional effort.

When asked about whether the show ever considered shooting for longer than three days in any location, perhaps giving them the ability to push toward these locations serving as something beyond an evocative backdrop to the narrative, Gero reinforced that the bare bones filming strategy devel-oped in conjunction with MasterKey was what made this kind of shooting successful, and moving the entire production to a city like Prague—which was considered for the show's fifth and final season—would have been a logistical nightmare on a broadcast schedule where "you're just always behind." Through the system developed by Giles and the individual com-mitment from Johnson, *Blindspot* was successful at generating spatial capital that distinguished it from its broadcast counterparts, but only by consciously restricting the terms of that spatial capital to ensure that they could get a return on investment from the risk of moving the production to a wider range of locations.

Conclusion

During *Blindspot*'s trip to South Africa at the end of the fourth season, there is one moment that stands out as a glimpse of a deeper form of spatial capi-tal: as the characters arrive in Cape Town, a group of singers are performing in the plaza. The episode does not dwell on their appearance, and they play no role in the plot of the episode, but their presence goes beyond symbolic capital that would be explicitly recognizable to the audience to a form of local culture that has the potential to be transformative. It emerged through the show's long-term planning of their strategic location shooting, as the choir was hired for the show after appearing in video footage captured on location by Johnson and Giles on their scouting trip. It is the kind of detail that would never appear in a virtual backlot set and would be unlikely to appear on a physical backlot transformed into Cape Town. Yet it is still purely symbolic, as the strategies developed by *Blindspot* to make shooting in international locations feasible meant that there was no time to dwell on spatial capital in a more meaningful way. *Blindspot* was respectful to the locations where they filmed, working with local officials to respect the sanctity of sites like Machu Picchu and working with the government of South Africa on adhering to local regulations under drought conditions, but the show's burden of spatial capital never moved beyond the beautiful vistas and recognizable landmarks of these cities to trying to tell stories about them. Mobile production makes it possible for broadcast series to map out new locations previously unavailable to them, but there is no incentive to push toward more meaningful investigations of place identity in a context defined by efficiency. Strategic location shooting does not change the burden of spatial capital of broadcast television traveling to global locations; rather, it gives producers a leg up at meeting the burden that other shows try—and often fail—to meet using new technology like virtual backlots or old-fashioned strategies like establishing shots.

That said, the labor involved in these efforts is defined by a personal investment in spatial capital, wherein editors turned cartographers like Brandi Bradburn or writers turned location scouts like Ryan Johnson redefine their place within the collaborative nature of television production in order to carry the burdens of spatial capital of their respective shows. This chapter has revealed this work to be potentially transformative, insofar as personal investments of time and energy by someone like Lafe Jordan can expand the capacity for a television series to represent a particular location, while others like Rhett Giles have invented entirely new roles within the television industry to facilitate an expanded geography of production. The challenge is that each of these laborers must ultimately position their value to their respective productions in accordance with their place within the production hierarchy. In the case of showrunners like Martin Gero, this is tied to their responsibility of delivering a series that is both on budget and on brand for a respective network. The technological and industrial shifts that enable mobile production are creating new opportunities for workers to engage in spatialized labor, but rather than dramatically expanding how television's spatial capital is understood, it is simply generating new tools to meet the existing burdens of spatial capital contingent on the existing tensions between economic and cultural capital that define commercial television production.

The textual strategies outlined in this chapter will continue to evolve. Giles expects that strategic location shooting will only become more common as mobile production remains rampant, while evolution in commercial camera equipment could mean more laborers could be shooting establishing shots at any time, in any location. The question is whether there will be similar opportunities to push the boundaries of spatial capital using these same practices, or whether opening title sequences and virtual backlots will continue to be used predominantly to embrace two-dimensional ideas of spatial capital based on principles of economic capital baked into the logics of television production. However, much as MasterKey's work pushed back against logics regarding the cost of location shooting, there remains space for workers to negotiate spatial capital from within these restrictions, in addition to new platforms emerging where such negotiations would seem less necessary. The following chapter explores how programs that straddle the boundaries of different television markets generate distinct burdens of spatial capital and push us to consider how issues of distribution further compound the challenges of spatial capital within the industry.

Notes

1 Interestingly, perhaps tied to production logistics, the three Tanner children remained inside the soundstage for their title cards in Season 4, further linking them to the home. Only in Season 8, when the actresses were considerably older, were they each linked to the broader space of San Francisco through on-location title cards.
2 The sequence also features a "Gator Xing" sign to signify Burt Reynolds, Hayes's pet alligator and itself a symbol of the series' regionality.
3 The establishing shot of the doctor's office changed in the show's second season, when the production began to use the office exterior to set scenes; accordingly, a new establishing shot of a house located on the Warner Bros. backlot was introduced, although there is never a diegetic acknowledgment that the office changed appearance or location.
4 The post-production coordinator can best be described as the head administrator for the post-production department. The post-production supervisor oversees and manages the entire post-production process, both administratively and creatively.
5 This was most apparent in *Hart of Dixie's* duplication of *Gilmore Girls'* "basket auction" storyline—from that show's second season—in season 2 episode "Sparks Fly."
6 Giles noted that some crews outgrew their business model after becoming too large and expensive, specifically citing the crew that worked on Netflix's *Narcos* (2015–2017).

References

Baudrillard, Jean. 1994. "The Precession of Simulacra." In *Simulacra and Simulation*, translated by Sheila Faria Glaser, 1–42. Ann Arbor: University of Michigan Press.

Blass, Dave. 2013. "Dave Blass on Derek Hill for 'Hatfields & McCoys'." *Variety*, February 1. https://variety.com/2013/scene/awards/dave-blass-on-derek-hill-for-hatfields-mccoys-1118065437/.

Bradburn, Brandi. 2014. Personal Interview.

Butler, Jeremy G. 2009. *Television Style*. New York: Routledge.

Byrne, Terry. 1993. *Production Design for Television*. Boston, MA: Focal Press.

Caldwell, John T. 1995. *Televisuality: Style, Crisis, and Authority in American Television*. New Brunswick, NJ: Rutgers University Press.

Couldry, Nick. 2003. *Media Rituals*. London: Routledge.

Gabrielle, Desirae. 2013. "*Hart of Dixie* Creator and Stars Dish on Audition Process, Ultra-Passionate Twitter Fans, and More." *Yahoo TV*, July 1. https://tv.yahoo.com/news/hart-dixie-creator-stars-dish-audition-process-ultra-173100005.html.

Gero, Martin. 2020. Personal Interview.

Giles, Rhett. 2020. Personal Interview.

Gray, Jonathan. 2010. *Show Sold Separately: Promos, Spoilers, and Other Media Paratexts*. New York: New York University Press.

Griffis, Noelle. 2021. "Music City Makeover: The Televisual Tourism of *Nashville*." In *Media Crossroads: Intersections of Space and Identity in Screen Cultures*, edited by Paula Massoud, Angel Daniel Matos, and Pamela Robertson Wijcik, 141–54. Durham: Duke University Press.

Harvey, David. 1991. *The Condition of Postmodernity: An Enquiry into the Origins of Cultural Change*. London: Wiley-Blackwell.

Johnson, Ryan. 2020. Personal Interview.

Johnson, Victoria E. 2008. *Heartland TV: Prime-Time Television and the Struggle for U.S. Identity*. New York: New York University Press.

Jordan, Lafe. 2014. Personal interview.

Lacob, Jace. 2012. "'Revenge': Emily VanCamp, Mike Kelley, Madeleine Stowe and Gabriel Mann on the ABC Soap." *The Daily Beast*, February 28. www.thedailybeast.com/revenge-emily-vancamp-mike-kelley-madeleine-stowe-and-gabriel-mann-on-the-abc-soap.

Lydon, Raf. 2013. "Raf Lydon on Glenda Rovello for '2 Broke Girls'." *Variety*, February 1. https://variety.com/2013/scene/awards/raf-lydon-on-glenda-rovello-for-2-broke-girls-1118065430/.

Lyons, Margaret. 2012. "*Revenge*: The Best Half-Terrible Show on TV." *Vulture*, April 18. www.vulture.com/2012/04/revenge-return-terrible-nolan.html.

McNutt, Myles. 2017a. "'Skip Intro': Netflix Could've Saved TV Title Sequences, but Now It's Killing Them." *The A.V. Club*, September 14. www.avclub.com/skip-intro-netflix-could-ve-saved-tv-title-sequences-1802926420.

———. 2017b. "Narratives of Miami in Dexter and Burn Notice." *Series—International Journal of TV Serial Narratives* 3.1: 73–86.

Means Coleman, Robin R., and Andre M. Cavalcante. 2013. "Two Different Worlds: Television as a Producers' Medium." In *Watching While Black: Centering the Television of Black Audiences*, edited by Beretta Smith-Shomade, 33–48. New Brunswick, NJ: Rutgers University Press.

Parmett, Helen Morgan. 2018. "Site-Specific Television as Urban Renewal: Or, How Portland Became *Portlandia*." *International Journal of Cultural Studies* 21.1: 42–56.

Reijnders, Stijn. 2011. *Places of the Imagination: Media, Tourism, Culture*. London: Ashgate.

Rhodes, John David, and Elena Gorfinkel, eds. 2011. *Taking Place: Location and the Moving Image*. Minneapolis: University of Minnesota Press.

Ryan, Maureen. 2011. "*Revenge* on ABC Is Sweet: Let Us Count the Ways." *AOL Television*, November 9. https://web.archive.org/web/20120112104056/www.aoltv.com/2011/11/09/revenge-on-abc-is-sweet-let-us-count-the-ways/.

Soja, Edward W. 2011. *Postmodern Geographies: The Reassertion of Space in Critical Social Theory*. New York: Verso.

Straw, Will. 2010. "Letters of Introduction: Film Credits and Cityscapes." *Design and Culture* 2.2: 155–66.

Warner, Kristen. 2015. *The Cultural Politics of Colorblind TV Casting*. London: Routledge.

3 Distributional limits on spatial capital

Not there, but anywhere

If there is one social reality where location matters, it is in the sale of property: this book draws its subtitle from the mantra "Location, location, location," an often-quoted description of the most important principle in purchasing real estate. Whether it is a family looking for the best school districts or a developer tracking moves toward gentrification, where a particular property is located is a matter of utmost importance. It is a principle so central that it is actually the title of a long-running Channel 4 real estate reality series in England (2000–present).

Along similar lines, location is a critical part of the reality programming on American channel Home and Garden Television (HGTV), which through franchises like *House Hunters* (1999–present) and *Fixer Upper* (2013–2018) has turned aspirational home improvement into a powerful cable brand. Although the core principle of these shows—someone is either looking to purchase or renovate a home—is consistent across the vast majority of the channel's programming, location is a key variable even within episodes of the same program. Shows like *House Hunters* and its spin-off *House Hunters International* (2006–present) crisscross the United States and the globe, showcasing not just individual homeowners but also different housing markets and how the same budget can offer vastly different options depending on where a buyer is located. HGTV even produced a series built on this question. *What You Get for Your Money*, which debuted in 2019, highlights two buyers with the same budget in different cities, giving viewers insights into how much spatial capital and economic capital intersect in the area of real estate. In 2020 during the COVID-19 pandemic, HGTV debuted *Flipping Across America*, which repackaged existing episodes of various house-flipping shows with the purported goal of understanding how far a dollar goes in different cities for real estate developers who purchase and renovate homes for profit.

However, one cannot generalize and say that location matters equally to all HGTV programming. Whereas series like the Laurel, Mississippi-set *Home Town* (2016–present) are rooted in local communities, and invested in developing spatial capital as part of their storytelling, there is a series like *Love It or List It* (2008–present) and its spin-off, *Love It or List It,*

DOI: 10.4324/9781003224693-4

Too (2015–present). These series never discuss location in specific terms: dialogue carefully avoids reference to what city an episode is filmed in, local business logos are blurred out, neighborhoods are spoken of only in vague terms, and while there is some spatial capital in establishing shots it typically requires close investigation to recognize where an episode may be taking place. Although shifts in the style of homes and the surrounding areas signal when these series might be filming in different locations, both *Love It or List It* and *Love It or List It, Too* uproot the principles of real estate from their relationship to geography, replacing it with purely relative notions of spatial capital like commuting distance to work, distance from one's current neighborhood, or distance from an unidentified "downtown." Location still matters to these series, but only in generic terms that restrict their capacity to embrace spatial capital in a way that has been so crucial for other successful HGTV series.

The explanation for this reveals another critical dimension of spatial capital, as concerns over distribution deploy the strategies used to activate and construct spatial capital (discussed in the previous chapter) instead to dislocate series like *Love It or List It* and *Love It or List It, Too* or, as the latter series is known in Canada, *Love It or List It Vancouver*. Both series were developed in Canada, in fact, and sold to HGTV to air in the larger and more lucrative U.S. television market. *Love It or List It*'s approach to spatial capital emerged during early seasons filmed in Toronto, Ontario, a fact that the series never acknowledged specifically; in the case of *Love It or List It Vancouver*, the series debuted on Canada's W Network, highlighting the real estate market in Canada's third-largest city, but that branding—and program components that explicitly deal with local landmarks as well as partnerships with Canadian brands—are excised when the show is shipped south of the border, and when it airs internationally. Embedded in this decision is the argument that the spatial capital of Vancouver is perceived as negative in the context of a global marketplace, and that the absence of spatial capital—which allows the show to be read as the U.S. Pacific northwest— is more valuable.[1]

This chapter investigates how the negotiation of spatial capital inherent to distribution shapes how space and place are articulated within specific programs, exploring how circumstances of production and storytelling overlap with the either presumed or explicit demands of international marketplaces. Spatial capital has always intersected with television distribution: local broadcast stations tailor programming to their respective markets, while cable and streaming have brought new changes to the reach of particular channels and programs both domestically and internationally. After locating spatial capital within those changes, I consider how international co-productions and "local" productions intended for—or even dependent on—international distribution are built on specific burdens of spatial capital. The case studies in this chapter reveal that although these series use similar strategies to the television shows discussed in earlier chapters, they focus as much on *dislocation* as on location itself, with the goal of disrupting a straightforward reading of their spatial capital. This is not to say that these series are devoid of space and place; rather, their burdens are designed to carefully engage with spatial capital in an imagined dialogue with a wider range of audiences and markets. In this chapter I push back against the notion that the result is a "non-place." I use the example of the U.S./Canada co-production *Orphan Black* as a series set in a "polysemic place," wherein spatial capital exists but in ways that allow different audiences to read the series as local in different markets.

The chapter then shifts to how these strategies, an evolution of long-standing practices in the development of international co-productions, apply in the case of original, local programming produced by Netflix in markets outside of the United States. Netflix is a central force in the emergence of "Peak TV," and their global reach and investment in programming developed in international markets like the UK, Spain, South Africa, and India—among others—have reshaped the television landscape and with it the relationship between spatial capital and distributional capital. The chapter maps how these programs are distinct from traditional international production and co-productions, especially given that they are designed to support Netflix's business in local markets but are able to do so without needing to compromise to secure global distribution, which is already guaranteed for any Netflix original. However, a case study of a range of local Netflix originals from Western and non-Western countries reveals a muddled relationship with spatial capital, wherein the perceived "universality" of a given story or genre dictates how textual strategies are deployed to either locate or dislocate a particular show from its country of origin. Netflix's original programming strategy is built—like real estate—on the importance of location. Yet critically, it is defined by an inscrutable approach to spatial capital that reinforces how distributional capital continues to limit and restrict how space and place function across television markets, even within a purported global network provided by the streaming service.

Location matters, in other words, but it must co-exist with dislocation to meet the distinct and often contradictory goals of so-called global programming in the contemporary television marketplace.

Global flows of spatial capital

When the cast and crew of *Blindspot* engaged in strategic location shooting in Venice, Italy, as documented in the previous chapter, the trip had an additional component on top of the three-day shoot for the third season premiere. Cast members were also responsible for a day of press and promotion alongside local journalists and local stations. *Blindspot* had been sold internationally by producing studio Warner Bros. Television based on the show's pilot, so the decision to shift toward foreign location shooting did not change the terms of those agreements; there was no additional financial incentive to shooting internationally from a profit perspective. However, the cast recording brief segments for local stations and glad-handing the local broadcasting community on behalf of the studio was—to creator Martin Gero—"a phenomenal way to help those partners that had been support-ing us for so long." He considers it a case of "diplomacy," which would no doubt help Warner Bros. make future sales in the Italian market when those local broadcasting partners saw how the studio supports them.

International distribution is critical to the success of a U.S. broadcast tele-vision series, although they enter that marketplace with a distinct advantage over shows from other countries: there is inherent cultural capital attached to American productions, which leverage a combination of factors—higher budgets, star power, conglomerate backing—to dominate the global tel-evision marketplace. Although scholars have pointed to the impact that this has on local media markets through the lens of cultural imperialism (Schiller 1976; Ramiro Beltran 1978), other scholars have identified such often problematic globalization as a complex exchange of cultural capital, positioning media as an interrogative force against modernity (Appadurai 1996), a foundation for a transnational cultural sphere (Hilmes 2011), and as an evolving flow of content across borders (Moran 2009b). There is no question that the United States' significant export of television content cre-ates an imbalance given that U.S. networks historically do not purchase programs from international sources; this imbalance is a potential threat to other countries' domestic output such that they—including neighboring Canada—institute policies mandating the broadcast of locally produced content. However, countries have historically been able to participate in the U.S. television industry in three key ways that complicate a purely cultural imperialist reading.

The first is through format sales, which allow for broadcasters in coun-tries like Israel or South Korea to sell the ideas behind a series rather than the series itself (Moran 1998, 2009a; Moran and Malbon 2006; Oren and Shahaf 2012). Although series like Showtime's *Homeland* (2011–2020, Israel) or ABC's *The Good Doctor* (2017–present, South Korea) are exam-ples of scripted program formats turned into U.S. productions, program formats are most common in reality television, with many of broadcast television's most enduring reality success stories—*Survivor* (2000–present, Sweden), *Big Brother* (2000–present, Netherlands), *The Voice* (2011–present, Netherlands), *American Idol* (2002–present, UK)—originating in other countries. These formats are often designed to be sold into the United States and other large markets; as such, they are devoid of explicit spatial capital that would complicate the process of developing a version in other countries. Scholarship has thus framed this process as one of localization, with producers gaining the ability to take regional and national differences into account as they develop their own take on the basic foundation offered.

The second is the inverse: foreign series based on program formats devel-oped in the U.S. marketplace. Although this in many ways reinforces the dominance of U.S. television, such adaptations create opportunities for local producers to engage with America's cultural influence: the documentary *Exporting Raymond* (2010) is a mistitled film about the Russian version of CBS sitcom *Everybody Loves Raymond* (1996–2005), as the resulting sitcom *The Vororins* (2009–2016) is not so much an export of American culture as it is a glimpse into how local broadcasting traditions confront and engage with the series' premise. Program formats, moving in both directions, do not displace America's position as the dominant cultural force in the global television marketplace, but the texts themselves present clear discursive struggles over that impact, such that a simple cultural imperialist reading fails to account for how spatial capital and distributional capital intersect therein.

Those intersections become explicit in the third form of participation, which is co-productions, wherein broadcasters from multiple countries partner to produce a particular series. Although co-productions are often developed independent of the U.S. marketplace, U.S. distributors often enter into co-production agreements for series based in Canada and the UK, and on rare occasion with other Western nations. Research into such co-productions has focused on the compromises in spatial capital that occur when a series is funded by production studios in multiple countries, particularly in cases where they share a common language. Returning to the example of *Love It or List It, Too*, Serra Tinic's research (2005, 2015) identifies how Canada's reliance on co-productions with the United States and other countries has shaped the depictions of Canada—and often the erasure of Canada—in original series, arguing in 2015 that "Canadian producers and their coproduction partners tended to erase culturally specific markers and follow the grammar of American network formulas and genres" (56). This is similarly reflected in research into Canadian franchises like *Degrassi* that became more entrenched with the U.S. market over time (Levine 2009). Such power dynamics can be seen in other contexts, as with the expanding influence of China in the media landscape. Major film studios have begun partnering with Chinese producers to bypass the country's quota system for theatrical releases, and in many cases will use strategic location shooting to produce and set portions of a film in China as a way to directly appeal to local audiences (Kokas 2017). This has led to blockbuster films such as *The Meg* (2018) outperforming North American box office results using these strategies (Frater 2018). Although the stricter rules facing China's television marketplace have led to less strategic location shooting work in these markets, U.S. producers rely on format sales and co-productions to leverage this growing market, tailoring their programs to appease Chinese authorities and U.S. balance sheets equally (Roxborugh 2018).

However, larger shifts in television distribution are reshaping how spatial capital and distributional capital intersect. For one, while content produced outside of English-speaking countries has historically struggled to receive distribution in North America, streaming services have opened the door for this content, whether as acquisitions for services like Netflix, Hulu, and Amazon Prime, or as the subject of specific streaming services built around foreign content, like the Warner Bros. run DramaFever, which distributed dramas from Korea and other Asian countries from 2009 to 2018. Such content has always been available through piracy and other forms of informal distribution, but its presence on formal streaming services made it accessible for a wider audience across the world (Lee 2018; Han 2019). Whether as a small niche within a larger streaming service not dependent on advertising, or as the center of its own service, this content has newfound economic capital in a streaming environment (Elkins "Algorithmic. . . " 2019a). While U.S. acquisitions of foreign content are still far outpaced by foreign acquisitions of U.S. content like *Blindspot*, the increased visibility of this content on streaming services creates a more identifiable form of cultural exchange.

The streaming services have also cleared the way for program development strategies that embrace this principle of cultural exchange, but outside of the traditional co-production models where it has been most visible. In 2015, the globe-trotting drama series *Sense8* (2015–2018) debuted, following a group of characters around the world who were mysteriously connected to each other despite their geographic distance. This included characters in Kenya, South Korea, India, the UK, Germany, Mexico, and the United States, with the show filming on location in each of these countries. The series is technically a U.S. production, but its global scale was consciously tied to the distributor that commissioned it: Netflix, which broke into original programming in 2012 with the Norwegian co-production *Lilyhammer* (2012–2014) and began commissioning content on its own in 2013. However, initially this content was only intended for the U.S. market, with production studios selling international rights to other broadcasters and channels in most global markets due to Netflix's lack of penetration into those countries. Beginning with 2014's *Marco Polo* (2014–2016), however, Netflix began commissioning series designed to not only serve their U.S. subscribers but also appeal to an increasingly large number of international subscribers, holding onto foreign rights in the process.

Sense8 was the epitome of this strategy: a U.S. series that was designed, from the beginning, to use the spatial capital of filming its first season in 11 countries and 16 cities as an appeal to both domestic and international subscribers, particularly those in the countries and continents where the production traveled. Shows like *Sense8* were a critical first step in Netflix's global expansion, which separated it from other streaming services that have made either no movement into international markets (Hulu) or minimal expansion (Amazon Prime), leading to extensive region-locking (Elkins 2018, 2019b). The year after *Sense8* debuted, Netflix fully committed to global expansion as its key business model (Villareal 2016), with the majority of its subscribers and the bulk of its subscriber growth being outside of North America as of 2020 (Kharpal 2020). Key to this growth has been an enormous investment into original content, now being produced for a global subscriber base that would subsequently reshape the types of programs being produced and—relevant to this book—the spatial capital therein.

Netflix's impact on television distribution has gone beyond its own original programming based out of the United States. First, in their role as a distributor of content from other countries, Netflix has dramatically simplified the process of gaining access to a global audience. Whereas previously a series looking abroad to secure financing would require a production company to make distribution deals in different markets ahead of beginning production, often resulting in co-production or co-financing agreements, Netflix is able to offer distribution in all of the territories where they operate. Rather than trying to sell a show to different broadcasters in every country, tailoring it to their respective needs, producers now have the option to sell to all of those countries through Netflix, making them a particularly valuable partner for local broadcasters in countries like the UK, with Netflix making deals to distribute series like BBC Two's *Black Earth Rising* (2018) around the world.

Netflix's ability to offer near-global clearance makes it a valued co-production and distribution partner for local broadcasters, but it has also leveraged its global reach to bypass local broadcasters and build relationships with local production companies in markets outside of the United States. Beginning with Mexico's *Club de Cuervos* (2015–2019), Netflix followed in the footsteps of major Hollywood studios to engage in their own form of "flexible localization" (Brannon Donoghue 2014, 2017), commissioning programs directly to air in growth markets with the hopes of building subscriber numbers in the show's country of origin. However, these series were not only being produced to debut on Netflix in that country—rather, Netflix applied its "Netflix Originals" branding to each series as they debuted globally, with dubbed audio and subtitles for multiple languages to give each series further reach. This development meant that studios historically producing television series for markets like Mexico—forced to cobble together distribution deals in other countries to expand the scope and scale of their development—were now producing content that Netflix subscribers around the world would be watching.

These shifts in the distribution of television are changing how spatial capital is constructed and deployed in these programs. Although traditional co-productions still exist, how series that straddle geographic borders navigate questions of spatial capital is shifting in response to the complex cultural exchange currently defining the global marketplace. Michele Hilmes (2014) identifies the emergence of the "transitional coproduction," where series are not only financed by multiple countries but also developed specifically to combine and reconcile their respective markets. Media scholar Serra Tinic (2015) points to the BBC America original series *Orphan Black* (2013–2017) as a new type of U.S.–Canadian co-production that reflects changes in their respective industries and also differs in that "there is no erasure of its cultural spatiality or domestic reference points." To understand this new era of global production, *Orphan Black* provides an instructive model for textual strategies of spatial capital that are applicable to this current configuration and which serve as a foundation for considering how Netflix's locally commissioned original content—distinct from but related to co-productions—fits within this shifting global television marketplace and the role of spatial capital therein.

Toronto, but not Toronto: *Orphan Black* and polysemic place

In the opening scene of *Orphan Black*, an aerial shot shows a train moving toward a city center (see Figure 3.1). Sarah Manning is asleep on that train until an announcement for "Huxley Station"—a fictional name—wakes her, and as she steps off onto the platform there is an announcement about the "next train to New York City." We next see Sarah at a payphone with signs for "York Street" in the background, speaking in a British accent, explaining to the person on the line that she's "back in town" and wishes to see her daughter, Kiera. She then sees a distressed woman on the platform and moves closer to discover that it is someone who looks remarkably like herself: it is, in fact, her clone, and the woman jumps in front of an ongoing train and kickstarts the series' science-fiction journey. But before she jumps, she stands before Sarah in front of a damaged poster advertising

Figure 3.1 A screenshot from the opening scene of *Orphan Black*'s pilot, where a train is shown approaching Toronto's Union Station with the base of the CN Tower in the distance. The camera moves upwards but stops before approaching the tower's iconic observation deck.

Screenshot by author.

local information with the top half of the poster that would reveal their location torn away, leaving only "Metropolitan and Surrounding Areas" behind.

This scene is an ideal introduction into the distinct negotiation of spatial capital operating within this U.S.–Canadian co-production. Based solely on this description, there is no reason to believe that this scene is not taking place in the United States. The announcement about New York City is the only explicit spatial capital in the scene, with background signage far less noticeable to an average audience member. The only thing we know for sure from this scene is that it is not taking place in New York City, but that bit of specificity leaves an open door for a viewer to believe that we are watching a story play out in a U.S. city by which New York City is accessible by train.

But for a Canadian audience, the scene has plenty of clues that suggest otherwise. In the opening aerial shot, the train is approaching a structure that looks suspiciously similar to the base of Toronto's iconic CN Tower, but the shot stops abruptly without continuing up the skyline to confirm the suspicion. The trains in "Huxley Station," meanwhile, bear a striking resemblance to the green-and-white GO trains of Toronto's public transit system, which includes a central hub at Union Station, off York Street; these trains are black-and-white, though, and bear different branding. In the following scene, as Sarah investigates her clone's belongings, she finds a driver's license that looks like an Ontario driver's license, but the province's name is missing, and the address is blurred out. It's a collection of circumstantial evidence that would tell anyone with a passing familiarity with Toronto that, at the very least, they are watching a series that was filmed on Canadian soil, although the question of its setting remains open.

Obviously, the producers of *Orphan Black* had tools at their disposal that could have been used to clarify this question of setting, if they had so desired: an explicit skyline in an establishing shot, an onscreen chyron identifying the location, and direct expositional dialogue could have easily been implemented to avoid any potential confusion. However, the producers of the show also had the ability to evoke less spatial capital: there was no need to mention New York City, they could have shot scenes to avoid the "York Street" signage, and the opening aerial of the train could have stopped short of revealing the base of the CN Tower. This liminality is consciously constructed, in other words, and requires a rethinking of the textual strategies available to producers in this context. Tinic argues that what separates *Orphan Black* from typical Canadian shows is that it lacks the "erasure" of specific Canadian-ness, but I contend here that spatial capital is too complex to be considered in terms of erasure. *Orphan Black* is neither erasing nor specifying spatial capital; rather, it is deploying spatial capital selectively and strategically, in ways that confound a singular reading but provide evidence to support competing claims.

The result, I argue, is a polysemic sense of place, defined by its ability to be read as local by different audiences in different markets. Constructing a polysemic place relies on generating a setting that is never explicitly identified as being a particular location but is rather constructed using strategies that nonetheless contain spatial capital to certain audience segments. Such places avoid actively acknowledging landmarks recognizable by a general audience member and associated with a particular location—like the CN Tower—along with any markers of municipal or national specificity pertaining to such locations. The goal is to create a setting that Canadians are able to read as local based on trace evidence that is either invisible to or ultimately insignificant to an U.S. or global audience, with the belief that those audiences will presume—based on the lack of explicit suggestion that the series is set in Toronto—that they are seeing an unnamed U.S. city. Polysemic places have been critical to Canadian productions with U.S. distribution partners in the past, with details like street names and neighborhoods used as a signal for viewers of shows like the ABC co-production *Rookie Blue* (2010–2015) north of the border. The reason that Tinic believes *Orphan Black* separates itself is because its choices run the risk of accumulating a greater amount of specificity than an average series, but I argue this is offset by the concrete spatial capital affirming a U.S. reading. This renders Orphan Black's "Toronto, but not Toronto" a heightened form of this polysemic deployment of spatial capital that showcases the nuances of spatial capital central to the textual dynamics of international co-productions.

The reasons for the series' commitment to polysemic place are a byproduct of the series' production context. Although shot in Canada and developed by a Canadian production company, Temple Street Productions, *Orphan Black* was actually first sold in the United States to BBC America after Canadian science fiction-focused channel Space passed on the series initially. Although Space—owned by national broadcaster CTV—subsequently joined on as a distributor once the show had been sold in the United States and was involved moving forward, it meant that they were now in "second position" when it came to the decision-making on the series. Accordingly, reporting suggests that the reason the show is not explicitly set in Toronto is that "BBC America . . . didn't want the show to be identified as taking place in Toronto" (Dixon 2014). In an interview with *Entertainment Weekly* (Ross 2014), showrunners Graeme Manson and John Fawcett confirm as much: when asked directly where the show takes place, and whether they are "specifically making it a very generic place," there are two answers. The first is that they believe it is in line with the story that they are telling, with Manson arguing "it adds a certain universality to the show that we're looking for. Since we don't mind the audience being off-kilter or off-step, it works for us." Fawcett, meanwhile, reframes this as a practical concern regarding their dual audiences: "To be honest, we don't want to say we're American and alienate the Canadians, or say we're Canadian and alienate the Americans. The bottom line is we're one big happy family." Their approach, in other words, may be dictated by distributional considerations of spatial capital, but they are also working to frame the decision as being consistent with the narrative burden of spatial capital within the series.

These ideas of universality and "one big happy family" are underselling the complexity of the negotiation of spatial capital happening in the early episodes of *Orphan Black*. Extending beyond the opening scenes analyzed earlier, the show features various elements that would seem to confirm that the show's Toronto filming location is also its setting. Cars display license plates—a classic tell of where a show is filmed or set—identical to those in Ontario, although always in ways that are identifiable to someone who recognizes the plates but not readable by someone who does not. When Sarah poses as her clone Beth to clear out her bank account, the manager returns with Canada's distinct multicolored Canadian bills, although the camera never lingers on them long enough to get a clear glimpse of any of the historical figures that appear on them. Similar clues—like a briefly seen printed boarding pass for a flight from Toronto to Baltimore and a business card featuring a phone number with an Ontario area code—are further breadcrumbs for Canadians to follow, and the second episode goes further by explicitly identifying that a third clone is living in the Toronto suburb of Scarborough. Combined, this evidence is enough spatial capital for someone to determine that the show is, in fact, taking place in Toronto.

However, this spatial capital remains untethered to cultural specificity if one lacks the underlying knowledge to interpret it. Without an explicit acknowledgment through dialogue or on-screen details that do not require pausing the image and zooming in to confirm that the show is taking place in Ontario, these details could easily go unseen. This is particularly true given that the series continues to combine these appeals to Canadian audiences with specificity intended to anchor the show in the United States. For instance, the fourth clone, Cosima, is a graduate student at the University of Minnesota, but the series never indicates any kind of cross-border travel when the characters converge. The polysemy of the series' spatial capital comes from creating a setting that eschews explicit acknowledgment of locality—the painted GO trains, the "Municipal Police" logos on the cop cars—but containing subtle appeals to its Canadian-ness. At the same time, this Canadian-ish space is punctuated by explicit acknowledgment of real, American cities in close proximity. It is an acknowledgment that for the show's location to be polysemic, it cannot simply be generic, as it must confront the different approaches to spatial capital among the show's audience. Whereas Canadian viewers are conditioned to seeing shows filmed in Canada but set in the United States hide many of the subtler details that *Orphan Black* includes, U.S. viewers are conditioned to see any show where characters are speaking English in what appears to be in North America as taking place in America, meaning that mentions of New York and Minnesota can reaffirm that belief without alienating a Canadian audience from believing that Toronto is finally allowed to play itself. While I have previously outlined cases where combinations of ignorance or logistics shape spatial capital, here the polysemic sense of place in *Orphan Black* is a carefully constructed confusion, controlled and ultimately deployed by the show's producers in accordance with their distribution partners.

Orphan Black may not be the first effort to generate a polysemic sense of place through the strategic deployment of spatial capital, as other Canadian co-productions have tried to walk a similar tightrope to varying degrees, but the series' distinct origins—ordered by an American cable channel funded by a British broadcaster's global distribution arm and produced by a Canadian company—result in an embodiment of distribution's impact on spatial capital broadly. Notably, after the series had been widely distributed and established its audience, the concern about perceived alienation from BBC America began to fade. By the show's fourth season, when its audience was now invested in the show's complex serial narrative, spatial capital was no longer considered a barrier that needed to be overcome. In a pivotal scene, the show for the first time features the full CN Tower, visible for an extended period, with no attempt at eliding its presence in the Toronto skyline. It serves as an implicit acknowledgment that polysemic places are a product of distributional negotiations of spatial capital. Once the initial burdens of the series' co-production were met in early seasons, there was less anxiety about embracing the show's filming location as its setting. It also creates a framework for evaluating spatial capital's role within new forms of global television development that bypass some of those initial burdens, drawing from these traditions of polysemy to confront new challenges that come from creating original programs for an always already global audience.

International and intra-corporate: Netflix originals and spatial capital

Netflix's original programming strategy with respect to international markets is built on similar rhetoric of polysemy as *Orphan Black*, insofar as these programs are simultaneously imagined as local and global programming initiatives in the same way that *Orphan Black* was successfully framed as both Canadian and American. In 2017, chief content officer Ted Sarandos claimed that "great storytelling knows no geographical bounds" while touting Netflix's expanding global production slate (Lodderhose 2017), developed through partnerships with production companies based in markets that include typical U.S. co-production partners like the UK alongside markets like Spain, India, and South Africa that have historically rarely shared such arrangements with Hollywood studios. But unlike those co-productions, Netflix is not collaborating with local broadcasters: they *are* the local broadcaster, meaning they are the sole forces negotiating the local interests and global demands of their subscribers. This intra-corporate approach to international programming creates a significant burden on programming executives, program creators, local production companies, and Netflix's marketing team to successfully navigate the creative and industrial challenges of producing programs for multiple markets on a larger scale than has ever been attempted.

Netflix's approach to this has played out within the trade press, and through development executives focused on not only international programs broadly, but also executives responsible for originals in individual markets or regions of markets. In doing so, Netflix fights against discourses of cultural imperialism that come with an American studio operating in the global marketplace—this is necessary given Netflix's need to develop positive relationships with government regulators and existing telecommunications providers that control the ability to reach new subscribers in expansion countries. In the case of Canada, which regulates broadcast content to force Canadian broadcasters to prioritize local programming over U.S. imports, Netflix promised a $500 million investment of both programming and production infrastructure into the Canadian film and television industry in order to stave off threats of regulation, a commitment that it met in 2019 (Vlessing 2019). Still, in 2020 the Canadian government moved forward with regulation that would force them to "invest in Canadian stories" in addition to these other commitments (Vlessing 2020), language that Netflix itself has used when framing its local production initiatives around the world. When Netflix announced its first Indian original series *Sacred Games* (2018–2019) in 2016, VP of international originals Eric Barmack said in a press release that "*Sacred Games* reinforces our commitment to bring the authenticity of local stories to Netflix members across 190 countries worldwide" (Ramachandran 2016). This language frames Netflix as a distributor of local stories, working to help writers and producers to execute their vision in their own market with the guarantee of reaching Netflix's global audience. However, Netflix would prefer to be able to produce these shows on the company's own terms, and without an explicit mandate that restricts their business interests. While self-determined, profit-driven contingencies on spatial capital are acceptable, government-determined and cultural-focused contingencies on spatial capital are not.

A similar discourse echoes in Netflix's efforts to develop original programming in Africa, beginning with 2020's *Queen Sono* based in South Africa. Speaking to *Variety* about their efforts to develop productions in countries like Nigeria and Kenya (Vourlias 2020), Netflix's head of African originals Dorothy Ghettuba notes that

> [W]e have come across great creatives and great producers who have, for the longest while, been working with what they have, and now we give them the opportunity with this platform and this backing from this company to really do these best . . . it's how do we shepherd them across the finish line?

This rhetoric consciously places Netflix as a better alternative to a traditional co-production model requiring a cobbling together of funds from local broadcasters. The choice to frame Netflix's role as shepherding frames this within economic terms—there is an implied "financial" before "backing"— but also positions the company within the ongoing creative and distributional support that allows a series to reach a much wider audience. Netflix is not just promising the continent of Africa that they are making a financial commitment to local production: they are promising access to global markets, a form of corporate service that Netflix hopes will offset any reservations regarding an American company expanding globally at such a rapid rate.

That being said, there is a second concurrent discourse in the way Netflix frames its original programming that speaks of the burden these series face creatively. On the one hand, Netflix did not come with the same demands that some local producers have faced when it comes to working with U.S. producers: author Vikram Chandra, who wrote the 2006 graphic novel that inspired *Sacred Games*, told the *Hindustan Times* that

> [U]nlike mainstream American channels where the absence of American characters makes everyone nervous, Netflix is unique and brilliant in its notion of global indies. . . . They didn't mind at all that we didn't have a CIA agent at the front of this series.
>
> (Choudhary 2018)

Chandra's separation between what were likely efforts to Americanize his source material during a previous film rights deal with Focus Features and the Netflix approach is meaningful, but just because Netflix's development is not U.S.-centric does not mean there are no burdens attached to the distribution agreement made with the company. In the case of *Queen Sono*, a *TIME* report on the series' development notes that the series' global reach "brought greater expectations and more pressure to translate a story rooted in South Africa for not just the continent but also global audiences" for creator Kagiso Lediga (Haynes 2020). Lediga asserts, "The more specific you are, the more authentic a story is," but adds that "the rest is trying to make it clearly understandable," suggesting a needed balance between the authenticity valued locally with the legibility that Netflix desires for a global audience.

It is here where authenticity meets universality in the development of Netflix original programming. In announcing one of their first local UK commissions, *Sex Education*, in late 2017, Netflix's vice president of original content Cindy Holland describes the show—commissioned from British producer Eleven Film—as a "distinctive, fresh and witty examination of the universally awkward teenage experience" (Vlessing 2017). Similar language of universality emerges in the announcement of Netflix's Spanish teen series *Elite* earlier in 2017, with Barmack quoted as being "excited to be working with producers and writers so relevant to the Spanish industry on a very different teen thriller that will push across borders and thrill a global audience" (Lang and Hopewell 2017). Although trade stories about these developments emphasize their relationship to Netflix's push into local commissions, and the *Elite* quote in particular pays deference to their relationship to local industry, the notion of "push[ing] across borders" and "universal experience" belies Netflix's interest in being able to package local originals alongside their U.S. originals. Barmack echoes this desire in the press release announcing the pickup for *Queen Sono*, stating that "taking talent like this and telling stories to the rest of the world puts Pearl in the same category as other strong female characters like Claire Underwood in *House of Cards* and Jessica Jones" (Vourlias 2018). This need for international series to simultaneously serve local audiences but nonetheless fit into the same categories as Netflix's domestic original programming points to how genre, narrative, and other forces shape foreign content for American consumption. Tinic (2015) frames this as "industry productions" in a Canadian context, even if Netflix is still allowing shows to debut in local languages or focus on domestic protagonists.

The intersection of authenticity and universality fundamentally shapes how spatial capital functions within these Netflix series. On the one hand, unlike many U.S. co-productions, these series are not under explicit pressure to "appear" American in the way that *Orphan Black* was, suggesting that these locally commissioned shows are spared the need for polysemy enforced by even the shrewdest co-productions. On the other hand, the theoretically global audience—and the likelihood of a program's continued success if it could successfully "push across borders" as Barmack suggests—of these programs functions as a crucial variable in how spatial capital is deployed or not deployed in these series. This makes the textual strategies discussed in the previous chapter and the polysemic model of *Orphan Black* critical tools for evaluating the distinct distributional burden required of a local production commissioned by a U.S.-based global streaming service. This analysis begins with the two non-Western series previously referenced that were the first produced by Netflix in their respective regions and where spatial capital is unavoidably specific but nonetheless bears the markings of universality that speak of the series' desired global reach.

Distinct settings, universal genres: *Sacred Games* and *Queen Sono*

Debuting in 2018 as Netflix's first original series in India, *Sacred Games* makes no effort to elide its setting: through dialogue, the series regularly anchors its story in India, in terms of both its modern-day police storyline in Mumbai and its historical counter-narrative that moves throughout the country. Flashbacks are regularly accompanied by on-screen chyrons locating the action in a particular setting, and the stories—detailing the rise of notorious gangster Ganesh Gaitonde, who is communicating with a Mumbai police officer in the present—intersect with the political and cultural history of the country. The show regularly films on location in and around Mumbai, creating images that are unmistakably rooted in the geography of the city, leveraging the spatial capital involved as opposed to attempting to mitigate or otherwise obscure it.

However, *Sacred Games* nonetheless approaches spatial capital differently than other series that film on location in the city where they are set. Whereas *Blindspot*'s strategic location shooting leaned heavily on establishing shots to place the characters within a larger landscape, *Sacred Games* is very tightly focused, avoiding wide shots of the city and rarely featuring establishing shots between scenes in its first season. This is despite the fact that because of the parallel narratives, the show is regularly moving from one location—and time period—to another, a situation in which transitional material is valuable. This absence can be read in two ways. It could be seen as a form of erasure: establishing shots would continually reinforce the show's Mumbai setting, which could be seen as alienating to global audiences who are focused on the modern story's parallels to U.S. and British spy series like the BBC's *Bodyguard* (2018), for which Netflix was the global distributor in the same year. However, it could equally be seen as a reminder that in a local context, establishing shots are not necessary: Indian audiences do not need to be reminded that the show is taking place in Mumbai, meaning that such reinforcement of spatial capital could appear redundant. The absence of establishing shots does mean that opportunities where spatial capital could have been developed or amplified are being ignored, but those shots would primarily be in service of a global audience, not a local one. Of the global Netflix originals analyzed in this chapter, *Sacred Games* is by far the most specific, leveraging familiarity with a global genre of counterterrorism but largely resisting deploying textual strategies that would reposition its inherent spatial capital in globalized terms.

Released two years later as Netflix's first original series based out of Africa, *Queen Sono* is much more invested in the strategies of spatial capital outlined in the previous chapter. The opening scene of the spy drama from South Africa loudly announces through an on-screen chyron that eponymous character Queen is in Zanzibar, and a drone shot moves from the ocean to a seawall, where the camera finds Queen walking her way toward her latest mission (see Figure 3.2). Throughout the series, new locations are announced with colorful chyrons that take up most of the screen, and the same chyrons are used when the series returns to Johannesburg, where Queen was raised, and where the backstory of her mother's assassination is set. While some of these chyrons are superimposed over specific scenes, many are set over traditional establishing shots of city skylines or drone shots of the respective locations, which include a combination of cities and regions (Joburg, Harare, Nairobi, Zanzibar) and countries (Congo, Kenya) over the course of the show's six-episode first season. Similar establishing shots are also used in episodes primarily set in Johannesburg, where the Special Operations Group for whom Queen works is based.

Figure 3.2 The opening chyron in the first episode of Netflix's *Queen Sono*. Similar chyrons are used throughout the series to represent countries and cities across Africa.

Screenshot by author.

Queen Sono's embrace of its varied location shooting is in part based on its status not simply as South Africa's first original series, but as the first original on the entire continent, clearly generating an active interest in highlighting the series' transnational production geography within the text itself. But it is also a by-product of its genre: the chyrons and establishing shots are in line with U.S. spy series like *Alias* (2001–2006), with globetrotting Sydney Bristow working undercover for SD-6 and traveling to locations around the world. Although the specific focus on African nations is distinct, and the location shooting differs from how a typical U.S. series would articulate spatial capital, *Queen Sono*'s relationship to those locations remains fairly indistinct from the touristic approach seen in *Blindspot*, despite the intended appeal to local audiences. The fact that this drama is rooted in Johannesburg means that the story remains specific to the African continent, but the need for the show to be "clearly understandable" for a global audience results in fairly generic spy conflicts—terrorists, corrupt government officials, and so on—driving the primary "plot" of any given episode of the series, with place primarily functioning as a narrative backdrop rather than a narrative engine for the series.

However, *Queen Sono*—like *Sacred Games*—does not work to hide the specificity of its setting, although where it chooses to embrace that setting is restrictive. In a review for *Indiewire*, one of a range of U.S. publications that reviewed the series when it debuted in 2020, Tambay Obenson

(2020) writes that the show's setting "allows the series to introduce themes that likely aren't being discussed during dinnertime conversations in many homes, at least in the West." He summarizes a collection of small moments that point to the cultural and political issues relevant to the African continent, concluding that

> [T]hese flourishes aren't necessarily there to move the plot forward, and sometimes do feel inorganic, but they help to contextualize the series' overall backdrop and might even educate audiences on ongoing debates that affect Africans and Africa, without the didacticism.

Sacred Games uses its flashback structure to tell a historical story rooted in Indian culture within a counterterrorism plot derivative of a U.S. series like *24* (2001–2010) in its contemporary narrative. By contrast, *Queen Sono* presents derivative spy narratives inflected by issues like neocolonialism and Africa's relationship with global institutions, details that Obenson frames as a way of speaking to African audiences and educating Western audiences simultaneously.

The result is a distinct form of spatial capital operating in these two non-Western productions, wherein genre is used as a universalizing function. Other details of storytelling and textuality are consciously deployed to engage with spatial capital enough to simultaneously appeal to local/regional audiences and preemptively defend against cultural imperialist rejections of Netflix's global programming strategy. The two series showcase the sliding scale of spatial capital within this strategy, with *Sacred Games* largely resisting further globalization whereas *Queen Sono* leans into its global appeal, likely because it is predominantly in English and thus perceived as more accessible. Obenson rejects this particular approach, concluding that *Queen Sono* is "version 1.0 of Netflix's African Originals" and arguing that it should strive to be "less of a derivative of an American procedural peppered with 'Africanisms'" and instead aspired to be "unapologetically African." But in *Entertainment Weekly*'s coverage of *Queen Sono*, the series is framed as a spy story "from a South African point of view," and that while "it may be similar to other espionage stories . . . it's told without America as a central figure," suggesting the low burden of spatial capital applied to the show from a U.S. perspective (Yohannes 2020). The series and the discourse around it showcase how Netflix's careful negotiation of the series' filming locations and storytelling communicates the desired brand messaging of their African programming initiative—spatial capital is deployed as part of that strategy. The distribution of *Queen Sono* and *Sacred Games* by Netflix set a specific burden of spatial capital that the company defined based on a balance of specificity and universality. Although the resulting representation may not have met all expectations, both series were successfully positioned in industry trade press as breakthroughs for Netflix's local production commitments. Each earned a second season renewal.

This sliding scale of specificity and universality can be seen across Netflix's original programming. However, shifting focus from these non-Western examples to series produced in Western markets highlights the risk of spatial capital sliding beyond polysemy into inscrutability.

"American influence, but [local] ingredients": *Sex Education* and *Elite*

In the opening scene of *Sex Education*, which debuted on Netflix in 2019, the camera moves from the living room of a family home to the bedroom upstairs, where teenager Adam and his girlfriend Aimee are—fitting given the show's subject—having sex. As they engage in conversation, both Adam and Aimee have what would be broadly described as British accents, strongly suggesting that the series in question is taking place somewhere in England. The scene's final line reaffirms this, as Aimee uses the term "spunk," an English slang term for semen; it was such a clear indicator that the line in question has been enshrined as the "Top Definition" for "spunk" on Urban Dictionary, affirming *Sex Education* as a beacon of English cultural representation where at least this bit of slang is concerned.

However, immediately after this scene concludes, the show's title card first appears and does so over a very different series of images. In the first, a lone rower travels down a still river, surrounded by trees as the title appears superimposed over the landscape. In the next shot, we see a wooded valley, with a small collection of buildings largely obscured by the trees around them, too far away to give any sense of specific architecture. The third shot doubles down on this generic set of images with a close-up shot of a random tree, easily capable of being placed in any number of different towns, cities, countries, or even continents. The concluding shot then finally anchors the images to a location featured in the series itself, panning up from a pine tree to reveal the house where Otis, the show's protagonist and teenage sex therapist, lives with his mother, an actual sex therapist. The house sits overlooking another generic river, and the camera shifts inside to Otis, waking up to start his day.

The juxtaposition between these two negotiations of spatial capital—distinctly British characters followed by a distinctly generic landscape—diverges from what has been seen in the case studies in this chapter thus far. Unlike *Orphan Black*, *Sex Education* cannot reasonably construct a sense of place that could be read as multiple different countries: the characters speak with accents that clearly mark the series as emerging from the UK, even if an average American viewer may not be able to distinguish between the distinct accents of the various countries and regions therein. However, the vague montage of images of the surrounding landscape are a far cry from the evocative drone shots that signal *Queen Sono*'s African backdrop, seemingly ignoring spatial capital despite engaging with textual strategies associated with it. It is not a simple case of the production trying to obscure a case of city-for-city doubling; the shots in question come from the series' production in Wales, which has emerged as a crucial production hub for UK productions, but the show is not trying to suggest it's *not* Wales. And yet throughout the show's two-season run, *Sex Education* never confirms that it takes place in Wales, or in the UK at all, choosing instead to articulate an "inscrutable place" that actively pushes back against any attempts to pin down a clear sense of spatial capital.

The specific choice to avoid setting the series in Wales, despite the show being shot there, could come down to the fact that the series' cast is largely English, meaning that the decision to take advantage of Wales' crew base and production facilities did not come with a perceived burden of casting the series with Welsh actors or working to give the characters Welsh accents. However, *Sex Education* does not simply generate a generic UK setting out of its collection of locations in Wales, as evidenced when Otis makes his way to school. Moordale High is a fictional high school, but it is also a dislocated one. In an early scene, characters Maeve and Jackson walk down a hallway in the school, passing by various other students (see Figure 3.3). However, the scene feels at odds with the school's exterior, which is a large histori-cal building. The hallway is filled with rows of yellow lockers that, while common in the United States, are unlikely to appear in British secondary schools. Jackson is wearing a "letterman jacket" bearing Moordale's logo, but the letterman jacket is a distinctly American convention, as is the idea of a school logo like the one that appears on backpacks and banners in the scene's background. In motion, the scene is still clearly placed in the UK

Figure 3.3 A scene from the first episode of *Sex Education*, featuring numerous pieces of spatial capital tied to American high school experiences—the school's logo, the lockers, the letterman jacket—that caused confusion for viewers.

Screenshot by author.

based on the actors' accents, but as a static image it would be mistaken for a scene from an American high school series.

This confusion is furthered by the establishing shots of students milling about outside the school. While the first scene where Otis and his friend Eric arrive features a group of students playing rugby, a later scene shows them throwing an American football, a choice that raised particular alarm bells for many watching the series from the UK. These details were all interrogated as part of a series of online articles confronting the show's relationship with spatial capital, in which creators and actors were asked to comment on these choices. In an article for *Radio Times* (Harrison 2019), creator Laurie Nunn and director Ben Taylor explain that these elements were consciously deployed as a nostalgic throwback to the John Hughes American high school films of the 1980s, acknowledging that this led to a contradiction of spatial capital. Taylor explains that "it was a stylistically deliberate choice early on that we dislocated it from geographically knowing exactly where it was," summarizing their approach as "Mid-Atlantic, American influence, but British ingredients." Nunn's argument for this choice is a creative one, wanting to set Otis's coming-of-age against the Hughesian aesthetic where "even though the films are riddled with anxieties and angst, you'd still look back at them as the best years of your life," as compared to a bleaker image of British high school typically depicted in media. Nunn and Taylor are arguing that the spatial implications of this creative choice were unavoidable, a necessary dislocation in order to successfully construct the nostalgic lens they felt was best for their story.

However, in the same *Radio Times* article, actress Gillian Anderson—who was born in the United States but spent much of her childhood in the UK—offers a different explanation. She agrees "there is a bit of both worlds . . . in the series," but goes a step further to say that "the hope is that Americans won't notice" the series' British setting if they see familiar iconography like the American footballs and letterman jackets, concluding, "I think Netflix feels quite strongly that they've hit on something with this amalgamation." Anderson, unlike Nunn and Taylor, is framing the show's American element as a cynical effort to expand the show's appeal to American viewers, effectively allowing Netflix to simultaneously leverage the series as evidence of its commitment to local UK production while also reaping the benefits of an increased value to U.S. subscribers alongside the added global value of a series that is perceived as an American cultural export.

It's the same logic that drove the polysemic spatial capital of *Orphan Black*, and of co-productions broadly, but *Sex Education* approaches this goal in a way that lacks any of the subtle elisions and redirections designed to allow the viewer to decide regarding where a series is set. *Sex Education* does not avoid establishing shots of the Welsh countryside, but it consciously avoids forms of spatial capital—such as pop culture references—that would be associated with Britain, whether through the dialogue of the characters or through the stories being told. When elements appear that could provide

clear instances of spatial capital, like a municipal bus line and the affiliated bus stations, the locations featured are entirely fictional: the name that
appears on the buses themselves (Poynton) is indeed a location in the UK
outside of Manchester, but Netflix told Buzzfeed—only when asked—that
the fictional Moordale is actually in the southwest UK, where no such location exists (Bryan 2019). The few locations that are explicitly mentioned
on buses or in dialogue—Lytton Hill, Ellencot—appear to be entirely fictional, despite the fact that an average American viewer would certainly
not recognize real place names from the UK if the creators had included
them. Whereas an enterprising viewer could "figure out" that *Orphan Black*
was set in Canada through a comprehensive Google search, *Sex Education*
is designed to be truly inscrutable, with no amount of Googling able to
"resolve" its dislocation of spatial capital.

As Anderson notes, however, this serves Netflix's larger global interests. It
is not necessarily clear whether this inscrutability was something that Netflix
encouraged the producers to explore, or whether Netflix's specific interest
in this project was due to the producers' goal to evoke American culture so
heavily and generate this confusion. However, the fact that Netflix's Spanish
original *Elite*—which debuted in October 2018, three months before *Sex
Education*—follows a similar pattern suggests that Netflix's development
process for local programming during this period carried a burden of spatial capital that led to such representations. *Elite* is positioned as a story of
class conflict, with three students from a working-class background given
scholarships to a prestigious international school after their own school is
condemned. The series' in medias res opening scene establishes the murder
mystery that structures the first season, intercut with one of the three students, Samuel, riding his bike passed the condemned San Esteban school in
what proves to be its only appearance in the series. The next scene follows
Samuel on his first day at the elite Las Encinas, which is established through
a drone shot: it is a large building, more reminiscent of an office building
than a school, with manicured grounds and a large pond spanned by a metal
bridge (see Figure 3.4). It is a shot that could just as easily be of an office
park in Florida as an international school somewhere in Spain; later in the
season, the show gestures to the existence of a "sister school" of Las Encinas located in Florida, which one imagines would look nearly identical. As
with *Sex Education*'s Moordale High, Las Encinas leans into iconography
of American high school series—hallways filled with lockers, school dances,
and so on—that is inconsistent with how an international school in Spain
would function.

Akin to *Sex Education*, *Elite* features various other establishing shots and
shooting locations that would not be mistaken for Florida, particularly in
the lower-class neighborhoods where Samuel, Christian, and Nadia live. But
while these locations feature cobblestone streets and Spanish architecture,
the larger establishing shots of the town where they live—which is never
named—are so wide that few details are visible. Although the characters

Figure 3.4 One of a range of establishing shots of Las Encinas, the private school
presumably located somewhere nearby Madrid featured in Netflix's *Elite*.
Screenshot by author.

reference other cities in Spain, they never specifically articulate their spatial
relationship to their location. The second season introduces two locations—
the Teatro Barcelo and an unnamed hotel rooftop—that are within the city
of Madrid, yet the series leaves this connection unspoken barring a hotel
sign for the (fictional) Starlite Madrid seen briefly at the top of the frame.[2]
Asked by *Variety* about the show's relationships to "themes [and] idiosyncrasies rooted in the Spanish culture," co-creator Carlos Montero explained
that "we didn't try to make a Spanish series nor for that matter an international one," arguing that while some stories were inspired by observations
about Spanish news or politics, this was not their focus (Granada 2019).
Here, Montero is suggesting that *Elite* sits outside of concerns of spatial
capital or that spatial capital is in some way not a valid framework for the
series. This choice echoes in the way the characters speak and act, with no
references to specifics of Spanish culture. When the writers included a joke
about the 2019 Eurovision Song Contest in its third season, it was one of the
first evocations of European popular culture in the series, reinforcing how
rarely the characters' perspectives on their situation are filtered through that
lens elsewhere in the series.

However, it is impossible for any series to be separated from its spatial
capital, particularly one like *Elite*. One key distinction between *Sex Education* and *Elite* is that the latter is a local language production, filmed almost
exclusively in what Netflix calls "European Spanish" outside of scenes in
the students' English class or in instances where certain characters—in particular Lucrecia, who is from Mexico—use English phrases. Historically,

such productions have failed to make significant headway in the American market due to a perceived aversion to subtitled content, but when considering spatial capital, it is also far more difficult to dislocate their sense of place if a distributor desired to do so. Whereas *Sex Education* is dealing with accented English, the use of Spanish in *Elite* creates a more significant barrier to the idea of Americans—to use Gillian Anderson's language—"not noticing" that the show is not set in the United States, which as evidenced by examples like *Orphan Black* carries a stigma for channels and networks. However, Netflix's local language productions are afforded an additional benefit to facilitate global distribution and potentially overcome this stigma: dubs in multiple languages, which for *Elite* includes English, German, Spanish, and French, with subtitles in Simplified and Traditional Chinese. While this makes the series more accessible, it also potentially removes a huge component of spatial capital that marks the series' Spanish roots. In the dubbed version, their English class is replaced with a French class, dislocating Spanish from the series' narrative given the absence of cultural specificity in dialogue or storylines as the series progresses. The subtitled version of the series can rely on language to articulate its setting, whereas the dubbed version—which could appear as the default for viewers in English-speaking countries, depending on how Netflix's algorithm determines their viewing patterns—fully dislocates the series' spatial capital, combining with the textual choices to create an inscrutable setting that privileges universality over specificity.

As with *Sex Education*, *Elite*'s creators acknowledge the influence of American culture on their show but suggest this was a form of cultural commentary. In an interview with *Entertainment Weekly* (Cadenas 2019), Montero responds to viewers who argued "the show presented a very 'Americanized' reality," saying that this was based on their research:

> It's not that we were trying to be American, it's that some very posh schools in Spain are doing things the American way because parents and students have all seen those U.S. movies and TV shows and that is their idea of a "cool" education. It's their way of attracting customers/students, almost as if the brochure for the schools had a [sic] "As seen on TV" sticker on it.

Rather than a nostalgic throwback to American popular culture, Montero frames *Elite* here as a critique of the impact of U.S. media abroad, concluding that "a lot of things 'American' about our show are in there because in Spain we also take a lot of things from American culture in our everyday lives." However, nothing about the text itself reflects this claim: the characters themselves never speak about this influence, nor critique it in any meaningful way. The show is entirely uncritical about the Americanization that allegedly permeates Las Encinas, despite the fact that the first season's focus on class conflict would have easily allowed those themes to emerge organically as the new students adjusted to the posh reality of the school. Whereas *Queen Sono* at least calls out local issues even if its story was not directly influenced by them, *Elite* ignores them entirely. As such, *Elite*'s inscrutable sense of place prohibits the show from speaking to spatial capital even when it would be thematically relevant and when it allegedly shapes the distinct blend of American and Spanish influences within the series' setting.

In both these cases, producers insist that Netflix did not specifically mandate an "Americanized" setting for the series, suggesting they were personally behind their decision to dislocate their settings despite the shows being commissioned locally for their respective markets. However, *Elite* and *Sex Education* were notably among the first "global originals" that Netflix revealed viewership figures for in early 2019, after years of refusing to release data publicly. Although other foreign originals like Italy's *Baby* (2018–20) and Turkey's *The Protector* (2018–20) drew ten million viewers—measured at the time as having watched 70% of one episode[3]—over their first four weeks, *Sex Education* and *Elite* each outpaced them: the former was on track to draw a projected 40 million, while Elite was seen in 20 million homes in the month after its launch in 2018 (Kafka 2019). Language would be a significant factor in the series' greater reach, given Netflix's large audience in Latin America and in English-speaking countries, yet the two series were also the most legibly positioned within American genre traditions in the stories they were telling, with no specific spatial capital to disrupt a universal—read: American—interpretation of their narratives. There is also a clear contrast between how shows produced in Western countries approach this universality compared to the non-Western examples of *Sacred Games* and *Queen Sono*. There would be greater cultural and political consequences to attempting to "Americanize" those series to the same degree as *Sex Education* and *Elite*, which were produced in countries that—as producers argue—already have an accepted cultural relationship to American popular culture. But regardless of how this relationship may be accepted, and whether it was Netflix who encouraged creators to Americanize their shows or the creators naturally developing that approach in producing a show for Netflix, the consequence is the same: dislocated spatial capital that bypasses polysemy into an inscrutable sense of place that deeply complicates an attempt to read the show as local despite Netflix's stated commitment to local programming initiatives.

Conclusion

In January 2019, when *Sex Education* debuted, it inspired two op-eds in *the Guardian* responding to its inscrutable relationship with spatial capital. In the first, writer Caspar Salmon (2019) argues that the show is "about as British as a high-school prom," declaring "you couldn't hope for a better encapsulation of Britain's new-found world status as crave adjunct to the

United States." Cultural anthropologist Grant McCracken (2019) offers an alternative view: rejecting the idea that Netflix is "flogging an American- ised version of British teenage culture to appeal to two markets at once," McCracken reframes *Sex Education* as akin to music's mashing up of gen- res, a "deliberate collision of cultural materials . . . to draw British and American cultures together for their contradictions and inconsistencies." To Salmon, "Britain's contemporary politics, culture and issues are being sold down the river," but for McCracken the inscrutability of its setting means "the story of adolescence has been rendered less predictable and given new life."

This discursive struggle clarifies that despite Netflix's distinct position as a commissioner of local content for global distribution, its original pro- gramming is embedded within historical struggles of spatial capital tied to international co-production. Distribution has always reshaped the burden of spatial capital for series dependent on international marketplaces to succeed, whether that means obscuring their country of origin to appear American or shaping their stories to veer away from cultural specificity into purportedly universal narratives. But whereas we have historically framed this conflict as one between different funding sources, with producers nego- tiating spatial capital to find a compromise between different broadcasters with different priorities, the burden of spatial capital set at Netflix lacks the same justifications.

A show like *Orphan Black* made the choices it did to maximize suc- cess as an ad-supported cable series in the United States, as determined by its American distributor. Failing to do so placed its longevity at risk—the resulting polysemy was a careful balancing act of spatial capital that was not entirely necessary to the show's success in Canada, but it allowed the producers to comfortably serve both BBC America and Canadian distribu- tor Space and leverage the show's prestige into not only an Emmy for star Tatiana Maslany, but also 35 Canadian Screen Awards, including four for Maslany. But the core of Netflix's stated commitment to local commissions is that this process of eliding or erasing spatial capital to ensure clearance in global markets is no longer necessary: Netflix is going to distribute the show in a huge range of global territories, alongside both original and acquired programming from countries around the world. Moreover, Netflix is not dependent on ad revenue to determine a program's success. And yet, with *Sex Education* and *Elite* in particular, Netflix's production process generated series devoid of cultural reference points where spatial capital is deployed in vague, often contradictory forms, with a seeming desire to appeal to an American market that has become a minority of Netflix's subscription base in recent years. Even in non-Western series like *Sacred Games* and *Queen Sono* where there is a greater acknowledgment of specificity, certain choices of how and where spatial capital is deployed speak of missed opportunities that we would normally associate with a co-production model to which Netflix need not subscribe.

The pervasiveness of forms of television spatial capital that privilege universality over specificity, even as the conditions of production change, points to how certain realities of the television industry persist even amidst periods of immense change. Although streaming television has often been framed as a disruptive influence on the industry, and is often experienced this way by audiences who might have previously had minimal access to programming from countries like India, Spain, or South Africa, Netflix's programming strategy remains built on ritualized forms of spatial capital learned from a pre-streaming era, institutionalized by production companies in countries around the world and by the programming executives Netflix hired to build their "global" empire. Netflix's huge influence on the television industry contains the potential to relocate the nexus of spatial capital away from a universalized, Americanized sense of place, in the same way that mobile production or new technologies give producers the tools to explore spatial capital in new ways. However, across these first three chapters I have outlined the self-imposed barriers placed on such geographies by the institutions in question. The burden of television's spatial capital is shaped by these forces, which go beyond budgetary restrictions or distinct conflicts between competing forces to a broad, industry-wide belief that even when a series is guaranteed global distribution, it must be restrained by a dislocated sense of place to be "successful" in that marketplace.

This chapter's focus on the textual function of spatial capital in relation to distributional capital offers a clear position regarding Salmon and McCracken's disagreement over *Sex Education*'s sense of place. McCracken's argument is in line with the producers' claims as to their intent, but the text's active refusal to even acknowledge its location functionally limits the impacts of such a claim. Even if a viewer engages with the series through the lens that McCracken suggests, the series lacks the spatial capital necessary for it to take on greater meaning. However, McCracken's argument reinforces that in considering the relationship between spatial capital and distribution, it is not simply the text that shapes this process: it is discourse like these articles—and the trade reports used throughout this chapter—that establish audience expectation, and it is the audience itself who interprets how the perceived burden of spatial capital is being met. Accordingly, the next two chapters consider what happens when spatial capital is dislocated from the text itself, whether in the way examples like these are framed by papers like *the Guardian* or how local and global audiences ultimately consume them.

Notes

1 In the final days of working on this book, an episode of the Canadian-produced *Vacation House Rules* aired which featured a vacation property where a prominent Canadian flag hung on a flagpole in the backyard. It was blurred out in every image, meaning someone was paid to remove any sign of the show's Canadianness for its American airing.

2 In the show's fourth season released in June 2021, a new group of characters move to the area from London and explicitly identify their new location as Madrid, following *Orphan Black*'s lead in becoming more geographically specific as the serial narrative invests viewers in the story and characters.
3 In the proceeding years, Netflix has shifted their metrics to watching only a few minutes of a given episode, making its reporting numbers inscrutable in their own right.

References

Appadurai, Arjun. 1996. *Modernity at Large: Cultural Dimensions of Globalization*. Minneapolis: University of Minnesota Press.

Brannon Donoghue, Courtney. 2014. "Sony and Local-Language Productions: Conglomerate Hollywood's Strategy of Flexible Localization for the Global Film Market." *Cinema Journal* 53.4: 3–27.

———. 2017. *Localising Hollywood*. London: BFI Press.

Bryan, Scotty. 2019. "Here's Why 'Sex Education' Looks So American, Even Though It Is British." *Buzzfeed*, January 15. www.buzzfeed.com/scottybryan/sex-education-american-british-feel.

Cadenas, Karensa. 2019. "How the *Elite* Showrunners 'Root for' but 'Plot for New Ways to Ruin' the Characters in Season 2." *Entertainment Weekly*, September 6. https://ew.com/tv/2019/09/06/elite-showrunners-season-2-marina-new-characters/.

Choudhary, Vidhi. 2018. "Sacred Games: How India's First Netflix Original Came Together." *The Hindustan Times*, July 7. www.hindustantimes.com/tv/sacred-games-how-india-s-first-netflix-original-came-together/story-qDGceqq9SR4jStYluu1vhM.html.

Dixon, Guy. 2014. "Toronto Lends Sense of Place to Orphan Black." *The Globe and Mail*, August 11. www.theglobeandmail.com/report-on-business/industry-news/property-report/toronto-lends-sense-of-place-to-orphan-black/article19994127/#dashboard/follows/.

Elkins, Evan. 2018. "Hulu: Geoblocking TV in an On-Demand Era." In *From Networks to Netflix*, edited by Derek Johnson, 333–41. New York: Routledge.

———. 2019a. "Algorithmic Cosmopolitanism: On the Global Claims of Digital Entertainment Platforms." *Critical Studies in Media Communication* 36.4: 376–89.

———. 2019b. *Locked Out: Regional Restrictions in Digital Entertainment Culture*. New York: New York University Press.

Frater, Patrick. 2018. " 'The Meg' Aims Big at China, but Will Audiences Bite?" *Variety*, August 8. https://variety.com/2018/film/news/the-meg-shark-movie-china-will-audiences-bite-1202897561/.

Granada, Emiliano. 2019. "Netflix's 'Elite' Creators Carlos Montero, Dario Madrona Talk Class Warfare, Rosalia, Season 2." *Variety*, September 5. https://variety.com/2019/tv/global/netflix-elite-carlos-montero-dario-madrona-class-warefare-rosalia-season-2-1203324485/.

Han, Benjamin M. 2019 "Fantasies of Modernity: Korean TV Dramas in Latin America." *The Journal of Popular Film and Television* 47.1: 39–47.

Harrison, Ellie. 2019. "Netflix's Sex Education Is Set in a British School—so Why Does It Feel so American?" *Radio Times*, January 14. www.radiotimes.com/news/tv/comedy/2019-05-17/sex-education-netflix-british-show-look-so-american/.

Haynes, Suyin. 2020. "Inside Queen Sono, Netflix's First African Original Series." *Time*, March 3. https://time.com/5792339/queen-sono-netflix-africa/.

Hilmes, Michele. 2011. *Network Nations: A Transnational History of British and American Broadcasting*. New York: Routledge.

———. 2014. "Transnational TV: What Do We Mean by 'Coproduction' Anymore?" *Media Industries Journal* 1.2: 10–15. https://quod.lib.umich.edu/m/mij/15031809.0001.203/-transnational-tv-what-do-we-mean?rgn=main;view=fulltext.

Kafka, Peter. 2019. "Netflix Is Finally Sharing (some of) Its Audience Numbers for Its TV Shows and Movies: Some of Them Are Huge." *Vox*, January 17. www.vox.com/2019/1/17/18187234/netflix-views-numbers-first-time-bird-box-bodyguard-you-sex-education.

Kharpal, Arjun. 2020. "Nearly Half of Netflix's New Subscriber Growth Came from Asia-Pacific." *CNBC.com*, October 20. www.cnbc.com/2020/10/20/netflix-nearly-half-of-q3-new-subscriber-growth-from-asia-pacific.html.

Kokas, Aynne. 2017. *Hollywood Made in China*. Oakland: University of California Press.

Lang, Jamie, and John Hopewell. 2017. "Netflix Announces Second Spanish Series, 'Elite'." *Variety*, July 13. https://variety.com/2017/digital/global/netflix-second-spanish-series-elite-zeta-audiovisual-1202494542/.

Lee, Hyunji. 2018. "A 'Real' Fantasy: Hybridity, Korean Drama, and Pop Cosmopolitans." *Media Culture & Society* 40.3: 365–68.

Levine, Elana. 2009. "National Television, Global Market: Canada's Degrassi: The Next Generation." *Media, Culture and Society* 31.4: 515–31.

Lodderhose, Diana. 2017. "Netflix Says Euro Content Key to Growth; Unveils New Co-Pros at Berlin Event." *Deadline*, March 1. https://deadline.com/2017/03/netflix-international-strategy-troy-black-earth-rising-the-spy-1202032904/.

McCracken, Grant. 2019. "Is Netflix's Sex Education US/UK Mashup the Future of TV?" *The Guardian*, January 29. www.theguardian.com/commentisfree/2020/jan/29/netflix-sex-education-us-uk-british-american.

Moran, Albert. 1998. *Copycat Television: Globalisation, Program Formats and Cultural Identity*. Bloomington: Indiana University Press.

———, ed. 2009a. *TV Formats Worldwide: Localizing Global Programs*. Bristol: Intellect Books.

———. 2009b. *New Flows in Global TV*. Bristol: Intellect Books.

Moran, Albert, and Justin Malbon. 2006. *Understanding the Global TV Format*. Bristol: Intellect Books.

Obenson, Tambay. 2020. "'Queen Sono' Review: Pearl Thusi Is Compelling in Netflix's Otherwise Unremarkable Espionage Drama." *Indiewire*, February 29. www.indiewire.com/2020/02/queen-sono-review-netflix-africa-original-series-1202213890/.

Oren, Tasha, and Sharon Shahaf, Eds. 2012. *Global Television Formats: Understanding Television Across Borders*. London: Routledge.

Ramachandran, Naman. 2020. "Netflix to Make 'Sacred Games' as First Original Series in India." *Variety*, June 5. https://variety.com/2016/digital/asia/netflix-sacred-games-series-india-1201789219/.

Ramiro Beltran S., Luis 1978. "Communication and Cultural Domination: USA-Latin American Case." *Media Asia* 5.4: 183–92.

Ross, Dalton. 2014. "'Orphan Black': Sarah Was Not Originally British (and More Fun Facts from the Creators)." *Entertainment Weekly*, April 16. https://ew.com/article/2014/04/16/orphan-black-creators-season-2/.

Roxborough, Scott. 2018. "In China, Western TV Companies Go Co-Production Route." *The Hollywood Reporter*, October 18. www.hollywoodreporter.com/news/china-western-tv-companies-go-production-route-1152752.

Salmon, Caspar. 2019. "Netflix's Sex Education Is About as British as a High-School Prom." *The Guardian*, January 22. www.theguardian.com/commentisfree/2019/jan/22/netflix-sex-education-british-high-school-prom.

Schiller, Herbert. 1976. *Communication and Cultural Domination*. White Plains, NY: ME Sharpe.

Tinic, Serra. 2005. *On Location: Canada's Television Industry in a Global Market*. Toronto: University of Toronto Press.

———. 2015. "Where in the World Is Orphan Black? Change and Continuity in Global TV Production and Distribution." *Media Industries Journal* 1.3: 54–59. https://quod.lib.umich.edu/m/mij/15031809.0001.310/-where-in-the-world-is-orphan-black-change-and-continuity?rgn=main;view=fulltext.

Villareal, Yvonne. 2016. "Netflix Announces Huge Global Expansion, Adding 130 More Countries." *The Los Angeles Times*, January 7. www.latimes.com/entertainment/envelope/cotown/la-et-ct-netflix-global-expansion-20160107-story.html.

Vlessing, Etan. 2017. "Netflix Nabs U.K. 'Sex Education' Dramedy." *The Hollywood Reporter*, November 28. www.hollywoodreporter.com/news/netflix-nabs-uk-sex-education-dramedy-1062037.

———. 2019. "Netflix Accelerates Canadian Investment as Streaming Competition Heats Up." *The Hollywood Reporter*, September 26. www.hollywoodreporter.com/news/netflix-accelerates-canadian-investment-streaming-competition-1243592.

———. 2020. "Canada to Force Netflix, Amazon Prime to Pay for Local Content." *The Hollywood Reporter*, November 3. www.hollywoodreporter.com/news/canada-to-force-netflix-amazon-prime-to-pay-for-local-content.

Vourlias, Christopher. 2018. "Netflix Orders 'Queen Sono,' Its First African Original Series." *Variety*, December 10. https://variety.com/2018/tv/news/netflix-orders-queen-sono-first-african-original-series-1203085465/.

———. 2020. "Netflix's Head of African Originals Lays Out Streamer's Plans for the Content (EXCLUSIVE)." *Variety*, February 28. https://variety.com/2020/digital/news/netflix-head-african-originals-lays-out-plans-for-continent-1203518648/.

Yohannes, Alamin. 2020. "Why You Should Watch Queen Sono, Netflix's First African Original Series." *Entertainment Weekly*, February 26. https://ew.com/tv/2020/02/26/netflix-queen-sono-pearl-thusi-highlights/.

4 Discursive hierarchies of spatial capital

"Like a character in the show"

For all intents and purposes, Netflix's move into original programming began in 2013, when they launched *House of Cards* (2013–2018) and *Orange Is the New Black* (2013–2019) as marquee, award-winning series that would eventually expand to the global originals discussed in the previous chapter. However, technically speaking, Netflix's first original series came a year earlier: *Lilyhammer* (2012–2014), featuring *The Sopranos* (1999–2007) star Steven Van Zandt as an American mobster in the Witness Protection Program sent to Norway, was produced by Norwegian broadcaster NRK, with Netflix coming onboard as the exclusive distributor in the United States. After Netflix joined as a co-producer following season one, the show ran for two additional seasons, filming on location in Norway, in addition to location shooting in New York and Rio de Janeiro. Although a footnote in Netflix's original programming history, and distinct from the local commissions that would define the company's global push later in the decade, the series was nonetheless early evidence of how Netflix's expansion into global markets intersects with spatial capital.

Thus far, this book has attended to how spatial capital manifests in television texts, and the production cultures that generate and/or limit that capital, but in considering Netflix's push into global original programming my analysis has increasingly delved into the role that discourse—industry trade journalism, criticism, promotion and marketing—plays in amplifying, reinforcing, and in some cases creating spatial capital around these programs. For a show like *Lilyhammer*, the series' Norwegian landscape is a key point of distinction outlined by reviewers: *The Hollywood Reporter*'s Tim Goodman (2012) writes that "the predictable fish-out-of-water angle is far more endurable when it is applied to a series shot on location that looks beautiful and mysterious every time you look at it," while *The Telegraph*'s Benji Wilson (2012) writes that the show earns a few more episodes because "the landscape was magnificent: this was a show you could watch on mute (and at times it was much improved that way)." This foregrounding of spatial capital in reviews—albeit as a lone bright spot in articles critical of the series—is part of a broader discourse of place echoed in the press for *Lilyhammer*. When the BBC acquired the series for the UK market at the same

DOI: 10.4324/9781003224693-5

time that Netflix bought the American rights, BBC Four's Richard Klein said the show "mixes sharp wit and American big city ways with the beauty of the Norwegian mountains and the folksy nature of a small town" (Tartaglione 2012). In a brief interview with *The Austin Chronicle*, Van Zandt pushes for this framing of the series: identifying his pride that this was the first Norwegian series to garner distribution in the United States, he notes, "I wanted [Norway] to be like a character in the show" (Hoffberger 2012).

This chapter argues that these discursive articulations of spatial capital are critical to understanding how space and place operate within the television industry, as paratextual efforts by producers, distributors, actors, and filming locations take the textual spatial capital identified in the previous two chapters and leverage it as a form of cultural capital. It specifically identifies the discursive framing Van Zandt deploys in discussing *Lilyhammer*—the idea of place being "a character in the show"—as a recurring theme in how a series' location is discussed by these stakeholders in the promotion of their series. The "city as character" discourse is a specific manifestation of spatial capital within the industry trade press, program marketing, and other industry spaces. It is not a new discourse: in the study of film, the city of Los Angeles has often been understood as a character, whether in Thom Anderson's documentary *Los Angeles Plays Itself* (2003) or in Alain Silver and James Ursini's book *L.A. Noir: The City as Character* (2005). In the context of television, meanwhile, it has been used in reference—among other series—to Atlantic City in *Boardwalk Empire*, Baltimore in *The Wire*, and New Orleans in *Treme*, while broader categories of place have gained the status of character in series like *Friday Night Lights* (Texas) or *True Detective* (Louisiana).

Its ubiquity demonstrates how any consideration of spatial capital must ultimately reckon with how such claims function concurrently with television's significant claims to cultural capital in what has been popularly dubbed the new "golden age of television" (Leopold 2013). I begin by deconstructing this framing of cities/countries as characters, which emerges in scholarly considerations of the cinematic city before being leveraged as shorthand for authenticity within popular discourse around film and, especially, television series during an era defined by "quality" and "prestige." I argue that the idea of place as character is not built on an understanding of how characterization functions narratively but is rather a conscious effort to locate a series within discourses of legitimation surrounding television authorship and cultural hierarchies that came to define television drama during this period. Using the Emmy-winning AMC drama series *Breaking Bad*—set and filmed in Albuquerque, New Mexico—as a case study, the chapter considers how the discursive negotiation of spatial capital continues long after a series debuts, with various stakeholders working to frame the city as a character to position themselves within a larger hierarchy of television value, despite the fact this is often at odds with the text itself.

In 2019, the *Los Angeles Times* claimed that "when TV show creators use that oft-quoted phrase: 'The city is like another character,' they rarely toss it off lightly" (Dawn 2019), but this chapter will argue that the opposite is often true: place's role as a character in television shows is a commonly and consciously deployed discourse used in order to translate spatial capital into cultural capital within the hierarchies that define the television industry.

Setting the scene: the city and media

This book has thus far considered the parameters of place within spatial capital broadly, but in the process its analysis has necessarily considered towns, cities, nations, and continents as natural frameworks through which we categorize and interpret space. Although there are circumstances—as in the cases of *Sex Education* and *Elite* in the previous chapter—where such bounded forms of spatial capital are either erased or elided, our natural inclination is to attach spatial capital to such signifiers, which is also true of scholarly literature on the subject. In an interview with Karen Lury in a 1999 issue of *Screen*, Doreen Massey is asked a series of questions tied to the relationship between film and television and three terms: space, place, and the city. The specific inclusion of the city as a category in and of itself reflects a subfield of "city studies" within investigations of cultural geography, although Massey resists the distinction. She explains to Lury that

> [M]y own position is that cities (of the kind which we have in mind here) are indeed particular forms of spatiality, but that particularity consists primarily in an intensification, a dramatic exaggeration, of characteristics that I would argue are intrinsic to 'space' more generally.
> (231)

Massey's observations regarding the intensified spatiality of the city—or, to put it in this project's terms, the intensified spatial capital tied to cities—speak of the rise of studies of the "cinematic city" as a specific concept with film and media studies. This book as a whole has demonstrated how, to Lury's point in framing the interview, "socially deterring factors such as gender, race and class are seen to be revealed, constructed, and contested in the way in which films and programs construct space and place" (232–3). Moreover, it has inevitably looked to bounded geographical entities in order to contextualize this analysis, in the same way that the creators of these shows choose or create—for example, *Hart of Dixie*'s Bluebell—cities or towns in which to set stories. Although our understanding of space and place need not necessarily be focused on these intensified locations of spatial capital, they offer a guiding post both within the process of production—where setting can serve as a key point of signification for the creators in selling the type of show they want to make—and within the process of reception, where our understanding of Bluebell's location is framed relative to the real towns and cities referenced around it, as I will explore in more detail in the next chapter.

Within media studies scholarship, the politics of the cinematic city have been explored in great detail, whether through theoretical discussions of the relationship between these two modern institutions or through in-depth case studies of specific cities as depicted on film (Donald 1999; Clarke 1997; Brunsdon 2007). However, there has been significantly less research into the televisual city, as discourses of the cinematic city have often centered on genres and discourses that reinforce the hierarchy between film and television. In the introduction to *Taking Place: Location and the Moving Image* (2011), John David Rhodes and Elena Gorfinkel suggest the idea that "movies take place" is "a cliche of both realist location shooting and avant-garde film practice" (viii). The explicit appeal to aesthetic filmmaking strategies reinforces that "cinematic" is not simply a term of distinction between film and television but rather an aesthetic judgment on the type of images depicting a particular location and a term historically disassociated from television. Only a single essay in Rhodes and Gorfinkel's collection relates to television specifically, suggesting that the relationship between location and the moving image remains predominantly seen through the lens of film.[1] This hierarchy emerges in Lury's conversation with Massey, where the former argues that "television is, of course, a medium that is determined by different commercial and public interests, and its ideological function is often to try and erase or obscure real multiplicity and difference" (234).

At first glance, this distinction—television as a more commercial medium than film, and thus more conservative in its representations—makes sense: this book has thus far identified economic capital as a fundamental contingency shaping spatial capital, with limited budgets and commercial imperatives serving as an implicit or explicit restriction on various series' efforts to represent space and place in complex ways. However, in the two decades since this conversation was published, television's business model has diversified significantly. One could argue that the commercial imperative continues to separate all ad-supported television content from the purest of independent film productions, yet the rise in basic cable channels appealing to niche audiences and the increase in production for premium cable channels and streaming services where subscription revenues offer greater creative freedom has made such generalizations insufficient. Although we can—and should—critique the ideological functions of the texts that emerge within these and other models, such restrictive framing of television's relationship to any form of ideology was already on shaky ground before two decades of industrial change has dictated a more nuanced engagement with the medium and its relationship with ideologies tied to place. This book has thus far confirmed that television faces inherent challenges in activating spatial capital but suggests that ongoing negotiation needs to be explored on a case-by-case basis and not used as a dismissal of the medium as a whole.

Such claims must then confront a larger body of work related to the cultural capital of television programming and its intersection with identity. Lury's discussion with Massey took place immediately prior to what has been discursively constructed as the modern "golden age of television," where series like *The Sopranos* (1999–2007) and *Sex and the City* (1998–2004) established new baselines for both hour-long dramas and half-hour comedies in part due to their attention to aesthetic detail. In the process, discourse consciously tried to distance these shows from other forms of television: William C. Siska (2011) goes so far as to posit *The Sopranos* as "Art Cinema," an effort to legitimate the text by elevating it beyond its status of television. In *Legitimating Television* (2011), Michael Z. Newman and Elana Levine deconstruct this effort, accurately assessing the legitimation of television as a discursive act that problematically elevates some television over other television, ascribing value in uneven and often problematic ways that seek to claim that television as a medium does not itself have claim to legitimacy. Rather, it is these individual programs being compared to cinema or literature that transcend the medium, leaving the generalized notion of television's inferiority—whether in reference to broad aesthetics or issues like spatial capital—intact.

This culture of legitimation is a double-edged sword as it pertains to the study of television's relationship with place. On the one hand, it has resulted in meaningful analysis of how series like HBO's *The Wire* (2002–2008) and *Treme* (2010–2013)—both co-created by David Simon and set in Baltimore and New Orleans respectively—embody ideologically complex depictions of their respective cities. These shows aired on a premium cable channel and were lauded by critics for their complex narrative structures and depth of characterization. Both were closely analyzed by scholars (Williams 2014; Morgan Parmett 2019) and serve as paragons of what I have identified as spatial capital. However, while Charlotte Brunsdon's *Television Cities: London, Paris, Baltimore* (2018)—which works to rectify the absence of work on the televisual city specifically—contributes to this analysis by focusing a chapter on *The Wire*, it also identifies how such analysis intersects with Newman and Levine's arguments regarding legitimation, pointing to the masculinist and classist nature of "quality television" distinctions that preclude analysis of how series lacking the same pedigree confront space and place. Beyond her valuable assertion of the television city's specific value equal to and distinct from the cinematic city, Brunsdon's book also pushes against how discourses of legitimation artificially exclude certain shows from being analyzed through this lens. Although analysis of *The Wire* and *Treme* is crucial and productive work, it remains analysis that is too often reduced to a narrow set of case studies of series that have concurrent claims to cultural capital to support analysis of spatial capital.

The interconnected nature of spatial capital and cultural capital within television discourse requires interrogation but extricating one from the other is challenging as shifts in television distribution have destabilized the terms on which Newman and Levine's argument is predicated. Netflix and other streaming services have disrupted the traditional binaries between broadcast and cable content, and as younger generations primarily consume broadcast and cable content through those streaming services, the rigid hierarchies— of cable being quality and broadcast not—built during the "golden age of television" are fading. The result should be a democratizing of all forms of television's cultural capital, including spatial capital, but in practice Newman and Levine's observation about discourses of transcendence and exceptionalism has continued to dominate. Rather than arguing that all series contain spatial capital, the destabilizing of industry hierarchies has simply allowed more series to claim to be exceptional, continuing to reinforce the existence of a hierarchy of spatial capital in the process. As the chapter's opening example of *Lilyhammer* demonstrates, individual series that wish to be perceived or framed in the same light as programs like *The Sopranos* or *The Wire* are leveraging the discourse that existed around those series, rather than generating new discourses. When directly connected to spatial capital, such efforts create a discursive environment where space and place function as forms of legitimation, whether ascribed to a particular program by critics in ways that reinforce preexisting hierarchies or aspired to by writers, actors, and distributors in an effort to tap into those same hierarchies. To explore this in more detail, the following section considers how the specific discourse of a city or location being "a character in the show" evolved from a point of scholarly consideration to a common refrain and highlights the subsequent impacts on how we understand television's spatial capital.

Place as character

In the *Critical Dictionary of Film and Television Theory* (2011), Ken Fox outlines a range of theories for understanding the functions of place in film and television (although, continuing a theme, his examples come exclusively from film). He considers a range of different ways that films have used place, whether metonymically or metaphorically, or in ways that authenticate narratives or cut against the narrative flow of a given film. However, he begins with a clear dichotomy: while "place as a backdrop" is identified as "the least sophisticated function," in which place "invest[s] a scene or an action with aesthetic or emotional significance," "place as character" offers scenarios where "the location becomes vital in the way the film's narrative develops" (413). Citing examples such as Monument Valley in the work of John Ford, or New York in *On the Town*, Fox argues that in these cases place is "more than just a backdrop: it defines the attitudes and actions of the characters" (413).

Fox is drawing his categories from filmmaker Mark Rappaport (1980), and thus the absence of television as a topic of conversation is unsurprising. However, in addition to being attached to various films—as evidenced in the aforementioned *Los Angeles Plays Itself*, where "Los Angeles as Character" serves as one of the discrete sections of the visual essay—it has earlier origins in literature (Fowler 2003). The notion of "place as character" forms a key framework for literary analysis, including a 2013–2014 class at Pitzer College titled "The City as Character in Literature and Film." This is logical given that in the context of the written word a sense of place is constructed through similar strategies as a book's characters or situations, with authors describing place in ways that work to activate the reader's imagination. Although the same may not be true for film and television, which rely more readily on visual signifiers of place, the discourse still emerges both broadly and tied to specific genres such as science fiction (Strick 1984). In all cases, "place as character" serves to signify an importance of place that is notable and meaningful within the context of a given text, either by how it is framed in a shot or described on the page.

However, distinct from the clarity of Fox's categories, the way that discourse is deployed in regard to television in particular is uneven. In most cases, the discourse is deployed to simply reinforce that a series chose to shoot on location, something that—as discussed in the first chapter—is not necessarily typical in television as mobile production dislocates a show's setting from where it is produced. In an interview for his lead role on *Instinct* (2018), a short-lived CBS procedural set and filmed in New York City, Alan Cumming explains that in contrast to his experience filming *The Good Wife* (2009–2016), where New York City doubled as Chicago, he's "glad the city is like a character in the show" (Derenzo 2018). He speaks to this as though "place as character" is simply the ability for a show to avoid the inconveniences of city-for-city doubling, which he describes as being forced to stop a take because "there's a taxi in the background." This discourse can also be used by series that confront the relationship between distribution and spatial capital outlined in the previous chapter: actress Kim Cattrall describes Toronto as a character in her Canadian series *Sensitive Skin* (2014–2016), noting that they consciously chose not to set it in "Nameless City, North America" as might have been expected (Jancelewicz 2014). Jamie Dornan, meanwhile, mixes Fox's categories entirely: in a *Mirror* interview for the Belfast-set BBC/Netflix series *The Fall* (2013–2016), Dornan acknowledges "There's no definitive need for it to be set in Belfast, but it's a great backdrop. Belfast is like a character in the show" (Stacey 2014).

These actors, collectively, are working to legitimize the shows they are working on by emphasizing their commitment to spatial capital. They are enforcing a clear hierarchy between filming on location in a show's setting versus relying on city-for-city doubling, but in the process, they are making no specific links to storytelling or indeed to characterization. Although it is unclear where specifically these actors picked up on this language, its deployment creates a largely empty point of articulation that fails to address the relationship between place and narrative—as discussed in the second chapter—in a meaningful way. It is much more focused on describing the actor's experience of shooting in a particular location, as when Blake Lively uses it to casually discuss shooting The CW's *Gossip Girl* (2007–2012) in New York (No Author 2008), or when Jerry O'Connell speaks of shooting the short-lived WGN America series *Carter* (2019) in such a "cute, quaint place" as North Bay, Ontario (Terrones 2019). This particular strain of discourse is ubiquitous enough that it was the target of a joke in the final season premiere of NBC's *30 Rock* (2006–2013). When Liz Lemon tells her boss Jack Donaghy that she has always seen New York as a character on diegetic sketch comedy series *TGS with Tracy Jordan*, Jack replies with a derisive laugh and his belief "that's idiotic." In January 2021, the discourse came full circle when Sarah Jessica Parker was confronted by TMZ in the streets of New York City regarding Kim Cattrall's absence from the newly announced revival of *Sex and the City* and told them that New York is, in fact, the fourth character on the show (Kakala 2021).

The shows where "place as character" is evoked by those involved with the productions—frequently actors, as noted here, but often also producers and crew members such as production designers—range in genre, location, and distribution. It can even extend to shows that are filmed solely in a studio environment: when Kevin James discussed the decision to shoot his multi-camera sitcom *Kevin Can Wait* (2016–2018) on Long Island— an expensive decision made due to James residing there—he spoke to their commitment to authenticity by suggesting the setting "plays like a character in the show," despite the fact it had limited access to the location shooting so often used to signal authenticity (Matthews 2016). This is a reminder that "place as character" is a discursive claim made here during initial press tours and interviews designed to legitimate the shows in question. These claims can be challenged by critics, or by audiences, and ultimately fail to translate into meaningful spatial capital or cultural capital as the series progresses; however, the fact that they continue to be made showcases the perceived value the claims could hold for the series' future success.

Shows like *The Wire* that have successfully capitalized on spatial capital provide a framework for other series aiming to tap into the discursive value of "place as character." When *The Wire* was remastered for high-definition in 2014, Baltimore's function as a character in the show reemerged in discourse around the release. Washington radio station *WTOP*'s website wrote in an overview of the remaster that "the greatest character in the show is the city of Baltimore itself" (Fraley 2015), while star Sonja Sohn remarked to *Digital Trends* that "I've heard where David [Simon, co-creator] has said Baltimore is a character in the show" (Mettler 2014). The successful reinforcement of this discourse that first emerged during the series' initial release could be attributed to marketing or promotion, but it is also linked to the show's narrative: in *WTOP*'s reporting, writer Jason Fraley connects the show's depiction of Baltimore to its evolution over five seasons, arguing it is a character due to how "its levels of corruption [were] dissected through a different prism in each of the show's five seasons." The series' gradual expansion of focus from its original interest in the police and the people they investigate to the dockworkers, politicians, educators, and journalists who populate the same story world charts a relationship between the discourse of place as character and the discourses of contemporary television seriality, which Jason Mittell (2015) has identified as emblematic of "complex TV."

Accordingly, any series that aspires to the spatial capital attached to place functioning as a character must do so relative to the burdens set by archetypal examples such as *The Wire*, which subsequently shapes how space and place are discursively framed across all television regardless of genre or format. To better understand how these claims are made in the promotion and marketing of a given series, and how they intersect with the cultural capital attached to serialized prestige dramas, it is helpful to investigate a series from HBO's rival, Showtime.

Montauk as a character in *The Affair*

Showtime's *The Affair* (2014–2019) focuses on the characters Noah, played by Dominic West, and Alison, played by Ruth Wilson, who meet and begin an affair. In promotion surrounding the series, four central characters emerged: Noah and his wife Helen (Maura Tierney), and Alison and her husband Cole (Joshua Jackson). In the series' press kit, made available to critics in advance of the show's premiere, two small hardcover books are split between the two couples in a reflection the series itself, which evocatively divides each episode between Noah and Alison's respective points-of-view on a series of events.

As with any new series, Showtime produced a range of paratexts ahead of the series' premiere, and as a character-driven drama series there was a video for each of the four characters with the actors describing their role within the story. However, there was also a fifth video on Showtime's website and YouTube channel, prominently displayed in the set of revolving images on the page. Although this video could have focused on one of Noah and Helen's four children who feature prominently in the series, or Cole's brother whose death serves as an anchor for the show's ongoing mystery, the video instead focuses on what promotional copy refers to as "an important character in the show": Montauk, the hamlet of East Hampton, New York, where the eponymous affair develops (Figure 4.1).

In the video, West acknowledges that this particular "characterization" is not distinct to *The Affair*; he points out, matter-of-factly, that "the setting is so often this sort of other character in the show." The discourse is particularly relevant to West given his involvement in *The Wire*, creating an intertextual connection productive for Showtime as they work to assert Montauk's role in the story. The video consciously connects to *The Wire*'s narrative complexity using the different perspectives offered by Noah and Alison's halves of the episodes to consider how Montauk itself shifts in our perception as we see it from two very different points of view. This represents a critical stage in leveraging this discourse successfully: rather than

Figure 4.1 A screenshot of the YouTube video released in advance of *The Affair*'s premiere, highlighting the show's Montauk setting alongside the show's other characters. Allison is seen here cycling toward the Montauk Point Lighthouse, a key part of the show's location shooting.

Screenshot by author.

simply reiterating that the series was shot on location in Montauk, as was common in the interviews with actors outlined earlier, the video elevates Montauk to fifth billing and invites viewers to think of it as an evolving part of the series' narrative structure.

For this discourse to function effectively, however, the text itself has to justify the discourse: one could not produce a video like this without showing footage that supports the claim, which does mean that there are certain burdens a show must address in order to lay claim to place functioning as a character, present in *The Affair* and the shows it aspires to be.

Filming on location: As discussed in the first two chapters, and evident in the interviews with actors, there is inherent spatial capital to shooting on location where a story is set, which often requires significant financial investment. The discourse of "place as character" is one of the desirable outcomes of this decision, insofar as it broadcasts a perceived investment in authenticity on the part of a show's producers. In his profile of AMC drama *Low Winter Sun* (2013), set and shot in Detroit, Michigan, *The New York Times*' David Carr (2013) argues that "*Low Winter Sun* gives Detroit a leading role," suggesting it is a "persistent character" not only in this show but also in a range of other television series, narrative feature films, and documentaries. Citing the city's reputation for urban decay, Carr's description makes it seem as though Detroit was cast in this role, which could be true given that the city was consciously chosen as the setting for a remake of an existing British series of the same name. But if AMC had chosen to shoot the film in Toronto instead, as the Detroit-set *12 Monkeys* (2015–2018) did two years later, Carr's profile would not have discussed its setting in these same terms; in fact, given Carr's interest in using the show as a framework to discuss Detroit's urban identity more broadly, his article might not have existed at all.

Accordingly, *The Affair* would have struggled to claim that Montauk functions as a character in the story if it had not also chosen to film on location. The use of real Montauk locations on Long Island—including, for instance, the local public library—reinforces the town's role in the story, serving as a point of distinction when compared with other series set in the Hamptons like ABC's *Revenge*, which as mentioned in Chapter 2 used virtual backdrops on sound stages and location doubling in Los Angeles to signify locations from the series' pilot that were already doubling North Carolina for the Hamptons. *The Affair*'s use of location shooting continually works against this, both in the primary shooting in Montauk along with further location shooting in New York City—where Noah's story begins and ends following the close of the summer—as well as on nearby Block Island, where Noah and Alison memorably travel together in the series' fourth episode. While it is possible for actors or distributors to latch onto this discourse without this kind of location shooting, especially in instances of fictional locations like *Hart of Dixie*'s Bluebell, the absence of this basic claim to authenticity undercuts such efforts immediately.

Active setting of scenes within the landscape: Shooting on location is not necessarily enough, however. USA Network's *Royal Pains* (2009–2016), like *The Affair*, shot on location on Long Island and focused its attention on the luxurious culture of the Hamptons as part of the channel's "Blue Skies" branding. However, due to the show's smaller—although large by basic cable standards—budget and a larger production order, *Royal Pains* spent less time on location, relying more on studio sets. The show had access to authentic locations to assert its spatial capital but was limited in how it could activate those locations, which—along with the different discursive framings of the United States as a basic cable channel as compared to Showtime as a premium cable channel—meant that similar discourses around its use of location never materialized. When the show was remembered as it concluded its eight-season run in 2016, a *Hollywood Reporter* story focused more attention on its use of strategic location shooting—with trips to Italy, Hungary, and Hong Kong—than its Long Island setting (Stanhope 2016).

Although spatial capital can undoubtedly be connected to the interiors of buildings, the reality is that we most commonly associate a sense of place with a landscape: Andrews and Roberts (2012), writing about landscapes and liminality, identify a landscape as a "visual index of an area of land . . . as viewed from a given perspective" (1). As a result, we can understand a series' relationship with spatial capital as its chosen perspective on the area of land in question, whether that is a heavily urbanized cityscape or an untouched natural landscape. From a production perspective, locations manager Rebecca Puck Stair remarks that "when landscape is in the shot, it's usually almost a character," an acknowledgment that the logistics of shooting a given scene on location are usually only undertaken if the presence of the landscape serves a specific purpose.[2] The effort required to activate spatial capital through setting a scene within a landscape implies a degree of importance to the production that shifts from "setting" as a passive process toward an active engagement with place as a character in its own right. Every scene that actively engages with spatial capital, in other words, implicitly communicates to the audience that the show's setting mattered to the various workers—the writers who wrote the scene, the location scout who matched it to a location, the cinematographer and director who mapped out the shot—involved.

In a case like *The Affair*, this conspicuous assertion of spatial capital comes primarily in the form of shooting a huge percentage of scenes on location in Montauk, which is further reinforced by the fact that the pilot episode repeats the same scenes twice from both Noah and Alison's perspectives. The use of locations like a farmer's market for crucial interactions between Noah and Alison work to map out the community over the course of the series' first season, while key locations such as Alison and Cole's beachfront home consciously move characters in-and-out of doors in the midst of scenes to foreground the home's place within the landscape.[3] Although the series does rely on some green screen work during driving sequences, other location-shot scenes feature characters traveling through the landscape, including Alison's trips through Montauk on her bicycle as well as Noah's morning runs. Both of these practices isolate the characters through solitary modes of transportation, with the camera tracking their movement within the landscape. It is these types of scenes—rather than interiors—that serve as the backdrop for the actors' discussion of Montauk's role in the story in the promotional video Showtime produced.

In highlighting these scenes, *The Affair* challenges previously discussed strategies in this book that work to construct spatial capital more indirectly, such as establishing shots. The more often such landscapes include the actors from the series, the more the show can claim to have invested in its setting in a meaningful way. For "place to be a character," it has to be inhabited by the show's characters on a consistent basis, an integration that is not necessarily consistent across shows that film in the location where they are set.

Place as a paratextual signifier: The discourse of "place as character" also depends on efforts like this chapter has explored so far—including interviews and promotional videos—to lay claim to the discourse and explicitly outline a perceived commitment to spatial capital by those involved. The "Montauk" video on Showtime's website is part of a broader promotional push for *The Affair*, one that continually foregrounds its Montauk setting. The two books sent to critics ahead of the series' release do not feature traditional key art of the show's characters on their covers; instead, they feature images of Montauk, or at the very least images designed to evoke Montauk (see Figure 4.2). For Noah and Helen, an image of a pristine private beach works to signify Helen's parents' privileged place within Montauk's elite residents over the summer months. By comparison, the image on Alison and Cole's book is of the rocky beaches near the Montauk Point Lighthouse, the oldest in New York and a significant symbol in other key art for the series, including a foreboding black-and-white landscape image superimposed with the series' title. These paratexts extend the role of place in a given series beyond the contexts of production and textuality, shaping the discourse around the text—the articles and reviews of its first season—based on a text's given spatial capital. In cases like *The Affair*, paratexts like the video or the press kit foreground Montauk's role in the story, which is then further reinforced by its place in the text itself.

Figure 4.2 The two books included as part of *The Affair* press kit, which was sent to critics and journalists ahead of its premiere in 2014.

Photo by author.

We can return to opening title sequences, discussed in Chapter 2, as an important paratext in this regard. Although *The Affair* is not explicit in terms of location, its foreboding beachside imagery nonetheless connects with the specificity of location, placing the characters—seen in often obscured or filtered images—within the same aesthetic space as the waves and beaches that come to signify Montauk in the other paratexts surrounding the series. While title sequences were earlier identified as a key outlet for spatial capital more broadly, they can specifically complete work designed to articulate distinct claims to place as character. In the opening title sequence to HBO's *True Detective*, which won the Emmy for Main Title Design in 2014, various landscapes from the show are superimposed on silhouettes of its characters and vice versa. The visual effects work to obscure the line between characters and the landscapes they occupy, a blurring that previews the series' prominent location shooting in Louisiana as well as director Cary Fukunaga's extensive use of wide landscapes throughout the eight-episode first season.[4]

It is here where the relationship between "place as character" and discourses of prestige television further converge. Returning to the discussion of paratexts from the second chapter, *The Affair* and *True Detective*'s lengthy credit sequences are common for premium cable but rare on cable or broadcast, limiting those shows' ability to construct such legible engagements with spatial capital within these spaces. Similarly, the types of behind-the-scenes paratexts that emerged ahead of *The Affair*'s release, which likewise coincided with the release of *True Detective*, are particularly tied to prestige television, performing cultural capital in line with the brand identities of premium cable channels. As part of a 12-minute behind-the-scenes feature that aired on HBO prior to *True Detective*'s release, Fukunaga suggests "the world that [the show] is set in becomes another character," setting up a sequence in which various members of the cast and creative team speak of the crucial role that Louisiana played in the series. Fukunaga describes Louisiana's mashup of lush green landscapes and industrial detritus as "the texture of our story," while series creator Nic Pizzolatto suggests "landscape is an important part of the story we're telling"; actress Elizabeth Reaser connects the series' use of place to Pizzolatto's authentic experience growing up in the region, while Michelle Monaghan specifically articulates their locations in south Louisiana from the typical—and, in her construction, artificial—use of New Orleans and Bourbon Street in signifying the state. Subsequent consideration of the challenging weather and the contributions of the art department in selecting and transforming locations highlights the intensive labor and sacrifice that went into accessing such crucial spatial capital in the interest of making place a character in the series. It is an example of a paratextual claim to spatial capital that would simply not be afforded to an average series on broadcast or basic cable.

Such paratexts work in conjunction with interviews, critical reviews, and other discursive spaces to reinforce the role of spatial capital as evidenced in the text itself—whether experienced before, during, or following a series' run, the reiteration of the "place as character" discourse in these locations can in some cases be more influential than the role of place in the series itself. When *Newsday* reviewed *The Affair* ahead of its premiere, their headline suggested that Showtime had been successful: "Montauk is the star of new Showtime drama" (Gay 2014).

Place as character as defensive

These three guiding principles that group together texts associated with the discourse of place as character help us understand the resulting engagement with spatial capital as a privileged one. The type of series that can afford to be produced in the same location as where they are set and invest the time and money necessary to place scenes consistently within the landscape—and that are likely to coincide with significant paratextual engagement with place—are selective. Series like *The Affair*, *True Detective*, and *The Wire* all contain meaningful negotiations of place that justify their use as examples of how spatial capital functions in dramatic television, but their dominance within these discourses has as much to do with their place within typical hierarchies of television dramas as it does with the shows themselves. In this way, we can critique how discourses of spatial capital are deployed and the way that "place as character" functions independent of the circumstances of production or the text itself. We can also investigate how it is often used to obscure some series' more muddled relationship with spatial capital.

Technically speaking, the discourse of "place as character" never explicitly claims that the show's setting is crucial to the story, but the rhetorical framing of place as a "character" strongly implies that it plays an active role in the narrative that does not actually materialize in all shows where this claim is made. Place's role in a given text is complicated and exists—as I noted in Chapter 2—on a spectrum between narrative backdrop and narrative engine, where plot and character are more consistently driven by a show's setting. This means that claims to spatial capital through place functioning as a character deserve greater scrutiny than they are often given by preview or review content.

The Affair, to its credit, embodies this spectrum of spatial capital within its storytelling. Its understanding of the class hierarchies of Montauk is framed by the distinct engagement with spatial capital in its two different narrative perspectives. In Noah's story, place functions as a narrative backdrop, a summer vacation in which he becomes swept up in a torrid Hamptons love affair that he leaves behind when he returns to New York City and the reality of his struggling marriage. Noah is ostensibly doing research for his book to be set in the region, but he never engages with the local dimensions of Montauk in any detail, never—for example—getting to the town meeting he plans to attend in the first season's third episode. For Alison, however, place is a narrative engine in that it drives both plot and character development. In the same episode, we bear witness to the town meeting from Alison's perspective, where her husband Cole appeals to the community to stop a commercial development by emphasizing his and Alison's roots in Montauk, building on an earlier scene at their beach house where Cole laments the lavish residential development being built by summer residents nearby. Noah's perspective offers insight into the upper-class tourists who flock to Montauk each summer and build such houses, whereas Alison's point-of-view emphasizes the working-class locals. The latter perspective may be complicated by Cole's family's drug-running business, yet their ties to the community run deeper, and the show's perspective on that community becomes deeper accordingly.

In such cases, "place as character" communicates that the story has been built around its setting, going beyond an evocative backdrop to an integral driver of both individual episodes and the series as a whole. However, the discourse is often used around series where this is a questionable claim given the realities of mobile production outlined at the beginning of this book. Although *True Detective* is positioned as a story intricately tied to its location in formal paratexts and within the series itself, HBO's behind-the-scenes feature chooses not to reveal that Pizzolatto originally set his story in the Ozarks, only moving it to Louisiana when the state's lucrative production incentives made it a more feasible economic prospect. This negotiation of spatial capital is crucial to understanding the mobility of contemporary television production, but the pragmatic balancing of spatial capital with the economic realities of television production is inconsistent with the artistic construction of place as character outlined in the paratexts. Pizzolatto describes Fukunaga's work capturing the landscape as a south Louisiana that "nobody's ever seen before" in ways that foreground their respective authorship over the series' sense of place. Yet the role of what Fukunaga identifies during a Television Critics Association press tour panel as the "realities of production" that pushed Pizzolatto to change the series' location is obscured, along with the role of location professionals whose contributions to the production are obscured in favor of Fukunaga's vision and the art department's execution of that vision. Although Fukunaga acknowledges in his answer to a press question about regional specificity that it was the original Arkansas landscapes that drew him to the series, he also carefully retains the show's ties to spatial capital, emphasizing how Pizzolatto "went to work in earnest to translate the story and bring some of those themes over" (Rosenberg 2014). In this way, they each retain an authorship over the series' construction of place and over the series as a whole, despite evidence that might challenge such discussion.

Here, then, "place as character" is being deployed defensively, leveraging the cultural capital of a prestige drama series in order to obscure the fact that the series' relationship to spatial capital lacks the same backing as archetypal series associated with the discourse in question. It becomes a critical tool in the negotiation of spatial capital for series that are positioned in complicated ways within the geography of television production outlined in the first chapter, albeit one that is more accessible for series with access to discursive spaces tied to award-winning, prestige television. To explore this process in more detail, the following case study considers the spatial capital of one of the most-acclaimed series of the twenty-first century, around which nearly all stakeholders actively tapped into—or attempted to tap into—these discourses to maximize the spatial capital for the series, its setting, and the subsequent projects set in the same location equally interested in leveraging place as character.

Albuquerque's starring turn: place as character in *Breaking Bad*

When AMC drama series *Breaking Bad* began the final episodes of its five-season run in the summer of 2013, the channel and the series' producer Sony Pictures Television purchased several billboards commemorating the occasion. However, these billboards did not go up in Los Angeles or New York City to promote the series to the largest possible audience: they went up in Albuquerque, New Mexico, where the series was set and shot. Featuring an image of series stars Bryan Cranston and Aaron Paul, who played meth producers Walter White and Jesse Pinkman respectively, information about the series' return date and timeslot were placed in small font in the bottom right corner of the image. In the middle of the image, meanwhile, was a direct message to the city itself: "Thanks Albuquerque! We had great chemistry together!"

These localized billboards reflect a mutually beneficial relationship between *Breaking Bad* and Albuquerque over the course of its production. As referenced in this book's opening chapter, Albuquerque has emerged as a location for television production in part based on the visibility and production infrastructure created by *Breaking Bad*, to the extent that New Mexico's 2013 legislation establishing increased production incentives was known as the "*Breaking Bad* Bill" (Couch 2013). The series—which tracked Walter White's journey from cancer-stricken schoolteacher to drug kingpin—brought legitimacy to New Mexico as a filming location, its status as an Emmy-winning and critically acclaimed series building significant cultural capital for the state and the city of Albuquerque. In fact, it is one of only a small number of series filmed outside of Los Angeles or New York to win the Emmy Award for Outstanding Drama Series, and was the first since PBS' *Upstairs, Downstairs* (1971–1975) to do so more than once.[5]

These billboards were far from the only location where the connection between the series and its setting was remarked upon. Writing for *The New Yorker*, Rachel Syme (2013) characterizes *Breaking Bad* as "a show organically tied to its shooting location," arguing as a native New Mexican that it represents

> the first story to truly commit the full spectrum of New Mexico to film: the grandiose visuals, the soaring altitudes, the banal office complexes, the Kokopellis and Kachina dolls, the seamy warehouses, the marshmallow clouds. The show seems to root itself deeper in the landscape with every new montage. It has become our newest monument.

Interviewing locals who have profited from the tourism of the series and reflecting on New Mexico's aspirations to function as a media capital, Syme confronts the series' "seediness and monstrosity" given its subject matter, arguing that "New Mexicans are proud of anything that draws us out of neglect, out of never really fitting in. We are just happy to be considered, even if it is for our underbelly."

Syme's is not the only piece of mainstream journalism about *Breaking Bad* that narrows in on its setting as a point of distinction: in other press, Albuquerque gains the status of a "character" in the series, as ascribed by those involved with the production and those analyzing its local impact. In a travel article focused on the series' setting in *The New York Times* (Brennan 2013), series creator Vince Gilligan describes Albuquerque as "a character in the series," a distinction that is further reinforced by Cranston in an interview with Albuquerque alt-weekly *Alibi*. He suggests Albuquerque has "become an important character to our show. The topography. Really the blue skies, and the billowy clouds, and the red mountains, and the Sandias, the valleys, the vastness of the desert, the culture of the people" (Adams 2011). The "characterization" of Albuquerque also emerges in a *Forbes* interview with series cinematographer Michael Slovis (St. John 2013), whose evocative images of that topography have become iconic of the series. *The Santa Fe Reporter*, writing about the series' finale, makes the distinction as explicit as possible: "While many TV shows use a city as a setting, none have used it like a character like *Breaking Bad* did" (Reichbach 2013).

Breaking Bad embodies the qualities common to series in which place is framed as a character: the series is very notably shot on location in Albuquerque, continually sets scenes within the landscape, and has its sense of place reinforced through paratexts like the "Ozymandias" video released during its final season, in which Bryan Cranston's reading of the Percy Bysshe Shelley poem is combined with a collection of distinctive time-lapse establishing images used throughout the series. The series' surge in mainstream attention and ratings in its final season also amplified the visibility of media tourism to Albuquerque, where the intense online appetite for coverage of the series resulted in numerous unofficial paratexts where websites such as *The A.V. Club* visited locations like Walter White's house and the car wash where he laundered his drug money (Adams 2013). The show has subsequently been held up alongside shows like *The Wire* as an exemplar of "place as character," effectively putting Albuquerque on the map in the space of television culture and even creating a "recurring character" that remained central to discourse surrounding spin-off prequel *Better Call Saul* (2015–present).

However, although creator Vince Gilligan and cinematographer Michael Slovis have both been positioned as the creators of *Breaking Bad*'s Albuquerque, it—like *True Detective*'s Louisiana—was the result of financial considerations. Gilligan originally set his story of a teacher-turned-meth cook in Riverside, California, but before shooting the pilot producer Sony Pictures Television and network AMC made it clear that the economics would not work in southern California. In a roundtable interview with Charlie Rose in the buildup to the series finale in 2013, Gilligan spoke of his reaction to the mandated move to New Mexico to take advantage of its production incentives:

> They said, "What's the big deal, you put new license plates on that say California instead of New Mexico, it'll be fine." And I'm glad they came to us with this idea, but I'm so glad I said "no, let's make it Albuquerque." Because the sad truth of it is, unfortunately, you can't swing a dead cat in this country without hitting a meth lab somewhere or other. . . . It could be California, it could be—no one state has the lock on it, unfortunately.

These comments raise two crucial points within the conscious engagement with the discourse of "place as character." First, similar to *True Detective*, Gilligan is acknowledging here that the basic concept of his series is untethered from the location in which it is set. Although the popular press articles cited earlier highlight how intricately connected *Breaking Bad* is to its geography, Gilligan is simultaneously claiming that it could have been set anywhere in the United States. Such a suggestion goes against the type of intricate, inherent place-based storytelling evident in shows like *The Wire* or *Treme* that originate with specific efforts to tell stories emerging out of Baltimore and New Orleans, respectively, and against the principles on which a strong connection between media and a particular city is typically constructed.

Second, Gilligan is legitimating his own labor by positioning himself as an agent of authenticity, contesting the studio and channel's support of city-for-city doubling in favor of setting the series in Albuquerque, similar to Fukunaga's emphasis on his and Pizzolatto's respective labor in translating *True Detective* from Arkansas to Louisiana. Andrews and Roberts (2012) argue "landscape is understood as something that is 'shaped' and 'produced,' and by which is thus contingent to human or natural 'processes or agents'" (1). In this case, Gilligan is placing himself as the figure more responsible for shaping the landscape, here constructing place as character through his conscious resistance to less authentic engagements with place.

Breaking Bad may not have originally been set in Albuquerque, but the fact that it was his decision to do so allows him to retain authorship, while simultaneously reframing the series' engagement with location in similar ways to how authors construct place as character within literature, despite the expansive amount of labor that goes into constructing those images relative to the descriptive language evident in literary works.

As evidenced by *True Detective*, the fact that *Breaking Bad* was not originally set in Albuquerque does not mean that the show cannot successfully claim place functions as a character within popular discourse. However, when the series as a whole is considered, the function of Albuquerque fails to live up to the claims that the show's relationship with its setting transcends other televisual examples. There is no question that the setting is consistently used as a narrative backdrop to heighten thematic impact or draw out character distinctions as the narrative unfolds, and that the lack of representations of Albuquerque onscreen made this more notable than if the show had been set in Los Angeles or New York. However, the series rarely delves deeper into the spatial capital involved with the show's setting in a way that elevates it to a narrative engine.

There is no question that there is conscious engagement with the landscape in *Breaking Bad*. In the series' pilot, for example, the bank where Walt withdraws the money to pay for the RV is consciously isolated, surrounded by desert and mountains. Placing Walt's scene with Jesse within the landscape as opposed to a crowded urban environment calls attention to the characters' efforts to be as discrete as possible, while also previewing their journey into the desert to complete the cook in question. That iconic location, located in the Navajo reservation of To'hajiilee, becomes crucial again at the end of the series when Walt buries his drug money in the same location and ends up in the middle of a shootout trying to ensure its safety. In one of the series' most powerful engagements with spatial capital, the opening scene of "Ozymandias" calls attention to this serialized use of location: beginning with a "flashback" to previously unseen moments from the events of the pilot, that scene ends with Walt in the foreground, and Jesse and the RV in the background, fading away. Then, following the series' opening title sequence, we see the same location, this time with the action from the previous episode—two vehicles, Aryan gunmen, Walt, his DEA agent brother-in-law Hank, and Jesse—gradually fade in, the location the link between the past and the present.

However, although To'hajiilee is central to the series' narrative as a setting, its sense of spatial capital is defined purely through its aesthetic and symbolic value to the story. It is a landscape that is given meaning through the storylines that unfold within it, but the location itself holds no agency over that story—in this case specifically, the Navajo Nation plays no significant role in the series' narrative, with the writers choosing not to engage with the cultural or political dimensions of those who own and govern the land in question. Although the episode is named after the reservation, and early speculation from *Vulture*'s Margaret Lyons (2013)—based on episodes of *The X-Files* (1993–2002), which Vince Gilligan wrote for, that took place on Navajo reservations—hoped that the episodes would explore the specifics of Navajo culture, *Breaking Bad* went no further in investing the series with the culture of the lands its characters occupied in these pivotal scenes. A Google search for "To'hajiilee," as of January 2021, features primarily coverage of the episode by that name, with the minimalist Wikipedia page for the reservation itself pushed to second in the search results by the more-detailed Wikipedia entry for the episode of the series that bears its name.

Breaking Bad is undoubtedly leveraging spatial capital in these scenes, tied to its use of Albuquerque filming locations distinct from shows filmed in other parts of the country. Yet the series' investment with place is limited by their selective engagement with spatial capital. Although the landscape is of significant value to the series, the place-making activities central to that community are less crucial. To'hajiilee's name is actually a relatively recent development, which may in fact be part of the reason for its low Google ranking: in 2000, local high school law students petitioned to have the reservation returned to its traditional name, which means "the place where the water is drawn up," from its then-present name "Canoncito"—Spanish for "little canyon"—which had been foisted on the tribe by President Truman (Nevada Government Session 1999). This is critical to the culture of this location, yet this information is less valuable to the series given that none of the show's main characters are of Navajo descent, and the root narrative of the series was—as noted earlier—understood to be unhinged to any one location within the United States. The series took full advantage of Albuquerque and the surrounding area to serve as an evocative and distinct backdrop for the series, but the resulting representations of place show limited engagement with the complexities of spatial capital, even if they are memorable for audiences and valuable for the future of local production in the region.

Albuquerque is not incidental to *Breaking Bad*: Gilligan could have chosen to use city-for-city doubling to retain his original Riverside setting for the series, and his choice to embrace the landscape is a clear effort to leverage spatial capital in a meaningful way. However, the discourse of place as character says less about the actual function of location within the narrative and more about its discursive value to Gilligan as a writer, to other members of the production, and to Sony and AMC as its producer and distributor, respectively. The specificity of framing it as a character, though, anchors that spatial capital within the area of above-the-line labor, despite the fact that it is below-the-line workers like location professionals who are actually responsible for turning a landscape or cityscape into a significant part of a story. It is a discourse that, accurately or not, roots location in the very genesis of the story itself, meaning that any labor from the show's location manager Christian Diaz De Bedoya and his team is framed as executing—rather than shaping—that vision to a greater degree than if the discourse was not present.

This is not to say that Gilligan and the executive producers of both *Breaking Bad* and *Better Call Saul* have elided Diaz De Bedoya's contributions to the series. In a fan Q&A on AMC's website (2011), Gilligan was asked how they find locations for the show. In response, he explains Diaz De Bedoya's role and outlines how the work locations does ahead of each season is critical to their creative process:

> At the beginning of the season, they also go out and photograph places that they think are visually interesting. Typically, we'll have a meeting at the beginning in which they show us these photographs and discuss them. Very often we'll get inspired by these possibilities location-wise and we will indeed write to certain places that they find for us.

In an interview with *Better Call Saul* co-creator Peter Gould in *The Hollywood Reporter* (O'Connell 2017), Gould identifies Diaz De Bedoya as the person on the show who has the most difficult job, noting that the members of the location team "have an almost impossible task: finding new, expressive locations in a city we've been shooting in for almost 10 years. He comes through for us every single day and does it with effortless good humor." Given these statements, this is not a case of the producers of the series actively trying to supersede the location team's role in the production.

However, because locations professionals are so far below-the-line, they are rarely allowed to articulate their own contributions to a given series in outlets of this nature and are rarely credited in reviews that hail the show's relationship to Albuquerque. If Albuquerque is indeed a character in the show, it depends on the locations team finding the right locations, but their labor is largely elided because it does not fit comfortably into the cultural hierarchies of where creativity rests in the collaborative production of television, and which the discourse of place as character situates further within the authority of showrunners and producers. In the aforementioned 2019 *Los Angeles Times* story about place functioning as a character in television series, which valorizes filming on location, Diaz De Bedoya discusses *Better Call Saul*'s use of Albuquerque, but only below Gould's larger statement about the production's view of the city's role in the story. When *Entertainment Weekly* did a large profile on the different locations used throughout the prequel series, they interviewed Gould and fellow executive producer Melissa Bernstein, but not Diaz De Bedoya, who is credited by Gould only for maintaining relationships with the distinct owners of two interconnected locations (Snierson 2020). Although AMC's website did interview Diaz De Bedoya's predecessor Scott Clark after *Breaking Bad*'s second season (2009), they never interviewed Diaz De Bedoya about his contributions to the series' acclaimed final seasons, and no video content for YouTube channels or DVDs were produced with any members of the locations team as they were for figures like cinematographer Michael Slovis.

The only space where Diaz De Bedoya was able to speak at length about his role in either series is the aforementioned paratext produced by *The A.V. Club*, a *Pop Pilgrims* video where hosts Erik Adams and Emily VanDer-Werff tour iconic locations from *Breaking Bad* with Diaz De Bedoya (see Figure 4.2). In the write-up accompanying the 2013 video, Adams notes the credit that Slovis and the show's directors like Rian Johnson often receive for the series' visual signature, but argues that "were it not for Diaz De Bedoya, his fellow location managers, and their intimate knowledge of ABQ, Slovis and Johnson would be shooting against a less idiosyncratic canvas." It is one of the rare instances where Diaz De Bedoya gets to speak of his role in the series at length, and in the video, he gets to—for the first time—be the one to make the all-important claim that Albuquerque is, indeed "a character in the show" as the person most directly responsible for ensuring the show has access to the locations that make that possible.

But by reiterating this discourse, Diaz De Bedoya is further distancing himself from both series' spatial capital, entrenching it within the creative class of workers that "place as character" ultimately benefits. Much as a certain class of show can more successfully assert place's role as a character

Figure 4.3 A screenshot from *The A.V. Club*'s "Pop Pilgrims" tour of *Breaking Bad* filming locations, with location manager Christian Diaz De Bedoya being interviewed in local restaurant chain Twisters, which became fried chicken franchise Los Pollos Hermanos in the AMC series.

Screenshot by author.

in the story, so too can a certain class of worker benefit from deploying this discourse, even in circumstances where the initial creative instincts of the series were not based on the location in question. When Josh Wigler (2015) previewed *Better Call Saul* ahead of its premiere, he wrote that "more than a year after Walter White's final curtain call, we're back in the Albuquerque of Vince Gilligan's mind," a rhetorical turn owed in part to how reiterating place as character places spatial capital within the power of Gilligan and showrunners like him.

Place as character as location marketing

Writers and directors like Gilligan and Gould—along with Fukunaga, Pizzolatto, and others—may be the most central to the discourse of place as character, but they are not its only beneficiary. For cities like Albuquerque that are central to these claims, the spatial capital generated by place as character can be adopted to appeal to media tourists as well as media producers looking for a location to film their next project. On the City of Albuquerque Convention and Visitors Bureau website during the show's run (2015), the bureau boasted "the city . . . stars as a character in [*Breaking Bad*] with filming locations throughout the metro area," and included testimonials from Gilligan and the series' cast that speak to the fact—in Gilligan's words—that "Albuquerque has meant the world for *Breaking Bad*." Here, the discourse of place as character serves as a form of tourism marketing, working to convince potential visitors to use the *Breaking Bad* map featured on the page to create their own personal tour of locations used in the series. A similar page for *Better Call Saul* reiterates the discourse, claiming that "Just as in 'Breaking Bad,' Albuquerque plays an integral role on 'Better Call Saul'—almost serving as an additional character in the narrative," also collecting reviews of the show that specifically highlight the Albuquerque setting. In both cases, the city is working to translate the spatial capital embedded within the text and highlighted by popular discourse into cultural and economic capital, in the process further centralizing figures like Gilligan, Gould, and Cranston, as opposed to the below-the-line workers responsible for finding the locations highlighted.

In addition to serving as a draw for potential tourists, the discourse is equally beneficial for Albuquerque's ability to attract other film and television productions. Much as an actor's resume is improved by high-profile roles, a television series where place is so often part of the discourse surrounding its success offers clear benefits to a fledgling production hub like Albuquerque. Although less descriptive, *Breaking Bad* and *Better Call Saul* are the first projects listed in the Albuquerque Film Office's brief "History of Film in New Mexico" section on its website, and *Better Call Saul* concludes the New Mexico Film Office's 2018 sizzle reel intended for producers in addition to featuring heavily on the Film Office's "for fans" page intended for would-be tourists. The cultural capital generated by *Breaking Bad* and then reinforced by *Better Call Saul* gave Albuquerque and New Mexico the capacity to leverage that success into media capital, whether to highlight the state with shows like The CW's *Roswell, New Mexico* (2019–present) that are set there, or by leveraging the higher profile brought by the AMC series to convince shows like USA's *Briarpatch* (2020) and Netflix's *Daybreak* (2019) to film shows set in Texas and California against the same backdrop. Although these cases of city-for-city doubling carry less spatial capital, the fact they were produced in Albuquerque showcases how *Breaking Bad*'s success—and the discourse of the city serving as a character within the show—has provided the industry a calling card that will carry the city forward for decades.

Accordingly, when other locations are working to establish their own claim to television's mobile production, the discourse of place as character that worked so effectively for Albuquerque is an easy shortcut. This type of aspirational location marketing comes from cities like Charleston, South Carolina, which has yet to emerge as a key hub of television production in the same way as its neighbor to the north, North Carolina. When CBS made the decision to film its 2014 summer legal drama *Reckless* in the city, where the show was also set, the South Carolina Film Commission latched onto the opportunity to claim their own *Breaking Bad*: in a press release sent out on behalf of the South Carolina Film Commission, recipients were invited to "meet Charleston: The Newest Cast Member on CBS' *Reckless*." Suggesting that "the city is central to the series' storyline," the press release outlined a series of prominent locations used in the legal drama, including the exteriors of Charleston's City Hall and County Courthouse, along with Fountain Walk, which stands in for the local police headquarters in the series. Duane Parrish, Director of the South Carolina Department of Parks, Recreation, and Tourism, says that they "are thrilled that the *Reckless* cast and crew have found a home in Charleston and welcomed it as a main character of the show."

The co-opting of this discourse as an explicit marketing tool for the purposes of promoting the spatial capital of a given location connects to Sadler and Haskins's (2005) articulation of the "postcard effect" of television representations of place. With small thumbnail images of the beautiful Charleston locations featured in *Reckless*, and suggestions that "the series really highlights all the city has to offer," the press release reinforces how state production incentives function as a form of product placement, with states subsidizing production in the hopes of generating meaningful benefit. The use of "place as character" here is a conscious form of legitimation, connecting the series—which was canceled after one season, and garnered little critical attention—to a larger tradition that Charleston and South Carolina felt would allow them to generate additional production benefits in the future.

The discourse also attempts to maximize a rare occurrence for Charleston, as few of the film and TV projects that have taken advantage of their incentives have explicitly set their stories in South Carolina. Any successful project that films in South Carolina is valuable to the state's reputation and profile: appearing onscreen is meaningful spatial capital and can translate to other forms of capital both within the film and television industry and among audiences. However, while there are numerous stories online about locations in Charleston that were featured in the Netflix series *Outer Banks* (2020–present), the fact that those locations were doubling for North Carolina complicated their ability to capitalize on the project in the same way that Albuquerque capitalized on *Breaking Bad*. A strong capacity for location doubling is beneficial to the purely economic considerations of leveraging mobile production, but it lacks the capacity for discursive framing of the production that leads to greater benefits for the region and its place within television culture more broadly.

Conclusion

Reckless' low critical standing and short summer run meant that Charleston's time as a "character" was short-lived. However, even if the show had not been canceled, the South Carolina Film Commission's claim to the discourse of place as character was suspect. The series certainly contains many of the hallmarks of the discourse identified in this chapter, such as shooting on location and conspicuously setting scenes in the landscape—one of the two leads, Roy Rayder, even drives a boat to work every day for maximum time highlighting the city's proximity to the water. But the series' claims to this discourse are as aspirational as Charleston's: it is a broadcast procedural drama, without the prestige of premium cable, the complexity of serialization, or any of the other cultural capital that intersects with spatial capital in cases like *The Affair* or *Breaking Bad*. As much as the nuanced function of place within a given series rarely matches up perfectly with the claims wrapped up in place being a character in these series, there is a higher burden attached to the discourse when a show is operating uphill within hierarchies of television value more broadly.

This chapter has considered how the place of spatial capital within television culture has been shaped by these discursive formations, wherein meaningful representations of location are enshrined within certain forms of television program and the rhetoric surrounding them. Although the textual strategies for accessing and generating spatial capital discussed in the previous chapters are foundational to any claim that a location is a character in a given series, their ability to generate meaningful capital within marketing and promotion, previews and reviews, and other spaces is dependent on factors that extend beyond the text. Whereas the previous chapter outlined how distribution shapes and controls how spatial capital is articulated within the text itself, this chapter has considered how the discourse of "place as character" works to renegotiate the existing textual representation after the fact to present it as a set of authentic creative choices as opposed to compromises made due to realities of mobile production, limitations of budget or time, or dictates from studios or networks. This project as a whole has demonstrated how workers throughout the collaborative space of television production contribute to spatial capital, yet when place becomes a character, that work becomes attached primarily to above-the-line workers, credited to writers and deployed by actors who have greater access to the discursive spaces where television's cultural capital is determined. Below-the-line stakeholders of spatial capital are marginalized by this discourse, with the value of space and place shifted to those with stronger claims to either creative or economic ties to the television industry.

This project has consistently framed spatial capital as a negotiation, and thus its ability to be distorted and reshaped within interviews, reviews, and promotional materials is inherent to its place within the circuit of television production. However, the stakeholders identified throughout this chapter—and throughout the book thus far—are ultimately not the final word on how spatial capital manifests within a given series. If representing a particular location functions as a burden of spatial capital, the discourse of "place as character" communicates that this burden has been met to a degree that elevates place beyond setting to a vital part of a given series. But that in and of itself increases the burden as the viewers at home—the audience for this discourse—experience it.

And so, in the case of *Reckless*, South Carolina's claims to spatial capital were judged by not only critics but also viewers. While Allen MacDonald tweeted that "#Charleston is a real character on #Reckless," user @Azriel-Neighbors disagreed: acknowledging "a good show should make the city a character," they go on to say *Reckless* is failing this test because "African American's [sic] certainly aren't represented in #Reckless. #Charleston has a large black population. There is one black character." It's a tweet that simultaneously reaffirms how spatial capital is discursively framed within television series, while also indicating the consequences of this framework when the negotiation of spatial capital exits the space of the industry and is tested by an active audience, which leads us into the fifth and final chapter.

Notes

1 The essay in question, Meghan Sutherland's "On the Grounds of Television" (339–361), focuses on the ontology of television viewership, looking exclusively at news broadcasts with limited ties to the fictional programming focused on in this project.
2 This was in response to an unrelated question—Stair raised the discourse herself in this instance.
3 This is particularly evident in the first season's third episode, in which the opening scene of Alison's side of the story begins inside their home and moves onto the balcony overlooking the ocean.
4 The seasonal anthology structure of the series is also notable here, as subsequent seasons would feature an entirely new cast of characters, including new locations.

5 HBO's *Game of Thrones*, filmed in Northern Ireland and a range of European locations, and *The Crown*, filmed in and around the UK, have since been added to this list. Only three other series not filmed in New York or Los Angeles have won Outstanding Drama Series: Hulu's Toronto-shot *The Handmaid's Tale* (2016–present), the first season of Showtime's *Homeland* (2011–2020) filmed in North Carolina, and CBS' *Northern Exposure* (1990–1995), which shot in Washington State. The rise in recent winners reflects the rise in mobile production.

References

Adams, Erik. 2013. "Pop Pilgrims: We Go on Location with Breaking Bad." *The A.V. Club*, August 8. www.avclub.com/video/we-go-on-location-with-ibreaking-badi-101337.

Adams, Sam. 2011. "The Colorful Mr. White." *Alibi*, August 4. http://alibi.com/feature/38033/The-Colorful-Mr-White.html.

Andrews, Hazel, and Les Roberts. 2012. "Introduction." In *Liminal Landscapes: Travel, Experience and Spaces in-Between*, edited by Hazel Andrews and Les Roberts, 1–18. London: Routledge.

Brennan, Emily. 2013. "Albuquerque's Role on 'Breaking Bad'." *The New York Times*, August 6. www.nytimes.com/2013/08/11/travel/albuquerques-role-on-breaking-bad.html.

Brunsdon, Charlotte. 2007. *London in Cinema: The Cinematic City Since 1945*. London: British Film Institute.

———. 2018. *Television Cities: Paris, London, Baltimore*. Raleigh: Duke University Press.

Carr, David. 2013. "Broken Men, Broken Place." *The New York Times*, August 2. www.nytimes.com/2013/08/04/arts/television/low-winter-sun-gives-detroit-a-leading-role.html.

Clarke, D.B., ed. 1997. *The Cinematic City*. London: Routledge.

Couch, Aaron. 2013. "New Mexico Governor Signs 'Breaking Bad' TV, Film Subsidy Bill into Law." *The Hollywood Reporter*, April 4. www.hollywoodreporter.com/news/new-mexico-governor-signs-breaking-433168.

Dawn, Randee. 2019. "The Magic of Hollywood Can Transport You Anywhere, but Sometimes Nothing Beats the Real Thing." *The Los Angeles Times*, May 23. www.latimes.com/entertainment/envelope/la-en-st-la-ny-chicago-tv-shows-20190523-story.html.

Derenzo, Nicholas. 2018. "The Hemi Q&A: Alan Cumming." *Hemispheres Magazine*, April 1. www.hemispheresmag.com/alan-cumming-the-hemi-qa/.

Donald, James. 1999. *Imagining the Modern City*. Minneapolis: University of Minnesota Press.

Fowler, Elizabeth. 2003. *Literary Character: The Human Figure in Early English Writing*. Ithaca, NY: Cornell University Press.

Fox, Ken. 2001. "Space/Place." In *Critical Dictionary of Film and Television Theory*, edited by Roberta E. Pearson and Philip Simpson, 574–79. London: Routledge.

Fraley, Jason. 2015. "HBO's 'The Wire' Now Available in Remastered HD." *WTOP.com*, January 5. http://wtop.com/tv/2015/01/hbos-wire-now-available-remastered-hd/.

Gay, Verne. 2014. " 'The Affair' Review: Montauk Is the Star of New Showtime Drama." *Newsday*, October 9. www.newsday.com/entertainment/tv/the-affair-review-montauk-is-the-star-of-new-showtime-drama-1.9480668.

Goodman, Tim. 2012. "Review: *Lilyhammer* Season 1." *The Hollywood Reporter*, February 6. https://www.hollywoodreporter.com/tv/tv-news/review-lilyhammer-Steven-Van-Zandt-Sopranos-Netflix-287367/

Hoffberger, Chase. 2012. "Steven Van Zandt: The Fixer." *The Austin Chronicle*, April 3. www.austinchronicle.com/daily/music/2012-04-03/steven-van-zandt-the-fixer/.

Jancelewicz, Chris. 2014. "Kim Cattrall on 'Sensitive Skin,' Making TV for Baby Boomers and Why She Took a 'Time Out.'" *The Huffington Post*, July 17. www.huffingtonpost.ca/2014/07/17/kim-cattrall-sensitive-skin-interview_n_5596431.html.

Kakala, Alexander. 2021. "Sarah Jessica Parker Talks Replacing Samantha on 'Sex and the City' Revival." *Today.com*, January 13. www.today.com/popculture/sarah-jessica-parker-talks-replacing-samantha-sex-city-revival-t205804.

Leopold, Todd. 2013. "The New, New TV Golden Age." *CNN*, May 6. www.cnn.com/2013/05/06/showbiz/golden-age-of-tv/.

Lury, Karen, and Doreen Massey. 1999. "Making Connections." *Screen* 40.3: 229–38.

Lyons, Margaret. 2013. "Predicting What Will Happen in *Breaking Bad*'s Final 4 Episodes from Their Titles." *Vulture*, September 5. www.vulture.com/2013/09/predicting-breaking-bad-final-four-episodes.html.

Matthews, Liam. 2016. "How Kevin Can Wait's Long Island Setting Breaks the Sitcom Mold." *TVGuide.com*, November 27. www.tvguide.com/news/kevin-can-wait-long-island-kevin-james-erinn-hayes/.

Mettler, Mike. 2014. "The Wire Cast Members Reminisce as an HD Christmas Marathon Kicks Off." *Digital Trends*, December 25. www.digitaltrends.com/movies/the-wire-goes-hd-for-christmas-marathon-cast-members-reminisce/.

Mittell, Jason. 2015. *Complex TV: The Poetics of Contemporary Television Storytelling*. New York: New York University Press.

Morgan Parmett, Helen. 2019. *Down in Treme: Race, Place, and New Orleans on Television*. Stuttgart: Franz Steiner Verlag.

Newman, Michael Z., and Elana Levine. 2011. *Legitimating Television: Media Convergence and Cultural Status*. New York: Routledge.

No Author. 1999. "A Memorial: Acknowledging the Name Change of the Navajo Nation Chapter Formerly Called Canoncito and Now to Be Known as the To'Hajilee Chapter of the Navajo Nation." *Nevada Government Session*. www.nmlegis.gov/Sessions/99%20Regular/FinalVersions/HM042.html.

———. 2008. "Blake Lively: The Gossip on Hollywood's Newest Star." *The Independent*, August 22. www.independent.co.uk/arts-entertainment/films/features/blake-lively-the-gossip-on-hollywoods-newest-star-904881.html.

———. 2009. "Q&A—Scott Clark (Location Manager)." *AMC.com*, June. https://web.archive.org/web/20160407123901/www.amc.com/shows/breaking-bad/talk/2009/06/scott-clark-interview.

———. 2011. "*Breaking Bad* Series Creator Vince Gilligan Answers Viewer Questions, Part II." *AMC.com*, October. https://web.archive.org/web/20160504131734/www.amc.com/shows/breaking-bad/talk/2011/10/vince-gilligan-interview-part-ii-2.

———. 2013a. "Ozymandias—As Read by Bryan Cranston: Breaking Bad." *YouTube*. www.youtube.com/watch?v=T3dpghfRBHE.

———. 2013b. "The Creator and Cast of *Breaking Bad*." *Charlie Rose*, August 9. https://charlierose.com/videos/17847.

———. 2015. "*Breaking Bad* in Albuquerque." *Albuquerque Convention & Visitors Bureau.* www.visitalbuquerque.org/albuquerque/film-tourism/breaking-bad/.

O'Connell, Mikey. 2017. "'Better Call Saul' Showrunner on Bringing Back Blockbuster Video, Avoiding Courtroom Cliches." *The Hollywood Reporter*, August 15. www.hollywoodreporter.com/news/better-call-saul-showrunner-bringing-back-blockbuster-video-avoiding-courtroom-cliches-1028394.

Rappaport, Mark. 1980. "Place in the Cinema: Mark Rappaport on Place." *Framework* 13: 26–27.

Reichbach, Matthew. 2013. "Morning Word: Thank You and Goodbye, Breaking Bad." *The Sante Fe Reporter*, September 30. www.sfreporter.com/santafe/blog-4811-morning-word-thank-you-and-goodbye-breaking-bad.html.

Rhodes, John David, and Elena Gorfinkel. 2011. "Introduction." In *Taking Place: Location and the Moving Image*, edited by John David Rhodes and Elena Gorfinkel, vii–xxix. Minneapolis: University of Minnesota Press.

Rosenberg, Alyssa. 2014. "Why the 'True Detective' Shot that Has Everyone Talking Is Overrated." *ThinkProgress*, February 11. https://archive.thinkprogress.org/why-the-true-detective-shot-that-has-everyone-talking-is-overrated-247aa38a7dd2/.

Sadler, William J., and Ekaterina V. Haskins. 2005. "Metonymy and the Metropolis: Television Show Settings and the Image of New York City." *Journal of Communication Inquiry* 29.3: 195216.

Silver, Alain, and James Ursini. 2005. *L.A. Noir: The City as Character*. Santa Monica: Santa Monica Press.

Siska, William C. 2011. "'If All This Is for Nothing': *The Sopranos* as Art Cinema." In *The Essential Sopranos Reader*, edited by David Lavery, Douglas L. Howard, and Paul Levinson, online ed. Lexington: University Press of Kentucky. http://davidlavery.net/Sopranos/Web_Only/Siska.pdf.

Snierson, Dan. 2020. "Go Behind the Scenes of Better Call Saul's Iconic Albuquerque Locations." *Entertainment Weekly*, March 9. https://ew.com/tv/better-call-saul-key-locations-albuquerque/.

Stacey, Danielle. 2014. "The Fall's Jamie Dornan Reveals: 'It's Fun Playing a Psychopath'." *Mirror*, November 12. www.mirror.co.uk/tv/tv-news/falls-jamie-dornan-reveals-its-4616724.

Stanhope, Kate. 2016. "How 'Royal Pains' Became a Royal Success for USA." *The Hollywood Reporter*, June 8. www.hollywoodreporter.com/features/royal-pains-cancelled-why-legacy-lives-on-899948.

St. John, Allen. 2013. "Working Bad: Cinematographer Michael Slovis on 35mm Film, HDTV, and How 'Breaking Bad' Stuck the Landing." *Forbes*, September 26. www.forbes.com/sites/allenstjohn/2013/09/26/working-bad-cinematographer-michael-slovis-on-35mm-film-hdtv-and-how-breaking-bad-stuck-the-landing/.

Strick, Philip. 1984. "The Metropolis Wars: The City as Character in Science Fiction Films." In *Omni's Screen Flights/Screen Fantasies: The Future According to Science Fiction Cinema*, edited by Danny Peary, 43–49. New York: Doubleday.

Syme, Rachel. 2013. "Walter White's Home Town." *The New Yorker*, August 7. www.newyorker.com/culture/culture-desk/walter-whites-home-town.

Tartaglione, Nancy. 2012. "BBC Acquires 'Lilyhammer'; Hit Norwegian Show Debuts on Netflix Today in U.S." *Deadline*, February 6. https://deadline.com/2012/02/bbc-acquires-lilyhammer-hit-norwegian-show-debuts-on-netflix-today-in-u-s-226229/.

Terrones, Terry. 2019. "Q&A: Actor Jerry O'Connell Talks About His Fun New Series, 'Carter'." *The Colorado Springs Gazette*, September 5. https://gazette.com/arts-entertainment/q-a-actor-jerry-o-connell-talks-about-his-fun-new-series-carter/article_351be526-9547-11e8-b9f0–372fe780689d.html.

Wigler, Josh. 2015. "11 'Better Call Saul' Non-Spoilers You Need to Know Before the 'Breaking Bad' Spinoff Premieres." *MTV.com*, January 27. www.mtv.com/news/2059897/better-call-saul-review/.

Williams, Linda. 2014. *On the Wire*. Durham, NC: Duke University Press.

Wilson, Benji. 2012. "Lilyhammer, BBC Four, Review." *The Telegraph*, September 12. www.telegraph.co.uk/culture/tvandradio/9537056/Lilyhammer-BBC-Four-review.html.

5 Spatial capital and social media

Amplifiers, arbiters, and the mountains of North Dakota

In 2018, Netflix quietly began development on a new drama series focused on a group of teens living on North Carolina's Outer Banks, a series of barrier islands that serve as a key tourist destination on the Atlantic coast. The show was co-created by Jonas Pate, who had recently moved to his home state of North Carolina after two decades in Los Angeles. This return to his roots was a key part of his inspiration for the project. According to *StarNewsOnline* (Ingram 2019), Pate "crafted the show and scenes with specific . . . locations he said would be ideal for filming" the show in Wilmington, which over the years has housed a range of television projects including *Dawson's Creek* (1998–2003), *One Tree Hill* (2003–2012), and Pate's own *Surface* (2005–2006). It only made sense, when considering spatial capital, that his show about the haves and have nots that co-exist in the "OBX"—as the Outer Banks are known colloquially—would take advantage of filming in a state with a long history of film and television production.

In early 2019, however, Pate turned to the media in an effort to correct what he perceived as a crisis of spatial capital. Despite his best efforts, Netflix was resisting filming what would become its 2020 series *Outer Banks* in North Carolina based on a political wrinkle: while North Carolina had access to the crews, facilities, and locations necessary to sustain the production, the state government also enacted the controversial House Bill 2 in 2016, one of many such discriminatory "Bathroom Bills" that were introduced in state legislatures in response to local efforts to expand protections for transgender individuals. Although the bill was partially repealed in 2017 after backlash from film and television producers, sporting leagues, and civil rights groups, restrictions remained in place that kept local jurisdictions from introducing their own anti-discrimination legislation through the end of 2020, which Netflix cited to Pate when they rejected his recommendation to film in North Carolina and instead sent him down the coast to Charleston, South Carolina, to scout locations.

In *StarNewsOnline*'s coverage of Pate's Hail Mary effort to have the show film in Wilmington by convincing the state to remove the restrictions ahead of schedule (Ingram 2019), the dynamics of television's spatial capital are on full display. Pate's emphasis on having written the script with specific

DOI: 10.4324/9781003224693-6

locations in mind points to the textual dynamics of spatial capital detailed in Chapter 2 and the burden of spatial capital he had built into the project that was not being met by Netflix's decision-making. Pate frames this primarily through economic terms in an effort to speak to the state legislature, arguing "this tiny law is costing this town 70 good, clean, pension-paying jobs and also sending a message to those people who can bring these jobs and more that North Carolina still doesn't get it." State Senator Harper Peterson is quoted supporting Pate's effort to keep this production from embracing the mobility detailed in Chapter 1, noting that "we have to get back and be competitive with other states," with the article emphasizing the $60m investment that would be lost if the series filmed in South Carolina instead. Although Pate does not go so far as to claim that the OBX would be "a character in the show," he does conclude by insisting "the show would be a postcard to North Carolina," which the article notes would serve the goals of the state's grant program by featuring "identifiable attractions or state locales in a manner that would be reasonably expected to induce visitation by nonresidents."

Ultimately, Pate's campaign failed. In May 2019, the show began filming on location in and around Charleston, and when it debuted in April 2020 the series told a story about North Carolina's biggest tourist destination that showcased the sights and sounds of the South Carolina city that brands itself as "America's No. 1 small city, 9 years and counting" instead. As with any case of city-for-city doubling, the argument is that the majority of Netflix's global viewers will not know that South Carolina's "Low Country" is standing in for the Outer Banks, or that the characters' day trip to the mainland to visit the University of North Carolina at Chapel Hill is really the Charleston Gaillard Center; in other words, there is no burden of spatial capital if the imagined average viewer has no frame of reference for either the location where the series is set or the location where it is produced, similar to the negotiations of spatial capital evident in international co-productions and global Netflix originals outlined in Chapter 3. However, this argument implies that viewers are in localized bubbles, which ignores the impact of discursive framings of spatial capital outlined in Chapter 4 that make the city-for-city doubling visible to a wide range of audiences, among other factors that are changing how spatial capital is understood, interpreted, and ultimately negotiated by audiences in a contemporary context.

This final chapter is an effort to grapple with how questions of spatial capital ultimately resonate within the space of television consumption, as the interplay between production, textuality, distribution, and discourse intersects with viewers who bring their own understandings of spatial capital to their experience watching a particular series. It argues that while television's compromised and contingent approach to spatial capital has often relied on a presumed localized audience without the reference points to challenge or question a series' sense of place, social media has broken down geographic boundaries of viewer reaction, making city-for-city doubling and other negotiations of spatial capital a more significant part of a broader discourse around series like *Outer Banks*. Media is often framed as disrupting traditional geographic boundaries, but I argue here that in the case of television's spatial capital, new forms of communication highlight those boundaries, reframing location as a lens through which viewers respond to television in online forums as a public service to either serve as spatial amplifiers in praise of a series' sense of place or critique the series in question as spatial arbiters.

The chapter will begin and end with new case studies (*Outer Banks* and the short-lived, North Dakota-set 2015 ABC series *Blood & Oil*), but the remainder will consider how the space of reception shapes the impact of the place-making strategies outlined throughout the book, returning to previous case studies like *Breaking Bad*, *Blindspot*, and *Orphan Black* to explore how their approach to spatial capital resonates among audiences both locally and globally. Using Twitter as a primary site of analysis in conjunction with other discursive spaces like news stories where audience responses are aggregated, I examine how contemporary shifts in the visibility of production and audience literacy regarding production practices are inspiring audiences to take on key roles in the interpreting of spatial capital, potentially disrupting the production strategies that have been revealed as common over the course of the previous chapters. Such analysis both reaffirms and challenges the principles of spatial capital outlined in the book thus far, raising important questions that the television industry must reckon with as it navigates continued changes to space and place's role in television production moving forward.

Audiences, amplification, and arbitration: spatial capital and social media

In the context of what this book frames as spatial capital, reception has most often been considered through the lens of fandom, specifically through the practice of fan pilgrimages. The clearest way to measure spatial capital generated by a television series is if it manages to inspire viewers to seek out the locations where the series was set or filmed, or (ideally) both. Couldry (2002) frames such pilgrimages as a crucial form of media ritual that reaffirms the cultural capital generated when a location appears in a film or television series, and Reijnders (2011) identifies this as the natural conclusion of his cyclical model of place's relationship with media. Such pilgrimages can include informal visits to public locations, guided tours organized by private companies, and official tours organized by the industry, but the result is the same: the spatial capital generated over the course of a project's production and the discourse around it is confirmed by fans reaffirming the value of that capital by seeking out the "real" places and immersing themselves in them (Garner 2016).

To understand the reception of spatial capital in a contemporary context, however, one must consider how social media has complicated our understanding of television fandom. Convergence culture has transformed the television industry (Jenkins 2006), with social media platforms like Twitter and Facebook imagined as virtual spaces where fans congregate to engage with their favorite series. This congregation has been critical to distinctions made between fans and "spectators" (Ross 2009), as online platforms give viewers the ability to connect with other viewers and articulate themselves as part of the fandom through the topics of their posts, their bios and profile images, and their use of official and fan-produced hashtags. Studies of "contemporary participative TV audiences" (Bourdaa and Delmar 2016) use such forms of engagement as synonymous with fan activity, with participation in spaces like Twitter defined as foundational both to what it means to be a fan and how fans are positioned within television culture as producers of fan material and advertisers for the programs themselves.

However, it is oversimplifying to think about social media activity around television purely through the lens of fandom. As Jonathan Gray has argued, anti-fandom (2003) and dislike (Gray and Murray 2015) are equal parts of audience response to media and are similarly compatible with the affordances of convergence culture (Click 2019). Moreover, social media platforms—unlike message boards and other historical spaces of fan congregation—are used by a wider range of viewers for a broader set of purposes, which can involve television even for those who may not choose to identify as a fan of a particular program. Posting about what one is watching or using an on-screen hashtag for a series is absolutely a form of fan activity. However, these practices in spaces like Twitter have become untethered from the type of fan community studied by Jenkins, meaning an intense fan dialogue sits alongside a stray tweet from someone who is only dipping their toes in that same conversation. Moreover, Ouellette and Wilson (2011) argue that convergence culture may not actually enhance the existing pleasures of TV, but it rather introduces gendered labor that blocks those same pleasures. We can study how specific fan-created hashtags or fan-created Facebook groups replicate traditional understandings of fan activity, yet social media broadly generates a space where so-called spectators are both exposed to and potentially incited to participate in ways that we may not normally associate with fandom, and which cannot be generalized.

Another way that our understanding of social media is often oversimplified connects with questions of spatial capital. Virtual spaces are frequently framed as being separate from offline ones, but scholars (Kendall 2002; Miller and Slater 2000) have pushed to consider the intersections between virtual and lived spaces. Such connections are sometimes affordances built into social platforms, which ask users to identify where they are from as part of bios and provide users the option to give apps their location and tag their posts with it. The search functions on social media also allow users to search based on specific geographic parameters, meaning that they have the capacity to function as local to users who choose to treat them as such, but nonetheless retain their ties to global reach. Although Meyrowitz's (1986) suggestion that technology eradicates the meaning of place has long proven specious, these affordances foreground that modern social media platforms not only connect people across geographic distance, but they also give them tools to articulate the meaning of that distance and create substantive dialogue between localized responses to breaking news, cultural events, and—in the case of this project—television series.

Therefore, in considering Twitter as a space where spatial capital is negotiated by television audiences, I focus on the intersection of responses that range in terms of their relationship to the show in question and their own spatiality. It is oversimplifying and utopian to imagine Twitter or any social media platform as a virtual public sphere (Papacharissi 2002). Nonetheless, there is the capacity to bring together a diverse range of perspectives around a certain topic, and its capacity to bridge geographic divides is particularly relevant in continuing the lines of questioning thus far introduced in this book. Television's relationship with space and place is predicated on a burden of spatial capital, and while industry forces work to restrict the terms of this burden, it is ultimately tested when the series enters into the space of reception and is exposed to a diverse range of viewers whose perspectives may not match with the imagined audience used to determine that burden. Twitter is a space where these individual perspectives converge, as fan and anti-fan communities alike around the world are exposed to localized responses from those with firsthand experience of the locations in question.

Amplifying and arbitrating Netflix's *Outer Banks*

In adding audiences to the groups of stakeholders invested in television's spatial capital, this chapter largely considers two general roles that audience members take in engaging with a series' sense of space and place. Although these roles do not encompass all responses, they are the two most dominant approaches observed across Twitter when examining the case studies analyzed throughout the book, among others.

The first of these roles is the **amplifier of spatial capital**. In these instances, viewers are posting in ways that confirm and then redistribute the spatial capital embedded into the text by producers in ways that suggest the show has met the burden of spatial capital in question. In the case of *Breaking Bad*, the subject of the case study in the previous chapter's consideration of the "place as character" discourse, social media posters who post photos they have taken in iconic locations featured on the show are reinforcing the links built by the show itself, alongside the discourse presented by producers and other stakeholders in interviews. User Bryan Johnson, in a September 2020 post, uses a combination of screenshots from the series and his own photos taken in Albuquerque to memorialize the show's final season, writing that "the city (and area) of Albuquerque was as much a character on #BreakingBad as the cast members were," noting he was proud to have been able to take these photos and be in the same spaces as the production. This document of media pilgrimage is strongly associated with fandom and is a common thread in posts referencing Albuquerque posted using the #BreakingBad hashtag. The presence of Albuquerque functioning as a character further solidifies the message here, with Johnson's tweet serving not simply to say "I was there" but also reiterating why spatial capital is an important part of the show's appeal to him and others.

Amplification primarily works to confirm a series' spatial capital, typically accepting without debate the burden of spatial capital being presented. In the case of a show like *Breaking Bad*, which was filmed and set in the same location, the majority of tweets referencing Albuquerque lean toward amplification, reaffirming the spatial capital articulated over the course of the series' run. Where things become more complicated, however, is in cases like *Outer Banks* where one location is doubling for another. This is not to say that there are not instances of amplification among social media responses: one user writes in praise of the show that "the diverse setting of the Outer Banks (hence the name) makes this show very refreshing," lending credence to the belief that an average viewer may not be aware enough of the spatial capital involved to challenge the show's sense of place. Another user praises its "fun action scenes in a beautiful setting," and while they may not be delving into the specifics of the show's geography, this praise for the show's sun-soaked landscape nonetheless suggests that viewers were either unable to see or willing to look past the geographic differences between the low country of South Carolina and the Outer Banks of North Carolina. Such acceptance is also replicated in reviews: *The Hollywood Reporter* writes that *Outer Banks* is "set in the Outer Banks of North Carolina," but "filmed with acceptable replication in South Carolina locations," which in an otherwise critical review suggests that the burden of spatial capital has been met (Fienberg 2020). Although Pate and the North Carolina film and tourism industries may lament that the subsequent rush of "*Outer Banks* Tourism" involves online articles and posts about visiting South Carolina instead (Puckett 2020), the fact that this discourse exists is nonetheless evidence of spatial capital having been generated, despite the location doubling involved.

However, there is another group of social media posters alongside these spatial amplifiers, whose work is confronting the complexity of spatial capital directly. An **arbiter of spatial capital** consciously positions their reaction to spatial capital through the lens of their localized knowledge: rather than solely responding to a given text and how it presents location, an arbiter is interpreting and presenting their verdict as a conscious, discursive contribution. As it relates to the burden of spatial capital, arbiters are asserting their own understanding of that burden as defined by their expectation of verisimilitude matching their personal experience with a location they have visited or lived in. Arbiters can also contribute to amplification if their "verdict" is that a show has met the burden of spatial capital, as in the case of one user's response to *Breaking Bad*. Writing that how the show handles Albuquerque is "underrated," they write that "I lived there for 13mos and the city as a 'character' is very ABQ." The emphasis here on the amount of time that the user lived in Albuquerque, and the use of its "local" moniker of ABQ, serve to assert their authority in this matter, suggesting to anyone reading the tweet—posted in 2011 using the show's hashtag—that they can take their word for how well the show engages with the city's identity.

That having been said, in most cases arbiters of spatial capital are compelled to post in an effort to challenge a series' relationship with spatial capital and thus primarily confront examples like *Outer Banks* where the burden faced by producers is more significant. Andrea Cavalier, a digital producer for NBC's *Dateline* based in New York, posted about her experience watching the show on her Twitter account in the weeks after the show premiered, writing that "I'm 5 seconds into #OuterBanks on @netflix and it's so blatantly South Carolina and not the OBX. It also makes reference to places in Wilmington and Wrightsville Beach, but it's so very obvious that it's not filmed there either." Similar to the aforementioned example regarding *Breaking Bad*, Cavalier asserts her local knowledge, using the localized "OBX" designation and pushing back against not simply the general geographical inconsistencies but the reference to specific cities and communities in the area. She further positions herself as an arbiter of spatial capital by using the show's hashtag and tagging Netflix, as though the goal of her tweet is to reach fans of the show and its producers to inform them that the burden of spatial capital has not been met. In addition, Cavalier's authority on spatiality is further reinforced by the fact that she is taking advantage of the spatial affordances of Twitter as a platform. Although the tweet itself is geotagged to Brooklyn and she identifies her location as New York, NY, Cavalier's bio on the site includes "NC ◊ NY," asserting her home state as part of her identity. Although other Twitter users posted similar tweets, with one suggesting the show filming in Charleston is "ridic" and another noting there were "too many palmetto trees, marshes, and brown water," the spatial markers tied to Cavalier's tweet makes it emblematic of how arbitration can play out on the platform.

Both amplifiers and arbiters of spatial capital need not necessarily have a significant audience to take on these roles. Rather than focus on the *result* of specific social media posts, I am interested in the positions taken by users in these initial tweets, which may or may not produce additional engagement in the form of likes, retweets, or replies. What matters is that the initial statement exists to be engaged with, whether through users searching hashtags added by the initial poster or simply responding to the tweet when it enters their feed. Given her public profile and moderate following of roughly 1,200 followers, Cavalier's tweet spurned further discussion: one agreed that "as [a North Carolina] resident there are so many inconsistencies," while another follower from Brooklyn replied that "it's the same whenever I watch movies or TV shows based in NYC." Although the tweet reached only Cavalier's own followers, earning no retweets, it nonetheless generated a dialogue about spatial capital that brought localized responses from both her current location and her home state.

Similar dialogue emerged on another arbitration of spatial capital from user @trasheqanon, who observed that "there's a TV show on Netflix called Outer Banks that wasn't even filmed in the f**king outer banks?????" In the replies to this tweet, which was shared by eight other users including one with more than 4,000 followers, users engage in a multifaceted dialogue on spatial capital. One user notes that they have heard the show features a ferry from the Outer Banks to the landlocked Chapel Hill and do not know if they can even watch, while another reports that they turned off the show after they saw palm trees. The most common response, though, is users informing the original poster that the show was filmed in Charleston, with several summarizing the political reasons why Netflix refused Pate's request to film in North Carolina as detailed at the beginning of this chapter. This tweet does not specifically engage in the spatial capital of Twitter, as @trasheqanon's bio does not indicate location and their tweets are not geotagged. However, it managed to reach enough people invested in the series' spatial capital to generate an extended dialogue on the topic, including a lengthy back and forth with a resident of Wilmington, North Carolina, where they break down the show's muddled understanding of the state's geography.

Such arbitration of spatial capital highlights the compromises made by Pate as he navigated the political–economic limitations of media capital presented to him, with the users ultimately coming to the verdict—collectively, in this case—that the show failed to live up to the burden of spatial capital they felt was fair even considering the circumstances. With tweets like these, Twitter replicates the discursive construction of spatial capital outlined in the previous chapter. Here, though, that discourse extends beyond stakeholders like film commissions or news outlets to users themselves, who are able to challenge the relationship between spatial capital and cultural capital in real time. If Pate's initial intent with *Outer Banks* was for the show's setting to function as a character in the show, the social media discourse became a litmus test for the effectiveness of this strategy, with a spectrum of responses from both North Carolinians and South Carolinians confronting the muddled geography of the series' narrative. The underlying argument for city-for-city doubling is that an average viewer will not be able to tell the difference; such an argument does not account for a social media environment where both amplifiers and arbiters of spatial capital draw attention to that doubling through their posts. Such posts can also indirectly feed this process, as posts from fans visiting sets in Charleston or recognizing the show's actors when on set in South Carolina reveal the negotiation of spatial capital and have the potential to spawn further conversation. Across these tweets, users either directly or indirectly take on these roles, as the discursive space of Twitter makes the negotiation of spatial capital throughout this book visible in ways that threaten the intended function of representations of space and place.

Both amplifiers and arbiters of spatial capital are asserting themselves as stakeholders in this discourse, alongside the film commissions, tourism bureaus, networks, producers, and laborers who have been featured in earlier chapters. In some cases, as with *Breaking Bad*, these new stakeholders largely reaffirm the existing burdens of spatial capital and serve to reaffirm the value of space and place to those series. However, as seen in the case of *Outer Banks*, situations where the creator of a text has consciously asserted its authenticity but struggled to navigate the contingencies of television's spatial capital to achieve that authenticity are primed to be disrupted by these new stakeholders. The result is a social media discourse where spatial capital is challenged, dissected, and ultimately arbitrated for those following the discussion. As such, representations of space and place designed to register with siloed, localized audiences are increasingly confronted by integrated audiences where localized responses come into conversation and conflict.

Maximizing and minimizing mobile production

Thus far, this book has considered how a culture of mobile production presents both challenges and opportunities for the negotiation of spatial capital. Although the political–economic realities of the industry force some series to use city-for-city doubling in order to maintain a setting that carries cultural capital while filming in locations that are more financially viable, mobile production is also central to the strategic location shooting that *Blindspot* used in order to gain access to international destinations. In such cases, the resulting textual strategies for engaging spatial capital are designed to overcome or emphasize those challenges: the initial metric of success is the ability to meet their established burdens while remaining on budget and on time, but the ultimate success of these efforts is determined by whether the value of these investments carries over to the audience.

In the case of *Killer Women*, which shot its pilot in Austin before moving to Albuquerque, the producers' approach to city-for-city doubling was immediately swarmed on by arbiters of spatial capital even before the show moved to New Mexico. The show's pilot spent much of its time set in San Antonio, using locations like Austin City Hall to stand in for the San Antonio Police Department, which drew the ire of many users. One writes that "#KillerWomen says it's in San Antonio, but all shots show Austin landmarks— even the [University of Texas at Austin] tower! Why not just be in Austin? #fail #KnowTexas." Not every user who noticed this doubling objected in such strong terms, but the half dozen or so users who made the observations using the show's official hashtag leveraged their knowledge to inform others watching the show about a gap of verisimilitude. Such arbiters can be reasoned with, however: one writes that while "#KillerWomen did such a bad job of trying to make Austin look like San Antonio," the fact they used a song by the band The Mavericks "makes it ok." There were also amplifiers of spatial capital among the tweets, with one writing to star Tricia Helfer that it "makes me homesick for #SanAntonio" and another excitedly tweeting, "Finally, a show that takes place in San Antonio!" But the latter amplification drew an arbitration, with someone confirming in the replies that "it was filmed in Austin ☹" and the original poster replying, "I guess it's the thought that counts."

However, it is notable that there was no effort to hide the city-for-city doubling as part of the show's social media footprint. Helfer, who was actively replying to fans on Twitter both on the night of the show's premiere and in the months before, posted a tweet about two of her pets joining her on set in New Mexico in September 2013, inspiring one of her followers—a film industry professional from Texas, per her Twitter bio—to ask, "Why NM and not Austin for #KillerWomen." Helfer replies directly, quoting the user's tweet and bluntly adding "Tax credits." She was similarly blunt when live-tweeting the premiere: one user asks if she had fun filming the pilot in Albuquerque, but Helfer corrects him, clarifying, "We were in Austin for the pilot and the next episodes were Albuquerque." Although Chapter 1 discussed how the show's production worked tirelessly to find locations that could double for Texas in New Mexico, Helfer bursts through the charade for the social media audience, perhaps realizing that there was copious evidence that they filmed in New Mexico from her own social media feeds and those of her fellow actors, who may have documented their trips to and from Albuquerque and their off-day activities around the city. Her tweet acknowledges that social media is a space where spatial capital will be negotiated and effectively arbitrates the situation herself, lest the facts complicate the show in the future.

Typically, however, those involved with a production seek to generate amplification rather than arbitration, specifically in instances where it benefits their efforts. In the case of *Blindspot*'s strategic location shooting, the spatial capital achieved by filming on location is easily amplified by fans, cast, and crew. Luke Mitchell, who played globetrotting villain Roman, tweeted during the show's third season a checklist of locations where the show had filmed, checking off Venice and Sydney while letting his followers know that Barcelona was airing that evening. A few weeks later, a Twitter user based in Barcelona tweeted excitedly about the show's arrival in their city, writing, "I still can't believe they budgeted for on location shooting." This was a common refrain, as the novelty of international shooting led many to take on the role as amplifier of spatial capital, either generating their own tweets or sharing any of the number of posts made by the official *Blindspot* Twitter account, the official *Blindspot* writers room Twitter account, creator Martin Gero's account, or the account of the individual writers who worked on the episodes, including unofficial location scout Ryan Johnson. In situations where location shooting has been deployed, and where time and energy—if not more money, as many Twitter amplifiers assumed—were sacrificed to make it happen, there is a clear investment in cultivating the amplification of spatial capital, which is not as common in situations where arbitration is a more likely response.

Such encouragement of amplification also serves to drown out potential arbiters of spatial capital who could emerge. The social media conversation around *Blindspot* is inherently American, centered around the broadcast airing in the United States and predominantly in English, meaning that if there are localized responses from those in foreign locations who might object to how their city or country was represented, they will be a minority and may not be considered as part of the same discourse. There are, in fact, several arbiters of spatial capital who emerged in response to the show's depiction of South Africa: one user whose bio is simply a South African flag writes "so many inaccurate statements about South Africa on #Blindspot," while another laments "smh on the way [Cape Town] South Africa is being shown on #Blindspot." However, these tweets came months after the episode aired in the United States, meaning that they were unlikely to be seen by the same audiences amplifying the show's use of the city's striking vista for the season finale. They are also focusing specifically on details that the *Blindspot* team's own tweets largely gloss over: their focus is on the location shooting itself, not on the narrative engagement with location, a shift in framing that pushes the audience away from critiquing the storylines themselves to focus instead on the work of the production crew. Although the spatial capital of city-for-city doubling is threatened by its negotiation on social media, strategic location shooting benefits from this same practice, with the social media exposure generated by this shooting a built-in part of its value to the show and its network(s).

Arbitrating polysemic places: distributional capital and social media

Ultimately, the burdens on shows that feature city-for-city doubling and strategic location shooting are fairly apparent: although not all shows necessarily meet the expectations for a successful doubling, and some location shooting may be mistaken for CGI, it is generally evident what each show needs to achieve, creating fairly straightforward forms of amplification and arbitration. The roles that audiences take on are also clear. Either they celebrate seeing a location rendered in a way that translates spatial capital into cultural capital, or they assert their own understanding of spatial capital— often based on having lived or living in the area where the show is set—in order to reject the sense of place presented within the series.

However, returning to the polysemic places of the third chapter creates a more complex negotiation, where amplification and arbitration are operating across borders and within a less clearly defined burden. The efforts to generate representations of place that can be read as local in multiple different contexts are threatened when social media conversation crosses those borders. Although language barriers will somewhat maintain siloed conversations regarding shows like Netflix's *Sacred Games* (India) and *Elite* (Spain), Netflix's simultaneous release strategy—compared to the staggered international airings of shows like *Blindspot*—means that when a series debuts, its official hashtags will be populated by viewers around the world. In the case of South Africa's *Queen Sono*, this meant that African viewers who were proud that Netflix was releasing its first original series produced on the continent were tweeting alongside American viewers, who may be experiencing South Africa and the show's other African settings for the first time. In this case, Netflix's promotional campaign heavily emphasized the landmark nature of the series' production, working to shape the narrative and pushing audiences to amplify its spatial capital. Although there are instances of users arbitrating the show's depiction of Africa, in particular a recurring trend questioning the casting of a lighter-skinned actress in the leading role, there was also a clear push encouraging amplification: one user writes to an imagined African audience, suggesting "let's just support #QueenSono it will open up doors to more series to be commissioned in Africa let's support our own people." Even if there is pushback to some of the more Westernized elements of the series, Netflix's discursive framing of the show succeeded in prioritizing amplification among the show's audience in response to the intense burden the show faced as the continent's first Netflix original.

By comparison, however, the inscrutable burdens of a show like *Sex Education* create a culture of arbitration, in which viewers turn to social media in order to puzzle through the show's interweaving of British and American cultural reference points. In a thread, user Polly Pallister-Wilkins—based in Amsterdam—catalogs her reactions to the series' spatial capital, puzzling over "a rural area where kids can cycle to school with no cars trying to run them over," and "a secondary school with no school uniform and an American style logo," before sharing a cell phone video of her television featuring the scene where students are throwing an American football and concluding that "this is just a litany of annoying weirdness." Some users serve as forceful arbiters, asserting that "we wear school uniforms up until 16" and "we don't have lockers," while others turn to social media hoping that others will arbitrate spatial capital for them. For example, one writes, "I feel SO culturally confused RN," and another asks outright "Why is #SexEducation so American?" These tweets were shared hundreds of times and drew dozens of responses from others who either shared their frustration or tried to offer explanations. One user wonders, "was this show originally American and remade for the UK? Or maybe written for the US but then made here?" Collectively, these responses were enough to inspire the journalistic discourse cited in Chapter 3, as outlets like *Buzzfeed* and the *Radio Times* generated articles exclusively to capture the huge number of people searching online for answers to the question of the show's setting.

As established earlier, the choice to present an amalgam of British and American high school culture was a conscious one by the creators of *Sex Education*, and at least one instance of spatial arbitration understood the implication: user @BarbaraDanish asks "Is the British school experience so shit that we're keeping the accents but making it American," which is effectively the explanation provided by producers. Ultimately, although it created initial confusion, the series' tongue-in-cheek dramedy tone meant that the explanations provided were largely accepted. In *Buzzfeed*'s article exploring the confusion, nearly 35,000 readers voted in a poll asking, "Do you find this American feel to *Sex Education* jarring or does it not matter at all"; 61% of users chose "it does not matter," with 39% suggesting "it annoys me." However, there is no indication that this annoyance greatly diminished those 13,000 viewers' experience. The show's continued success for Netflix globally supports the argument that the arbitration of spatial capital on social media did not play a significantly negative role in the discourse around the series even if it demonstrated one way that social media responds to polysemic places.

In the case of *Orphan Black*, however, an absence of certainty contains a much more fraught negotiation of spatial capital. Although the show's producers acknowledged in interviews that its ambiguous setting was due to the co-production arrangements between the Canadian production company and U.S. distributor BBC America, the show lacks the tongue-in-cheek merging of cultures that helps explain *Sex Education*'s choice, leaving viewers to embrace existing narratives of Canadian series being unable or unwilling to acknowledge their Canadian-ness. Thus, the series' effort to present a polysemic sense of place that could be read as Canadian in Canada and American in the United States was fundamentally dependent on how the show's viewers interpreted it, and the show's 2013 debut placed it at the peak of Twitter's role in the promotion and viewing of television content.

In considering the Twitter response to *Orphan Black*'s polysemic sense of place, there is evidence of the spatial amplification among Canadian audiences that proves the theory that the lack of formal acknowledgment of a Canadian setting could still be read as Canadian by local audiences. Across Twitter posts both during its initial debut and in the years following the show's premiere, numerous viewers tweeted their excitement that the show was, in their eyes, set in Toronto. One user writes that "it's about time a show shot in Toronto is set in Toronto," while another expressed that the show being "actually SET in Toronto" made them "inexplicable [sic] happy." Another notes that "after seeing so many films and shows shot in Toronto and failing to convince me otherwise, glad to see TO as TO," and another connects the show with *Continuum* (2012–2015), a Vancouver-set Syfy/Showcase co-production that, unlike *Orphan Black*, was explicitly set in a Canadian city. Together, these tweets reaffirm the producers' belief that based on the absence of television series actively embracing their Canadian settings, the polysemic approach to setting developed by the show's producers was able to satisfy at least some Canadian viewers' burden of spatial capital for "local" programming. These amplifiers are embracing *Orphan Black*—which they all posted about using its official hashtag, making their tweets part of the larger discourse—as a show made in Canada and set in Canada, even though the text is never explicit about the latter point.

But there is a concurrent discourse of arbiters of spatial capital who responded to the show's spatial capital with more skepticism. One user noted that "#OrphanBlack tries desperately to look like it's in America, but you can blatantly see Toronto in parts," while other users got more specific: one user, whose tweet is tagged as being from Orlando, Florida, writes "Dear producers of #OrphanBlack: if you're going to pretend you're in NYC, at least show the right skyline. That was clearly Toronto." This is one of a number of tweets that explicitly accuse the show of doing a poor job of pretending to be set in New York City, a claim that does not actually match the text of the show. The show never claims to be in New York, and in fact the opening sequence analyzed in Chapter 3 explicitly positions the location as being *not* New York City through a station announcement for a train departing for the city. But these tweets reveal how ubiquitous bad cases of city-for-city doubling are, and how much viewers have internalized international co-productions defaulting to an American location. The show's polysemic approach to location is meant to allow for multiple interpretations, but these social media users are actively rejecting the polysemy based on both the spatial capital of the text itself and, perhaps more importantly, their embedded belief that *Orphan Black* cannot actually be set in Toronto because of how spatial capital is negotiated in shows filmed in Canada but distributed in the United States. In other words, they are so committed to their role as an arbiter of spatial capital that their response to polysemy is to challenge and ultimately reject ambiguity as part of a larger trend of misrepresentation.

The contentious nature of this discourse ultimately transforms all tweets, even those initially designed as amplification, into arbitration of spatial capital. Although some assumed this role unsolicited, in other cases the polysemy of the text drew users seeking a resolution, calling on arbiters of spatial capital to step forward. One user says they're "being driven nuts by trying to figure out what damn city it's set in. NYC? Ontario. Argh!" while another asks directly "where is #orphanblack supposed to take place," concluding that they can only be certain it's "not Los Angeles." Another turns to Twitter, asking "seriously what f**king city IS THIS!" and using the show's hashtag, clearly hoping that someone would put them out of their confused misery. There are no doubt other viewers who largely accepted their own reading of the polysemic sense of place in *Orphan Black*'s pilot, but there is a significant body of social media conversation explicitly committed to trying to resolve the show's location, potentially at the expense of the other elements of the story being told. Toronto-based writer Anthony Oliveira, watching the show a year after it premiered, worked through his existential struggle with his followers, eventually settling on the plane ticket prop mentioned in Chapter 3 and concluding "That's a prop someone MADE. So I'm going with this show is SET in Toronto. So I don't go crazy." His live, ongoing negotiation of the show's spatial capital was inherently positioned as a collaborative effort, welcoming comments from his followers and bringing together viewers from different subject positions—and likely, different sides of the border—to engage with the debate at hand.

The collaborative nature of this process is specific to television. Whereas the negotiation of spatial capital in film operates similarly in terms of audiences responding to cases of city-for-city doubling or location shooting, the discourse does not last for as long a period, with the audience reacting to new evidence as the series progresses. As *Orphan Black* continued to air, more users turned to social media to resolve their confusion, with new evidence presented. The ongoing arbitration of *Orphan Black*'s setting became itself a vital paratext for those participating, a dialogue in which users could crowdsource additional information from local experts. In response to one viewer's question about the show's setting, which tagged the show's official BBC America account searching for an answer, a Twitter user answers that the show is set in Toronto, pointing to the detail surrounding Alison's residence in Scarborough, a suburb of Toronto. The initial user writes "Oh! Well then it's just my own ignorance. Thanks for paying attention & helping the rest of us get a clue!" In another case, a group of users debate the show's polysemy in a more granular fashion: while one user asserts that "they don't SAY that it's Toronto, it's just obviously being shot there," and another confirms that "it seems like one of those shows that's made in Canada for tax reasons, not for actual setting," another notes, "you'd think, but multicolored money. And they say Alison lives in Scarborough." Others in the thread had not caught either of those details, but the subsequent social media conversation drew them to the surface, creating a collective understanding if not necessarily a clean resolution. Another user writes that "apparently there were lots of other details on #OrphanBlack revealing [it] is, in fact, set in Toronto! I clearly don't pay enough attention." But other viewers are paying attention, collectively generating an online space that breaks down the borders between local and global responses to the series. If there was a belief when the show debuted that the polysemy of its setting would allow for siloed American and Canadian responses that each read the show as local, those efforts were fundamentally disrupted when social media users from Canada took on the responsibility of educating viewers from America on other countries in order to resolve the perceived confusion.

One user, Alfonso Espina, tweeted various idiosyncrasies in the show's setting using the show's hashtag beginning in 2014, at one point asking, "can the writers officially admit #OrphanBlack is based in Toronto already?" Two years later, in 2016, he tweeted that "#OrphanBlack never does a good job of disguising Toronto," and when an American follower tweeted that they thought the story was supposed to be set in Toronto, Espinosa explained that "they've never confirmed it for American audiences. We're used to being fake NYC up here for films anyway lol." This serialized negotiation of spatial capital charts the show's evolving relationship with setting, including the scene in its fourth season where the show for the first time revealed the CN Tower, when Espinosa excitedly tweeted "The CN Tower!!!! #OrphanBlack FINALLY embraces Toronto." His was one of a range of tweets from the week that episode aired celebrating the resolution of spatial ambiguity, with one tweeting that "TORONTO WILL NOT BE DENIED." It would not be until the show's fifth and final season that there would be diegetic acknowledgment that the show took place in Canada—which Espinosa also tweeted about excitedly—yet the social media dialogue around the show had already provided paratextual certainty for its most engaged fans. The decision to acknowledge that the show took place in Canada—long past the point it might have driven away an American viewer unwilling to watch something set in a foreign country—resolved five seasons of textual ambiguity and reaffirmed the result of five seasons of paratextual dialogue that had transformed its polysemic sense of place into a form of cross-border crowdsourcing among arbiters of spatial capital.

Burden or bust: North Dakota, Utah, and the arbitration of *Blood & Oil*

Each of these case studies showcases how audiences invest in the negotiation of spatial capital, and while this practice happens with any series it is particularly strong in cases where the burden of spatial capital takes on greater stakes. *Orphan Black* inspired such impassioned amplifiers of spatial capital because the historic erasure from Canada in U.S. co-productions has trained Canadians to recognize when shows resist this practice, while the discourse around *Queen Sono* was heightened based on its landmark status as Netflix's first African original series. Although arbiters of spatial capital could emerge around a show set in New York City, the stakes of those representations are far less significant given how often the city is depicted on television. Similarly, while social media users could turn to social media to lament that a show is doubling Atlanta for Los Angeles, this carries less weight than a case of Austin doubling San Antonio, or New Mexico doubling Texas, states and cities that are seen on television less often and that are fighting to assert themselves in a culture of mobile production. The choices that amplifiers and arbiters of spatial capital make on social media are shaped by their understanding of this burden, which shifts with each series and—as seen with *Orphan Black*—over the course of a series' run.

Those who take on these roles can play a meaningful part in the determination of spatial capital for any series, including those identified throughout the book, but this chapter concludes by considering how they are particularly critical in instances where the burden of spatial capital is largely ignored by the production despite the stakes at hand. Returning to the second chapter, the negotiation of spatial capital is often contingent on independent laborers assuming the burden of representing space and place themselves, sometimes in situations where the show's producers may not necessarily share the same sense of responsibility. Although the criticisms faced by shows like *Outer Banks* for incongruities between its purported setting and the locations chosen out of political–economic necessity imply that certain details were overlooked by those in the production, the fact that creator Jonas Pate fought to shoot the show in North Carolina and the political reasons for Netflix's refusal absolved him of the burden of spatial capital in the discourse that emerged on social media. The same is not true for this chapter's final case study, an instance where one of the most significant burdens of spatial capital in recent broadcast television history was mishandled and ultimately held to account by the social media conversation around the series.

In January 2015, ABC selected the pilot scripts which would be produced for the upcoming 2015–2016 season, and among them was a show titled *Boom*. According to *Deadline* (Andreeva 2015), the series

> examines the biggest oil discovery in American history—bigger than Texas and as big as Saudi Arabia—which has triggered a geopolitical shift and an economic boom in North Dakota on a scale not seen since the 1849 California Gold Rush.

Promising a "classic tale with modern twists," featuring a "colorful ensemble of roughnecks, grifters, oil barons, criminals and fellow prospectors against a stark and beautiful backdrop," the logline was enough to convince ABC to produce a pilot, the first step in a lengthy journey for a project that had been in development for several years. Numerous steps would follow before the show was eventually picked up to series as *Blood & Oil* to debut in fall 2015. However, a crucial one was determining which location would serve as that "stark and beautiful backdrop" in a culture of mobile production.

Although critical for any production, the burden of spatial capital for *Blood & Oil* was especially significant: there had never been a television series set in North Dakota before. The absence of the state from maps like the poster identified in the book's introduction is conspicuous and something to which the show's creators were inherently drawn. During the show's panel at the Summer 2015 Television Critics Association Press Tour, co-creator Rodes Fishburne reportedly

> noted the Dakota oil boom is similar to the 1840s gold rush in San Francisco, adding he'd never seen any TV show set in North Dakota. So, he said, he was excited with the idea of this 'new place' super-imposed on the classic tale of boom.

> (de Moraes 2015)

This excitement, however, came with extreme responsibility: not only was *Blood & Oil* under pressure from North Dakotans to represent their state accurately in its first on-screen "starring role," but the series would also have an atypical amount of power in shaping viewers' understanding of a location given the dearth of representations in television and other media.

The North Dakota setting may have held spatial capital for the show's producers, but the subsequent burden was never going to be met using location shooting in North Dakota given the limited media capital attached to the state. On the website for Film Production Capital, one of the companies that helps productions navigate incentive systems, they rank states on a zero-to-five-star system based on their available incentives, with five stars—reserved for Georgia, Louisiana, and Massachusetts as of January 2021—indicating "the best state to film." By this metric, North Dakota is one of 18 states with zero stars, and in the space reserved for details of incentive systems, the website simply notes that North Dakota has "no current incentives." Although the website for Film North Dakota (2021b) currently features information about permitting and regulations as of January 2021, arguing that "North Dakota's striking landscape is a storyline that can enhance any story," in a 2016 update the same website featured only information about the "grains and other crops [that could] provide a striking background for road scenes," with a chart breaking down each crop's height and when it is at its most photogenic. Both versions of the site, however, acknowledge that there are no incentives for filming in North Dakota, meaning the "new place" Fishburne was excited about is incompatible with the culture of mobile production.

It is also geographically incompatible with many of the production hubs that typically draw mobile production, which eventually led the show's producers to choose Utah, a "two-star" filming location according to Film Production Capital. For Utah, *Blood & Oil* marked a new claim to media capital, almost a decade after the last broadcast series to film in the state—The WB's *Everwood* (2002–2006)—was cancelled. The director of the Utah Film Commission celebrated the announcement of the series' commitment to film its first season in Utah, noting that in addition to jobs and economic impact it would bring "a lot of credibility to our state's film industry" (*The Location Guide* 2015). Pearce is quoted elsewhere as suggesting that *Blood & Oil* "puts Utah on the map," an acknowledgment of the significance of this series to their future ability to lay claim to mobile productions while competing with neighboring New Mexico among other states with overlapping geography (Van Valkenburg 2015). In other words, while there was a burden attached to *Blood & Oil*'s depiction of North Dakota, there was also a burden attached to *Blood & Oil* as evidence of Utah's capacity to sustain ongoing television production, whether through locations like the town of Ogden—which doubled for the downtown of the fictional Rock Springs—or through new facilities like Park City Film Studios, which opened in summer 2015 in time for *Blood & Oil*'s arrival to film the remainder of its first season and, according to Pearce, "played a key role in attracting [the show] to Utah" (Ivins 2015).

All cases of city-for-city doubling create a conflict of spatial capital, but the conflict is more significant in cases where both the location being depicted and the production location are underrepresented in their respective contexts. *Blood & Oil*'s status as the first show to be set in North Dakota means that those who live or grew up in the state are more likely to see themselves as stakeholders, while workers involved with the production in Utah understand how significant the series could be to ensuring they can continue to work in their state in the future. Although the first chapter indicated how nascent media capitals are dependent on their ability to double for other locations in order to draw mobile productions, the reality is that Utah's ability to double North Dakota is not a particularly marketable skill compared to, for example, New Mexico's ability to double Texas, or Atlanta's ability to double Los Angeles. Thus, from the perspective of the Utah Film Commission, the fact that *Blood & Oil* was set in North Dakota was not necessarily significant—it was predominantly an opportunity to showcase the diversity of Utah as a filming location, rather than focusing on the doubling work involved.

This perhaps explains the landscapes of the series' pilot, which was filmed in Utah in March 2015 and served as the source material for the series trailer that was released when the show was picked up to series. In an early scene, a young couple moving to North Dakota to take advantage of the oil boom are seen driving to start their new life when two tractor trailers crowd the road ahead of them, the car crashing and leaving their dream of opening a laundromat in shambles as they are forced to walk into town with their luggage (see Figure 5.1). This scene is mostly designed to set up the series' plot, but it is evocatively set against a backdrop of snow-covered mountains, whether in the shots of the truck on the road, the driving plates used for shots on the interior of the car, or in the panoramic shot of their walk into town with the rolling hills and mountainous peaks prominently featured. The same mountains feature throughout the trailer, whether in the backdrops of the ranch owned by oil tycoon Hap Briggs or the oil fields themselves. They are striking images, and at least one Twitter user sought to amplify this message. Tagging four of the actors in the show, user @lali016 from Argentina writes, "Where did u guys shoot? The landscape is awesome!" Although this tweet went unanswered, the fact is that many of the shots in *Blood & Oil* would be an excellent advertisement for Utah's filming locations and may have played a role in convincing Paramount Network's *Yellowstone* (2018–present)—a ranch drama set in Montana—to base its first three seasons in Utah given its similar backdrops.

However, there is one small problem with these images from the perspective of the show's setting: there are no mountains in North Dakota. The most prominent peak in North Dakota, White Butte, is only 546 feet above the surrounding landscape (Peakery), and the state ranks as the third flattest

Figure 5.1 A screenshot from the *Blood & Oil* pilot highlighting the beautiful scenery of its Utah filming location and its seeming ignorance of the geography of the show's North Dakota setting.

Screenshot by author.

in the country after Florida and Illinois (Howard 2014). As a result, these images of snow-capped mountains in the backdrop of the first television series ever to be set in North Dakota proved an immediate controversy, as arbiters of spatial capital took to Twitter in order to make clear to anyone paying attention to the show that ABC had gotten this one wrong. Even before *Blood & Oil* premiered, its trailers sparked users to use the show's hashtag and some combination of the show's official account and other ABC accounts. One user speaks to them directly, informing @ABCNetwork, "there are no snow-capped mountains anywhere near the Bakken [Oil Fields]," adding both the show's hashtag and the hashtag #locationscoutfail. Another user writes, "THERE ARE NOT MOUNTAINS IN NORTH DAKOTA, just an FYI," while another asks, "has anyone in production of @bloodandoil been to ND?! There is no such things [sic] as mountains there," adding the hashtag #awkward. By the time the series was set to debut in late September, the mountains had become a running joke among North Dakotans, so much so that the "ExperienceND" account launched by the state's department of commerce to "connect with those who love our state and those who are on a journey to call North Dakota Home" tweeted about it with tongue firmly in cheek, asking "who's watching #BloodAndOil this Sunday on @ABC featuring our #NDLegendary mountains?" alongside a screenshot from the series' trailer with the mountains in the background.

This mass arbitration of spatial capital reached its apex on the night of the show's premiere when users live-tweeted their reactions to the show, and the mountains were a dominant subject of conversation among users framing their viewing through North Dakota. Although these responses echo the early ones, with many tagging ABC and the show's official Twitter account in the hope of correcting this error, the arbitration also comes with an acknowledgment that users are not surprised by what one user terms "#HollywoodGeography" while directing his complaint to "ignorant Hollywood douchebags." Other users seem to accept that the producers knew the geography was wrong, but simply didn't think that enough people would care: one user writes that "the producer's [sic] of #BloodAndOil must think North Dakotans don't have TV and wouldn't notice the mountains #wellwedo," while another laments, "c'mon @ABCNetwork people do have televisions here—at least pretend." These users are not simply pointing out an inaccuracy; they are specifically arguing that the reason the inaccuracy occurred was because their viewership as North Dakotans was not considered important enough for the show to strive for verisimilitude, given that North Dakota is the fourth least populated state, and its entire population would not even crack the Top 40 television markets in the country as of 2021 (Media Tracks, 2021b). Rather than simply arbitrating spatial capital in terms of the show's representation of North Dakota, these users are also arbitrating how their value as viewers was not respected by the production's choices, calling out their failure to meet the burden attached to being the first series set in North Dakota.

Evidence emerged later that confirm the arbiters' suspicions regarding the lack of care taken in depicting North Dakota in *Blood & Oil*: in an anecdote opening a 2015 *Vice* article about the show's struggles to make a soap opera out of the oil boom, writer Nathan C. Martin relays a story of a friend who worked as a location scout on the series and asks about the challenges of finding "locations in one of the most beautiful parts of the country to film a show that's supposed to be set in one of the ugliest." The location scout's response speaks to the disinterest in verisimilitude:

> I initially left out all the photographs of sites that had mountains in them, since North Dakota has no mountains. But the director saw them anyway and said, "These are great! The mountains are gorgeous! Who cares if North Dakota has no mountains! This is a fictional show!"

Although it is not necessarily clear if this anecdote relates to the series' pilot, the first two episodes of *Blood & Oil* were coincidentally directed by someone who has already been identified as a stakeholder of spatial capital in this chapter: Jonas Pate, the creator of *Outer Banks* who fought so hard for his show to be shot in the same location where it was set. We know from his experience with *Outer Banks* that spatial capital matters to Pate, whose brother Josh co-created *Blood & Oil*, but the fact that he would allow the mountains to play such a prominent role in the backdrop of a series set in a state with no mountains reinforces that individual workers approach these questions through the lens of their own experience. Although Pate felt strongly that his own show set in the state where he grew up deserved to be shot in the locations where he had consciously set the story, he did not feel as strongly about a show set in a state to which he likely had no connection. The responsibility thus fell to the residents of North Dakota to turn to social media to hold Pate and his team accountable for their choice.

The recourse available to these arbiters of spatial capital is, admittedly, minimal: there is no evidence to suggest that the tweets from North Dakotans played any role in *Blood & Oil*'s meager ratings performance, the trimming of its initial episode order, or its eventual cancellation after only a single season. A *Reuters* reporter based in North Dakota and the local *Grand Forks Herald* both wrote stories aggregating and gathering additional local responses to *Blood & Oil* (Scheyder 2015; Johnson 2015), but the discourse earned no further media attention, meaning that the arbitration was unlikely to reach the majority of the show's viewers. However, by using the official hashtag emblazoned on the screen during the show's broadcast airings, North Dakotans were not simply speaking to a localized audience. In other words, their objections to the mountains, or the lack of narrative complication stemming from a Black sheriff in North Dakota, or the overabundance of women compared to reality were part of the reception of the show for its connected audience. These tweets did not solely come from television fans who we think about as the connected audience; instead, they emerged from a diverse range of stakeholders who turned to social media and took on the role of arbiter of spatial capital out of the belief that it was their responsibility to do so. If they had not, it is unlikely that I would be writing about this case study at all given that when I saw the same trailer, as someone with no knowledge of North Dakota, I did not think twice about the mountains of North Dakota. Even though that only suggests that one perspective was transformed by the work of these localized audiences, it points to how the final judgment on the burden of spatial capital rests in the hands of those whose investment in that location is strongest, and how they use the tools available to them to invest others in the same issues.

Conclusion

Audience reception has played a role in negotiating the spatial capital of every television series referenced thus far in this book, whether celebrating a successful translation of place into a form of cultural capital or criticizing a struggle to represent marginalized locations. Collectively, the social media conversation outlined throughout this chapter is evidence that in a contemporary environment, the contingent, compromised, and complex construction of spatial capital within the process of television production cannot be hidden. Audiences will see when actors are traveling to Vancouver instead of Los Angeles to shoot a show set in the latter city, and the show's official hashtag allows local audiences to broadcast their objection to specious geography to ignorant viewers in other parts of the world. That these audiences take on these roles of amplifiers and arbiters of spatial capital is an indication that place matters to television viewers.

However, the reality is that the more marginalized a location is within the hierarchies of cultural capital, the more likely it is that the burden of spatial capital will be ignored and that efforts to hold television shows accountable for this will also be marginalized. Shows set in major cities like New York or Los Angeles will draw more arbitration of spatial capital, because there are more viewers with some level of familiarity with those cities either as tourists or as viewers of media texts set in those locations. However, because there are hundreds of shows set in those cities, any one representation of the city carries less weight, making the consequences of failed burdens of spatial capital less significant. Meanwhile, in cases like North Dakota where there is a greater need for arbitration based on a lack of representations, the fact that only a small percentage of ABC viewers have firsthand knowledge of those areas means there is less conversation, and thus less incentive for networks or distributors to engage with issues of spatial capital. If there is no one directly involved with the production who themselves takes on the role of arbiter of spatial capital, or if that person is unable to assert their authority over the departments responsible or the decision-makers who have final say, local audiences only hold power in matters of spatial capital if they also hold cultural capital to match viewers in major cities.

In cases where those individuals exist, however, this chapter's opening case study suggests that accountability may be retroactively achieved through audience response. After *Outer Banks* premiered on Netflix in April 2020, arbiters of social media—including the North Carolina Ferry System (see Figure 5.2)—focused their energy on the suggestion that the Outer Banks were connected to the landlocked Chapel Hill by ferry, so much so that the *Associated Press* aggregated details from a *Raleigh News & Observer* article on the subject (Price 2020). With the *Associated Press* noting that "the mistake has prompted jokes on social media targeting a show which has attracted an international audience during the Coronavirus pandemic," the *News & Observer* went directly to Jonas Pate for an explanation. Identified as a native of Raeford and a resident of Wilmington, Pate sought to rectify his personal failure to respect the region's geography, explaining that in the script, there was a ride-sharing trip between the coast and Chapel Hill. Pate reveals that the scene was never shot, and that in editing the episode no one involved realized what the scene's absence would imply to an unaware audience. Notably, the episode in question—"Spy Games"—was one of the episodes Pate did not direct himself, and while he is ultimately responsible as the showrunner, he would have had less direct involvement in the production of the episode as a result. He told the paper that "I don't want people to think that we don't know Chapel Hill isn't near the coast," suggesting

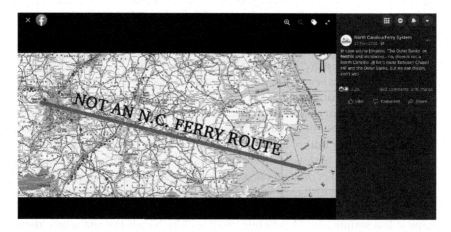

Figure 5.2 A screenshot of the image posted on Facebook by the North Carolina Ferry System in response to *Outer Banks'* failure of spatial capital. The post was shared over 3,000 times.

Image appears with permission of North Carolina Ferry System. Screenshot by author.

that the accountability from arbiters of spatial capital had reached him and made him feel as though he needed to take responsibility.

Although Pate suggests he might be "overthinking this," the fact that he felt it necessary to speak with a major news outlet and insist that "we bleed North Carolina" suggests that spatial capital can be asserted by viewers, even if that may not necessarily transform how that spatial capital is valued during the production itself, and even if Pate did not hold himself to the same standards telling stories about North Dakota five years earlier. This chapter's identification of amplifiers and arbiters of spatial capital does not imply that the only way these roles have an impact is if they impart direct change on television's spatial capital. Although some may frame their goal as fighting back against "#HollywoodGeography," others are simply seeking to provide clarity to other viewers, asserting themselves as stakeholders and reinforcing that spatial capital is ultimately contingent not only on industrial forces that are constantly in flux but also on cultural discourses that shape how a text exists in the world.

This book has considered how the contingency of spatial capital requires constant negotiation by stakeholders who must adapt their own labor and their own place within industrial and cultural hierarchies to balance the efficiencies of the television industry with the burdens of spatial capital attached to particular texts, all within an ever-changing culture of mobile production. This chapter has used examples like *Outer Banks* to consider how audiences position themselves as stakeholders within this process. However, the show's spring 2020 debut coincided with a massive fluctuation in spatial capital that demonstrates the precarity of this work and the challenges facing television's spatial capital in the future.

References

Andreeva, Nellie. 2015. "ABC Picks Up 4 Drama Pilots." *Deadline*, January 30. https://deadline.com/2015/01/abc-drama-pilots-1201363429/.

Bourdaa, Mélanie, and Javier Lozano Delmar. 2016. "Contemporary Participative TV Audiences: Identity, Authorship and Advertising Practices Between Fandom." *Participations* 13.2: 2–13.

Click, Melissa, ed. 2019. *Anti-Fandom: Dislike and Hate in the Digital Age*. New York: New York University Press.

Couldry, Nick. 2002. *Media Rituals: A Critical Approach*. London: Routledge.

de Moraes, Lisa. 2015. "Don Johnson: 'Blood & Oil' Not 'Dallas' Redux—TCA." *Deadline*, August 5. https://deadline.com/2015/08/don-johnson-blood-oil-dallas-chace-crawford-tca-1201492212/.

Fienberg, Daniel. 2020. " 'Outer Banks': TV Review." *The Hollywood Reporter*, April 14. www.hollywoodreporter.com/review/outer-banks-review-1290064.

Garner, Ross P. 2016. "Symbolic and Cued Immersion: Paratextual Framing Strategies on the *Doctor Who* Experience Walking Tour." *Popular Communication* 14.2: 86–98.

Gray, Jonathan. 2003. "New Audiences, New Textualities: Anti-Fans and Non-Fans. *International Journal of Cultural Studies* 6.1: 64–81.

Gray, Jonathan, and Sarah Murray. 2015. "Hidden: Studying Media Dislike and Its Meaning." *International Journal of Cultural Studies* 19.4: 357–72.

Howard, Brian Clark. 2014 "The Flattest U.S. States? Not What You Think." *National Geographic*, March 15. www.nationalgeographic.com/news/2014/3/140314-flattest-states-geography-topography-science/.

Ingram, Hunter. 2019. "Netflix Series Creator Still Pushing for Wilmington Shoot." *StarNewsOnline*, January 7. www.starnewsonline.com/news/20190107/netflix-series-creator-still-pushing-for-wilmington-shoot.

Ivins, Jessica. 2015. "ABC's 'Blood & Oil' to Be Produced at Park City Film Studios." *KSL.com*, July 14. www.ksl.com/article/35496641/abcs-blood-oil-to-be-produced-at-park-city-film-studios.

Jenkins, Henry. 2006. *Convergence Culture: When Old and New Media Collide*. New York: New York University Press.

Johnson, Ryan. 2015. " 'Blood & Oil's' Snow-Capped Mountains Only Beginning of Show's Inaccuracy." *The Grand Forks Herald*, September 25. www.grandforksherald.com/entertainment/3846769-blood-oils-snow-capped-north-dakota-mountains-only-beginning-shows-inaccuracy.

Kendall, Lori. 2002. *Hanging Out in the Virtual Pub: Masculinities and Relationships Online*. Berkeley: University of California Press.

Martin, Nathan C. 2015. "What TV Won't Tell You About the Wealth, Violence, and Boredom of North Dakota's Oilfields." *Vice*, November 4. www.vice.com/en/article/9bggyz/the-real-blood-and-oil-of-north-dakotas-oilfields-114.

Meyrowitz, Joshua. 1986. *No Sense of Place: The Impact of Electronic Media on Social Behavior*. New York: Oxford University Press.

Miller, Daniel, and Don Slater. 2000. *The Internet: An Ethnographic Approach*. Oxford: Berg.

No Author. 2015. "*Blood & Oil* Becomes First TV Drama in Ten Years to Film in Utah." *The Location Guide*, June 12. www.thelocationguide.com/2015/06/ng-television-blood-oil-becomes-first-tv-drama-in-ten-years-to-film-in-utah/.

———. 2016. "North Dakota Film Production." *North Dakota Tourism.* https://web.archive.org/web/20160305040320/www.ndtourism.com/information/north-dakota-film-production.

———. 2021a. "Film North Dakota." *North Dakota Tourism.* www.ndtourism.com/FilmNorthDakota.

———. 2021b. "Nielsen DMA Rankins 2021." *Media Tracks.* https://mediatracks.com/resources/nielsen-dma-rankings-2021/.

———. 2021c. "White Butte." *Peakery.com.* https://peakery.com/white-butte-north-dakota-3506ft/.

Ouellette, Laurie, and Julie Wilson. 2011. "Women's Work: Affective Labor and Convergence Culture." *Cultural* Studies 4–5: 548–65.

Papacharissi, Zizi. 2002. "The Virtual Sphere: The Internet as a Public Sphere." *New Media & Society* 4.1: 9–27.

Price, Mark. 2020. "Creator of Netflix's 'Outer Banks'—Who's from NC—Explains Show's Geography Snafu." *Raleigh News & Observer*, April 23. www.newsobserver.com/news/local/article242223351.html.

Puckett, Lauren. 2020. "Here's Where to Find the *Outer Banks* Set Locations in South Carolina." *Harper's Bazaar*, May 22. www.harpersbazaar.com/culture/film-tv/a32634199/outer-banks-netflix-filming-shooting-locations/.

Reijnders, Stijn. 2011. *Places of the Imagination: Media, Tourism, Culture.* Farnham: Ashgate.

Ross, Sharon Marie. 2009. *Beyond the Box: Television and the Internet.* Oxford: Blackwell.

Scheyder, Ernest. "Snow-Capped Peaks of 'Blood & Oil' Get Panned by North Dakotans." *Reuters*, September 25. www.reuters.com/article/us-television-bloodandoil-reaction/snow-capped-peaks-of-blood-oil-get-panned-by-north-dakotans-idUSKCN0RS2HQ20150928.

Van Valkenburg, Nancy. 2015. " 'Blood & Oil' TV Series May Return to Ogden." *The Standard-Examiner*, June 11. www.standard.net/news/blood-oil-tv-series-may-return-to-ogden/article_cab2908a-c72f-5ac5-bbd2-1bdcfc5d79a0.html.

Conclusion
Location, relocation, dislocation

Billed as Netflix's first "African Original series," *Queen Sono* debuted globally on February 28, 2020. Although its impact was fairly muted by the standards of Netflix megahits like *Stranger Things* (2016–present), the show garnered enough of an audience that two months later, on April 28, Netflix announced that they had renewed the show for a second season. Promising that viewers "will see Queen search for the truth as her newfound need for revenge takes her on a mission across Africa," Netflix's press release emphasized the spatial capital of this global original series: Dorothy Ghettuba, the head of Netflix's original international series, is quoted as saying that in the first season "we saw grit and glamour, strength and vulnerability, as well as the past and present, converge into a powerful narrative that explored the complexities and nuances of the African experience" ("Netflix Renews. . . " 2020). She asserts that "the first season of *Queen Sono* marked the beginning of our journey to introduce the world to exciting stories that are made in Africa," with the second season renewal promising to continue a journey that, according to creator Kagiso Lediga, shows "the appetite for African stories." The release noted that the second season was expected to begin production in late 2020, touting the place of *Queen Sono* amid upcoming series that form "Netflix's wide range of diverse, quality entertainment made in Africa to be enjoyed by members around the world."

Roughly seven months later, however, it emerged that Netflix's appetite for *Queen Sono* had changed: a report from South Africa's *Channel24* in November confirmed that Netflix had, in their words, "made the difficult decision not to move forward with season 2 of *Queen Sono*" (Eloff 2020). Although Netflix offered no specific explanation for this decision, Lediga's statement to *Channel24* explains that "we wrote a beautiful story that spanned the continent but unfortunately could not be executed in these current trying times," a not-so-subtle allusion to the fact that *Queen Sono*'s first season debuted on Netflix roughly two weeks before Hollywood and much of the global entertainment industry shut down in response to the COVID-19 pandemic. Overnight, the qualities that made *Queen Sono* a productive engagement with spatial capital—its striking location shooting, its transnational storytelling—became liabilities. Television production

DOI: 10.4324/9781003224693-7

went dark for months, and even when it reemerged it was with costly and complicated COVID procedures that led to a wave of cancellations of previously renewed series that were no longer considered valuable enough to expend these additional resources (Goldberg 2020).

Many of these shows were Netflix Original Series, and while shows like teen drama *The Society* (2019) and wrestling comedy *GLOW* (2017–2019) were "un-renewed" due to a complex calculus of cost and scheduling, there is a simpler answer for *Queen Sono*: shooting a globe-trotting spy drama during a global pandemic where travel is restricted—and the virus remains rampant—is both expensive and potentially reckless. Although an approved vaccine was imminent at the time that Netflix officially acknowledged their choice not to move forward with *Queen Sono*, they were unwilling to wait until it would be safe to film again, instead choosing to cut their losses and, per their spokesperson, "continue to work closely with South Africa's creative industry to keep producing more compelling 'Made-in-South Africa' stories."

Spatial capital and the COVID-19 contingency

This book has outlined the contingent factors that impact television's spatial capital, identifying an ongoing negotiation of modes of production, textual strategies, shifts in distribution, and audience consumption patterns that shape how a text is able to engage productively with questions of space and place. Although case studies like the rise of mobile production or the introduction of Netflix's "global originals" have reinforced how this negotiation is constantly in flux, with spatial capital continuously being located, relocated, and dislocated in response to industrial and cultural hierarchies, the COVID-19 pandemic threw this precarity into sharp relief. In some ways, television was less impacted by the pandemic than other media: whereas film studios were forced to scrap planned releases and push films into 2021 and beyond based on the closure of movie theaters, the television industry's mode of distribution was uninterrupted, and if anything became more vital to audiences locked down in their homes for weeks or months throughout 2020 and into 2021. From a production perspective, however, the cyclical nature of broadcast network production was disrupted significantly. Martin Gero was in Vancouver filming a reboot of *Kung Fu* for The CW when it became clear that COVID-19 was going to shut down production, forcing him to scramble his crew to film enough material to convince the network to pick up the show despite not being able to finish filming the pilot. Although Gero was successful and *Kung Fu* was picked up for the 2020–2021 season, the pandemic delayed the start of production of all broadcast series, forcing networks to go into fall with no new series and no new episodes of returning hits.

For streaming services like Netflix, however, their year-round release patterns meant that a large amount of content had been banked in advance, such that they were able to continue releasing original series through the end of 2020 and into 2021 with minimal interruption. It also meant that series like *Queen Sono* or Italian teen drama *Summertime* (2020)—which debuted in the heart of the U.S. lockdown in late April—that offer global audiences a glimpse of exotic locales were likely far more valuable to Netflix than they were before, given that international travel was effectively halted. Spatial capital is, by its nature, contextual to the circumstances of its audience, and at a time when feature films were delayed and vacations were postponed, a sunny glimpse of Italian high schoolers in a resort town on the Adriatic coast carried more value than it might have otherwise. Netflix does not release granular ratings data for its original series, but it seems plausible that the globe-trotting nature of *Queen Sono* meant that tens of millions of Netflix subscribers stuck in their homes who might have never discovered the show otherwise perhaps tuned in as a form of surrogate tourism. If the "curve" of COVID-19 cases had been successfully flattened over the course of 2020, season two of *Queen Sono* may have gone into production after having garnered a fanbase of viewers who found the show only because its perceived value shifted when its travel-by-proxy premise became more desirable.

As history shows, the curve of COVID-19 was not flattened in time for *Queen Sono*'s second season to go into production, and its cancellation supports the cynical thesis that has long driven conversations about spatial capital in the television industry. *Queen Sono*'s spatial capital mattered to its future until the point that it was too logistically challenging—read: expensive—for the show to produce its globe-trotting narrative safely, seemingly proving that economic capital remains the dominant force in the consideration of how and where television is produced. This project has articulated the complex ways spatial capital intersects with media capital, and how individual creative forces, distributional shifts, and discursive factors can shape and reshape the value attached to space and place in the industry. However, the COVID-19 pandemic undoubtedly saw the financial realities of production assert their place in the hierarchy. The un-renewal of *Queen Sono* showed that although the show's status as Netflix's first African original was valuable to their global expansion, the specific articulation of spatial capital in the series was no longer compatible with the global landscape. Netflix is careful to emphasize that they are no less committed to African original programming, but that programming is more likely to look like teen drama *Blood & Water*, Netflix's second African original that debuted in May 2020. The show follows the lead of Spain's *Elite* by presenting a Westernized high school story that, while set in Cape Town, lacks the investment in spatial capital that became a liability for its predecessor. The fact that *Blood & Water*—almost exclusively in English, mostly landlocked in Cape Town, filmed in the same high school that stood in for a Los Angeles high school during filming of Netflix's *Kissing Booth* trilogy—was not un-renewed at the same time as *Queen Sono* boils down to the reality that a commitment to spatial capital is costly and incompatible with the realities of COVID production.

However, the central thesis of this book is that spatial capital does not sit in a static or straightforward relationship with economic and cultural capital operating within the television industry. It is in a constant state of negotiation, the inherent mobility of production forcing the various stakeholders of spatial capital to rethink their accounting, rearticulate their labor practices, and reimagine strategies for new forms of distribution as circumstances require. In some cases, it is true that the pandemic disrupted existing practices in foundational ways based on the economic and logistical hurdles it created. In the COVID era, meeting the burden of spatial capital through strategies like strategic location shooting became a significant roadblock: Gero shared during his interview for this book that at least one of the shows he had under development at Universal as part of an overall deal would be planned as an international show filming in multiple global cities. Although that may have seemed plausible for 2021 during our conversation in May 2020, by the end of 2020 it was clear that the pandemic was too widespread for that series to be produced in the short term. With productions no longer able to be as mobile, companies like MasterKey that built their business around helping series leverage strategic location shooting were short of clients, joining the rest of the industry in patiently waiting for a vaccine that would hopefully restore the momentum they had achieved before an unprecedented global event made their service untenable for all but the most cash-rich productions.

Although no one in the television industry would suggest that they ultimately benefited from COVID-19, a full accounting of the stakeholders in spatial capital reveals how the virus forced a reevaluation of ingrained hierarchies, underlining—and in some cases challenging—the arguments in this book as the virus reshaped the foundations on which understandings of space and place are constructed within the U.S. television industry.

Borders of spatial capital in the COVID-19 era

For most productions, COVID-19 complicated the development of spatial capital from a production perspective: Showtime dramedy *Shameless* (2011–2021), which historically used strategic location shooting in Chicago to supplement interiors and other location work in Los Angeles to set itself in the former city, was forced to abandon this plan in order to re-enter production in the fall of 2020. This required the series to build a facsimile of a Chicago street on which the Gallaghers lived and supplement with visual effects work to enable continuity between seasons. Such efforts rely on technology like virtual backlots, which suddenly became the only option for shows that might have previously spent money to hire a company like MasterKey. Even for shows that film in the cities where they are set, necessary COVID restrictions complicate the hiring of extras and the use of public space, creating new challenges for below-the-line workers who work to leverage the spatial capital of filming on location. However, as the book has demonstrated, these workers have always been dealing with some form of limitations on their ability to activate spatial capital—COVID-19 was just the latest wrinkle that required them to hide mountains (or at least attempt to hide mountains until a director tells them not to bother).

In the area of distribution, though, COVID-19 did more than create a new challenge: it also created a new opportunity. When the Toronto-set original series *Coroner* (2019–present) debuted on Canada's public broadcaster CBC, it had already sold its global distribution rights to NBC Universal, who would go on to air and sell the rights to the series in a range of territories. However, despite a strong Canadian launch and a familiar star to American audiences in actress Serinda Swan, the series was never picked up for American distribution, a common fate for Canadian dramas that are not active co-productions with American studios and consciously produced with that goal in mind as it pertains to spatial capital. But when it became clear during the May upfronts in 2020 that no broadcast network was going to be able to launch their new or returning series in the fall due to the pandemic, networks were desperate for new original programming and changed their mind about Canadian series that had no doubt been pitched to those same broadcasters in previous years. The CW, which was already airing Canadian series *Burden of Truth* (2018–present), purchased the broadcast rights to *Coroner*, airing the show's first two seasons beginning in August 2020 and announcing in October that they had also purchased broadcast rights to the upcoming third season picked up by CBC in May of the same year. The CW was not the only network to turn to Canada to fill their schedules with programming shot and set in Toronto: NBC acquired CTV drama *Transplant* (2020–present) for their fall schedule and added Global's medical drama *Nurses* (2020–present) to its winter programming for a December debut. Faced with a shortage of original programming, the spatial stigmas attached to these Canadian dramas—which historically only air as summer filler even when they do secure U.S. broadcast distribution—no longer carried significant weight. The fact that the shows might not have been produced to meet the burden of spatial capital attached to co-productions like *Orphan Black* no longer mattered in a COVID-ravaged industry.

As a result, the logics over which series were able to travel across the U.S.–Canada border changed dramatically in 2020. This was especially true for *Trickster* (2020), a CBC drama series that debuted in the midst of quarantine in Canada. The show is based on Eden Robinson's coming-of-age novel *Son of a Trickster*, which focuses on an Indigenous Canadian teenager coming to terms with his Haisla heritage through his connection to the magical trickster spirit Wee'jit. In Canada, the series' debut marked a rare Indigenous narrative on broadcast television, with most programming featuring Indigenous storylines and characters relegated to the narrowcast Aboriginal People's Television Network (APTN) cable channel. The show's success in Canada—including a prominent spot in the Toronto Film Festival and an early second season renewal—was already a significant moment for the place of Aboriginal stories within the spatial capital of Canadian drama, but The CW's decision to pick up the first season to fill its January 2021 schedule was even more significant given the absence of Indigenous narratives on U.S. television. Only days before The CW announced their acquisition of *Trickster* in October 2020, NBC announced it had ordered the pilot for *Sovereign*, the first Native American family drama in network television history, a milestone that points to how stories about Indigenous people have played little-to-no role in the televisual depiction of the contemporary United States to that point. Unfortunately, controversy surrounding the claim to Indigenous heritage by the series' showrunner Michelle Latimer led to a muted U.S. release for *Trickster* and the show's cancellation in Canada (Dowling 2020), but the fact that a story about Indigenous Canadians would make its way across the border is groundbreaking. If the show had been successful, it could have been a bellwether for future projects with similarly localized storytelling.

However, "could" is the operative word here. For Canadian producers, the loosening of the historical border restrictions on Canadian-set shows offered a brief glimpse of hope, but the chances of this becoming a new normal were always slim. And when production was able to resume in the United States in time for the 2021 pilot season, and the networks were confident they would have content for their fall schedules, the subsequent schedules saw no significant progress for Canadian content being picked up for U.S. distribution. As for the shows that slipped through during this moment of industry crisis, the results were mixed: *Coroner*'s third season was slotted into The CW's summer 2021 lineup, and NBC picked up *Transplant* for a second season, but as of the Canadian premiere of *Nurses*' second season in June 2021 NBC had not committed to airing it. COVID-19 may have demonstrated the inherent contingency of spatial capital by creating a context in which existing concerns over Canadian content were no longer relevant, but the about-face from U.S. networks once the industry had implemented necessary protocols to return to production reinforces that the industry's understanding of spatial capital has a status quo. And as evidenced in the example of Netflix's push into global programming, even industry-wide changes like streaming and "Peak TV" that permanently alter spaces of production and distribution have continued to replicate existing principles of spatial capital. The pandemic revealed how the borders of spatial capital can shift swiftly when necessary, but it also reinforced how foundational principles of the television industry will reassert those borders when circumstances allow.

Distribution was not the only place where the U.S.–Canada border was relevant in the television industry during the COVID-19 pandemic. At the same time as more Canadian shows were crossing the border, the actual physical border between the two countries was closed to all but essential travel, destabilizing the culture of mobile production that has reordered where television is produced. The role of borders in the fallout from the pandemic cannot be overstated, as different countries approached the containment of the virus in ways that forced local governments to take dramatic action to keep outbreaks in neighboring regions from spilling over. During summer 2020, the failed U.S. government response to the virus was a stark contrast with the situation in Canada, where the first wave of the virus was largely mitigated by a concentrated federal effort that included shutting down their border with their southern neighbor. Whereas the U.S. response left states to fight among themselves to secure necessary medical supplies—and struggled to establish meaningful relief for out-of-work Americans in all industries—Canada moved more swiftly to establish a social safety net that kept cases from exploding in large cities like Vancouver and Toronto compared to major U.S. locations. As such, in late summer 2020 as the television industry hoped to return to production, major U.S. production centers were either embroiled in significant COVID outbreaks (Georgia) or heavily restricting any return to production due to rigid state leadership (California, New York), while Canada appeared to have avoided the worst of the pandemic.

Although mobile production is predicated on the destabilization of media capital, COVID-19 further complicated the calculus of deciding where a show is filmed, as concerns over tax incentives were combined with considerations of testing capacity and quarantine procedures. In October 2020, the *Hollywood Reporter* wrote that British Columbia was home to 61 film and television productions, 50% more than the 40 that were filming in Vancouver that spring when production was shut down, owing to the fact that the province "weathered the global pandemic better than rival locales like the southern U.S. states and New York City, which had U.S. film and TV producers choosing early on to shift projects to Vancouver" (Vlessing "Hollywood. . . " 2020a). Vancouver's film commissioner David Shepheard suggests in the story that British Columbia's containment of the virus made them the industry leader in post-COVID production, arguing that

> [T]he industry has been looking at British Columbia to see how to manage its way and those studies that are eager to get into production have been looking all around the world to where they can get into production quickly, with Vancouver eager to accept their business.

Americans crossing the border to work on these shows in British Columbia—actors, directors, other personnel—were still subject to the mandatory 14-day quarantine instituted by the Canadian government for those traveling to Canada from outside of the country, but in neighboring Alberta the government moved to simplify this process. In another *Hollywood Reporter* story, the Albertan government touted a "game-changer" with a rapid testing plan that required only a 48-hour quarantine after a rapid test at the Calgary International Airport, with talent able to be on-set within 48 hours if they tested negative (Vlessing "Why Rapid. . . " 2020b). The story somewhat ghoulishly frames the pandemic as an opportunity for Alberta to compete with British Columbia and Ontario, citing plans to make their incentive package more competitive and touting "great crews" and "great vistas." Suddenly, a province's testing strategy and rules related to travel were becoming a new metric in shaping a culture of mobile production alongside the tax credits or crew depths that have historically dictated those conversations, with stakeholders on the ground in Alberta seeing their opportunity to lay claim to media capital with projects that might have otherwise filmed in other locations, expanding their profile within the industry at a time when production was slowly restarting in other locations.

However, beyond its initial disruption of production, COVID-19 also amplified the precarity of mobile production, as the situation related to the virus can change suddenly and dramatically. Although Canada's numbers for COVID-19 remained better than those in the United States, the second wave of the virus in fall 2020 hit the country more significantly than the first, creating problems for television production. In British Columbia, production of ongoing television series was halted multiple times due to testing shortages, as rising cases among the public led to long delays in test results that made it impossible to follow the return-to-work safety requirements that had been set by SAG-AFTRA (Andreeva 2020). Even with these setbacks that were eventually resolved, "Hollywood North" was still a safer production location than Los Angeles, which ran out of ICU capacity in late 2020 and saw all production halted in January 2021 at the recommendation of Hollywood guilds and local health officials (Andreeva 2021). But the situation remained volatile, meaning that any series considering starting production in 2021 would need to look beyond Vancouver or Calgary if they were searching for a space where COVID-19 would be less of a risk factor.

One such location was located on the other side of the country in Atlantic Canada, which comprises Nova Scotia, New Brunswick, Prince Edward Island, and Newfoundland and Labrador. A combination of geographic isolation and low population density made it easier to contain the first waves of the pandemic given swift border closures and a relatively small amount of international travel under regular circumstances. By July 2020 the four provinces had COVID-19 under enough control to create the "Atlantic Bubble," which allowed for free travel between the provinces but retained strict limits of travel to other parts of Canada and outside of the country. Although there were subsequent outbreaks in the fall based on violation of strict isolation rules, ultimately ending the "Bubble," provinces like Nova Scotia were able to keep total cases of COVID-19 to under 100 as cases were skyrocketing in the United States. In November 2020, a *New York Times* op-ed by Stephanie Nolen touted the province's response to the virus, framing it as a "Covid-Free World a Few Hundred Miles from Manhattan."

Hollywood, it turns out, had already noticed. In September, with only a handful of cases of COVID-19, Nova Scotia was back in full production working through a backlog of projects that had been scheduled to shoot over the summer, but they reported receiving 50% more inquiries from the United States than in a typical year at the time (Gow 2020). As with Alberta, the province saw this as "a golden opportunity to boost the reputation of Nova Scotia's film industry on the global stage," with Screen Nova Scotia's Laura MacKenzie expecting the pandemic to be a boon to future production. In November 2020, the provincial government extended the Nova Scotia film incentive fund, with MacKenzie noting that the extension was in part based on the recent uptick of production interest due to the province's low COVID numbers. Speaking to the potentially full 2021 production slate, MacKenzie stated, "if we can keep our province safe, then this industry can be relied upon to be a big part of economic recovery because so many productions want to come here now" (Ryan 2020). She also framed this opportunity in light of the province's previous incentive program being scrapped in 2015, forcing many workers to leave the province in search of work and setting back Nova Scotia's efforts to compete with other provinces for mobile productions. The pandemic, then, became the province's opportunity to rebuild its film and television production reputation, with the belief that attracting productions "can hopefully instill enough confidence in those that left that they might be able to soon return and work year-round."

From Nova Scotia's perspective in late 2020, COVID-19 was a reset moment for the province's status as a space for production, but the precarity of spatial capital was such that this moment was short-lived. As was the case with the borders of distribution, the borders of production that were impacted by the virus throughout 2020 were not destroyed: they were simply stored away temporarily. Although Nova Scotia had lined up a full 2021 schedule of productions, that growth was contingent on the province's status as the safest location in North America: when a surge in cases beginning in April fueled by Easter holiday travel and the Alpha variant from the UK prompted the province to enter a full lockdown at the same time U.S. states were opening up due to rising vaccination rates, Amazon Prime series *The Summer I Turned Pretty* (2022) abandoned their plans to shoot the first season in the province (Chandler 2021). This loss of an ongoing television series that may have filmed for multiple seasons—as mentioned back in Chapter 1, the "holy grail" for a nascent media capital—represented a huge blow for Nova Scotia. However, the truth is that the culture of mobile production meant that even if the show had filmed its first season in Nova Scotia due to the pandemic, Amazon might have chosen to move production to Wilmington, North Carolina for any number of other reasons. In an environment where changing incentive programs, shifts in exchange rates, and the needs of actors could all lead to a change in production location, COVID-19 was just one more variable, and no state, province, or country could count on any growth to be sustainable in such an unstable context.

Locating, relocating, and dislocating spatial capital

The state of television's spatial capital in the wake of COVID-19 mostly affirms what this book has shown throughout its chapters: the negotiation of spatial capital is an inherently contingent process, predicated on long-standing political–economic realities of the U.S. television industry and on the way those involved with the production understand and address the burden of spatial capital within a particular text within that reality. Generally speaking, in an industry that privileges cost-effective and efficient modes of production to support commercial mandates baked into broadcast media and continue to carry over into cable and streaming even if other mandates could apply in those contexts, there is a perceived ceiling on spatial capital. Even as the geography of television production expands, and as producers gain additional tools to signify location, and as new forms of distribution emerge, there remains the sense that only exceptional texts can truly approach television's potential spatial capital.

That having been said, even if COVID-19's dislocation of spatial capital is a blip, it is still nonetheless a meaningful one for Canadian producers and territories like Nova Scotia. Every show that crosses the border has the chance of being the show that breaks down existing logics of what types of shows are able to "travel," and every production in a given territory could become the calling card that convinces the industry to invest more resources and turn Calgary or Halifax into the new Albuquerque with studios like Netflix investing in infrastructure. Mapping these fluctuations in spatial capital reminds us of the logics and limitations that delineate how television engages with space and place, but it also reveals fault lines in those logics that could become more pronounced in the future as circumstances continue to change. The impacts of COVID-19 may have been temporary, but the industry likely thought the same when productions started "running away" from Los Angeles, unaware they were seeing the early moves toward a truly mobile television production culture. The precarity of television's spatial capital makes it difficult to gauge when changes are foundational rather than circumstantial, making it all the more important to track these fluctuations carefully.

However, it is also critical to acknowledge which factors contributing to television's spatial capital are truly in flux in such situations. When Vancouver was experiencing its COVID-19 production boom in late 2020, reporting made note that an increase in shows being filmed in Vancouver was not leading to an increase of shows that were being *set* in Vancouver (Banse 2020). As productions leveraged their mobility in response to the pandemic, writers did not see this as an opportunity to invest in the culture of their new filming locations: *The Summer I Turned Pretty*, for example, was never going to move Cousins Beach to Nova Scotia and become a "Canadian show" when it was intended for the U.S. market. Much as strategic location shooting became feasible only through the conscious limitation of a production's investment in place identity, and much as productions that do shoot in the city where they are set will often privilege legible location shooting that registers with critics or audiences over deeper investigations of space and place, the default for the television industry is to see spatial capital not as an end in itself, but rather as a means to address concerns of economic or cultural capital. In simpler terms, while the negotiation of spatial capital fluctuated as a result of COVID-19, the baseline burden of spatial capital of the television industry did not.

Throughout the book I have highlighted individuals who have worked within television production to expand a text's relationship to spatial capital, whether as part of their job description or as a personal responsibility. Although we must remain critical of the limits placed on their work either by their superiors or by their own internalized understanding of television economy, in each of these instances these individuals—location professionals, editors, and writers, among others—generated spatial capital that would not have existed if not for their labor. But they were not the only ones who shaped spatial capital: after a series is produced, this process becomes the domain of more stakeholders—critics, marketers, audiences—who seek to amplify or arbitrate the value of location to the text. A text's spatial capital is contingent on where it is shot and where it is set, and the limited burdens of spatial capital embedded in that process, but it is not exclusively determined by those decisions: it is instead negotiated by each of these stakeholders, a process that always contains the potential to puncture long-standing truths about where television takes place even if this remains a rare occurrence.

Accordingly, it is impossible to say for certain how COVID-19—or any other change agent in the media industries—will impact television's spatial capital as I write this in the fall of 2021. Although there may have been a time when one could say the acquisition of spatial capital was a standardized process of translating a Hollywood backlot into a given location through established strategies, the past three decades have seen a dramatic shift in where television is produced, how television is distributed, and how we consume television that has forced negotiations of spatial capital to be intensely reactive. What COVID-19 has highlighted is that the answer to the question of "where television takes place" is a shifting target, with the answer being located, relocated, and dislocated by forces that may include the uncontrolled spread of a deadly virus. And to truly address this question, we must go beyond outlining the industry's standard operating procedures, and explore the ongoing, spatialized labor that takes place across all stages of television's journey from the space of production to the space of reception.

The answer to "where television takes place" will no doubt evolve further in the years to come as spatial capital continues to be located, relocated and dislocated, but what COVID-19 demonstrates is that the work required to answer this question—the work I have modeled within this book—will remain unchanged.

References

Andreeva, Nellie. 2020. "U.S. TV Production in Vancouver Largely on Pause Over COVID-19 Test Results Delays." *Deadline*, September 29. https://deadline.com/2020/09/production-in-vancouver-on-pause-ovid-19-test-results-delays-1234588472/.

———. 2021. "Los Angeles Production Grinds to a Halt Amid COVID-19 Surge; Netflix Is Latest Major Studio to Pause Filming." *Deadline*, January 4. https://deadline.com/2021/01/los-angeles-production-shutdown-covid-19-surge-netflix-is-latest-major-pauses-filmng-true-story-family-reunioni-1234664678/.

Banse, Tom. 2020. "Lights, Camera, Action!: 'Hollywood North' Revved Up Despite Covid—and Because of It." *Kuow*, November 16. www.kuow.org/stories/lights-camera-action-hollywood-north-revved-up-despite-covid-and-because-of-it.

Chandler, Feleshia. 2021. " 'Quite a Blow': Amazon Series Pulls Out of N.S. Due to COVID-19 Restrictions." *CBC Nova Scotia*, May 14. www.cbc.ca/news/canada/nova-scotia/film-amazon-halifax-nova-scotia-1.6026761.

Dowling, Amber. 2020. "Michelle Latimer's Identity Crisis Is Raising Impossible Questions for Canada's Indigenous Filmmakers." *Variety*, December 23. https://variety.com/2020/film/global/michelle-latimer-indigenous-trickster-inconvenient-indian-1234873888/.

Eloff, Herman. 2020. "Queen Sono's Second Season Cancelled Amid 'Current Trying Times'." *Channel24*, November 26. www.news24.com/channel/tv/news/queen-sonos-second-season-cancelled-amid-current-trying-times-20201126-2.

Goldberg, Lesley. 2020. "Making Sense of TV's Wave of 'Un-Renewals.' " *The Hollywood Reporter*, October 9. www.hollywoodreporter.com/index.php/live-feed/making-sense-of-tvs-wave-of-un-renewals.

Gow, Steve. 2020. "COVID-19 May Give a Boost to Nova Scotia's Film Industry." *Halifax Today*, September 24. www.halifaxtoday.ca/local-news/covid-19-may-give-a-boost-to-nova-scotias-film-industry-2736934.

No Author. 2020. "Netflix Renews Queen Sono for Season 2." *Netflix*, April 28. https://about.netflix.com/en/news/netflix-renews-queen-sono-for-season-2.

Nolen, Stephanie. 2020. "I Am Living in a COVID-Free World Just a Few Hundred Miles from Manhattan." *The New York Times*, November 18. www.nytimes.com/2020/11/18/opinion/covid-halifax-nova-scotia-canada.html.

Ryan, Haley. 2020. "Nova Scotia Film Fund Extended Amid COVID-19 Business Boom." *CBC Nova Scotia*, November 5. www.cbc.ca/news/canada/nova-scotia/nova-scotia-film-incentive-fund-extended-amid-covid-19-business-boom-1.5790219.

Vlessing, Etan. 2020a. "Hollywood Production in Vancouver Hits New High Amid Pandemic." *The Hollywood Reporter*, October 26. www.hollywoodreporter.com/news/hollywood-production-in-vancouver-hits-new-high-amid-pandemic.

———. 2020b. "Why Rapid COVID Testing Could Make Alberta Hollywood's Next Production Hub." *The Hollywood Reporter*, November 13. www.hollywoodreporter.com/news/why-rapid-covid-testing-could-make-alberta-hollywoods-next-production-hub.

Acknowledgments

As the culmination of over a decade of thinking and writing, the people I need to acknowledge are spread across time and space, so it seems fitting to map them.

In Madison, at the University of Wisconsin, a community of scholars whose contributions to this project—which began in earnest in Vilas Hall—are immeasurable. Jonathan Gray, for always knowing when I was about to overextend myself, but never stopping me from exploring those ideas long enough to create groundwork for expanding the scope for this book. Derek Johnson, for investing the time to turn teaching into a collaborative process and for modeling a balance of scholarship and pedagogy I strive to emulate. Michele Hilmes and Eric Hoyt, for their valuable insights as members of my dissertation committee. Mary Beltrán, Jeff Smith, Sue Robinson, Jeremy Morris, and Lori Kido Lopez, for creating a nurturing environment to learn how to be a scholar. And all my fellow graduate students that I shared space with at Vilas Hall, City Bar, and beyond, whose advice, commiseration, curiosity, and camaraderie are foundational to this book and everything I do in ways that I thought could not be more apparent than they were at the time. Time has proven me wrong.

In Norfolk, an environment at Old Dominion University where I feel so fortunate to have the opportunity to work and research. Avi Santo, who pushed me over numerous hurdles on the way to this book's publication and whose friendship and guidance have been constant regardless of his role. My colleagues in the Department of Communication and Theatre Arts, in particular Tim Anderson's steadfast support and Fran Hassencahl's late-night office check-ins. Allison Page, for being a cherished comrade and confidant and for both copyediting this book and giving me editorial control over my acknowledgment in her own. Dan Richards, for his generosity of insight and shared commitment to never getting good enough at golf that it becomes too serious. Jeremy Saks and Annemarie Navar-Gill, for making time for community even if it isn't Community Day. Andrea Battle-Coffer, Christina Johnson, D'an Knowles Ball, and Kristen Sahut, for supporting myself and my colleagues in all of our pursuits. And all my students, for keeping me on my toes and pushing my thinking on the media industries. This is especially true for my graduate students, who I subjected to iterations of this project, and who always offered great insights. My thanks also to Keith and Sarah Darrow for the good times and game nights.

In Wolfville, my professors in the English Department of Acadia University, in particular Kevin Whetter—who indulged my desire to write an honors thesis on *Battlestar Galactica* and had no idea what he was unleashing— and the late Herb Wyile, whose pointed refusal to let me write about the distinction between single-camera and multi-camera engagement with the landscape of the Canadian prairies became the germ of an idea that eventually turned into this book (he was right, that chapter was already doing too much).

Across Nova Scotia, all my friends and family, who supported my move across the border over a decade ago and have always been so welcoming when I return home. My brother Ryan and sister-in-law Janet, for being so engaged with my work, and fostering and encouraging—respectively—my relationship with popular culture. And my parents, Randy and Verna, for never once questioning my becoming a media scholar, even when it meant leaving the country. The trust they have placed in my judgment as I have navigated a career in academia is more critical than they could know, and that I've succeeded in these pursuits is due to their decades of unwavering encouragement.

Of course, support knows no borders, and completing this project during the COVID-19 pandemic has reiterated how much I have depended on virtual communities throughout the course of my career. Across Twitter and other social media platforms, I remain overwhelmed by the network of scholars, critics, and viewers that I've managed to become a part of, and my approach to studying this topic and the media industries broadly is helped every day by their willingness to join me in discussion. While there are too many to name, I must thank a few directly. Jason Mittell, without whom I wouldn't have understood how to go about becoming a media scholar and whose insight on this project and continued friendship have been invaluable. Emily VanDerWerff, Erik Adams, Keith Phipps, Danette Chavez, and all of my colleagues past and present at *The A.V. Club*, for giving me space to put on my TV critic hat while never asking me to take off my mortarboard first. Alan Sepinwall and Daniel Fienberg, for treating a grad student pretending to be a TV critic as one of their own.

I must also specifically acknowledge the groups of friends and colleagues who have helped sustain my sanity during the isolation of the pandemic. To my Fantasy Box Office pals, for pivoting when the box office closed to Slacking our way through cinema's greatest hits even if we peaked in week one with *Angry Birds 2*. To the Osgoode Ballroom brigade, for recapturing the energy of a late-night eviction by blathering around and helping each other survive an impossible year. And to Evan, Kit, Alyx, Sarah, and Chi Chi, for a never-ending stream of notifications that was the highlight of any day, before, during and after the stresses of the last year and a half.

Without these moments of levity and community, I don't think this book would have been finished, but it also wouldn't have materialized without the support of my editorial team at Routledge. My thanks to Suzanne Richardson for sharing her firsthand experience with spatial capital in our first meeting and for channeling her righteous anger at *Sex Education*'s inscrutable setting into support for this project at each stage of its journey. My thanks also to Tanushree Baijal, Alyssa Turner, and before them Sukriti Pandey, for their assistance in getting the project to the finish line, along with everyone involved in the production of the manuscript.

During its early stages, this project was supported by the Social Sciences and Humanities Research Council of Canada. The industry research within this project would not have been possible without the generous participation and assistance of the following: Shawn Ryan, Martin Gero, Ryan Johnson, Rhett Giles, Rebecca Puck Stair, Michael John Meehan, Brandi Bradburn, Lafe Jordan, Luke Pebler, Margaret Nagle, Tony Salome, and the Location Managers Guild of America. My thanks also to Todd Manzer for his hospitality during my time in Los Angeles. I would also note that portions of Chapter 1 were published in "Mobile Production: Spatialized Labor, Location Professionals, and the Expanding Geography of Television Production," 2015, *Media Industries* 2.1: 60–77, while parts of Chapter 4 appeared in "Narratives of Miami in Dexter and Burn Notice," 2017, *International Journal of TV Serial Narratives* 3.1: 73–86.

Index